AN INFLUENCER'S WORLD

AN INFLUENCER'S WORLD

A Behind-the-Scenes Look at

Social Media Influencers

and Creators

BY CAROLINE BAKER AND DON BAKER

University of Iowa Press, Iowa City

University of Iowa Press, Iowa City 52242
Copyright © 2023 by the University of Iowa Press
uipress.uiowa.edu
Printed in the United States of America

Design by Ashley Muehlbauer

Printed on acid-free paper

Library of Congress Cataloging-in-Publication Data
Names: Baker, Caroline, 1969– editor. | Baker, Don, 1972– editor.
Title: An Influencer's World: A Behind-the-Scenes Look at Social
Media Influencers and Creators / by Caroline Baker and Don Baker.
Description: Iowa City: University of Iowa Press, [2023] | Includes index.
Identifiers: LCCN 2022040096 (print) | LCCN 2022040097 (ebook) |
ISBN 9781609388959 (paperback) | ISBN 9781609388966 (ebook)
Subjects: LCSH: Social influence. | Social media.
Classification: LCC HM1176.I55 2023 (print) | LCC HM1176
(ebook) | DDC 302/.13—dc23/eng/20220922
LC record available at https://lccn.loc.gov/2022040096
LC ebook record available at https://lccn.loc.gov/2022040097

*For Cole, our inspiration, and the one
who keeps us on the cutting edge.*

*And to Carol Presno, an authentic, loving mother
whose influence has always been to keep writing.*

CONTENTS

AN INFLUENCER'S WORLD

VOICES OF THE DIGITAL CONTENT REVOLUTION

Social media influencers and creators have the unique experience of living with one foot in the real world and the other in a digital world where they hold the power. Every day, they are torn by the paradox of being adored by millions of followers while being trolled by haters.

What's the psychological toll of chasing the next post, going from adored to despised in the number of seconds it takes to read a comment? What got influencers to where they are now, and what helps them in the fight to remain relevant? How do they create an authentic brand that catches fire while still leading an authentic, healthy life?

Even the *New York Times* declares: "Don't Scoff at Influencers. They're Taking Over the World!"[1] Influencers are part of a $15 billion industry that keeps exploding. While the future is uncertain, it is projected to reach $85 billion by 2028.[2] It makes sense that there is intense curiosity surrounding the industry and the intriguing people who drive it. The spotlight is on.

Some of the most successful influencers and content creators tell a story with their posts, but even more fascinating is the story behind the posts. It's a lifestyle that's fast, exotic, voyeuristic, surreal, and sometimes mundane; it's the opposite of anything as old-fashioned as nine-to-five. It's the real world of an influencer. Some influencers and creators swim in money, drive exotic cars, vacation on luxury yachts, and live in mansions; others struggle to earn a living in the industry.

The purpose of the book is to get an insider's look at the influencing industry by showcasing a diverse set of voices from within the industry. It's an unconventional, holistic view that explores the business, history, culture, and psychology of influencing. To get the full picture, we've interviewed dozens of CEOs and other leading industry executives, brands, agents, talent managers, sports and entertainment insiders, academics, mental health professionals, celebrities, reality TV stars, and trending influencers.

TV reality shows have depicted the lifestyle of influencers and allowed people to peer into their world—shows like Hulu's *D'Amelio Show,* focusing on the turbulent lives of TikTok stars Charli and Dixie D'Amelio, and Netflix's *Hype House,* about the controversial influencers who are part of an infamous TikTok collective. These are, however, highly filtered and solely for entertainment; they do not offer insider analysis and perspective that add breadth and depth to the topic.

From a historical angle, we look at the rise of digital influencers/ creators and influencer marketing agencies. From a business perspective, we explore the process of influencers developing their personal brand and how they stay on top. On the flip side, we showcase brands that have had major successes with influencer marketing and how they go about doing it right. We also look at discrimination, bias, and pay inequities, which cast a shadow over the industry.

Then we dive into the culture by getting up close and personal about influencers' lifestyles, including dealing with the drama of content houses and cancel culture, along with the dark side of influencing, including stalking and sexual misconduct.

We look at all of this through a psychological lens that includes exploring the business of likes and hate, managing self-esteem and mental health issues associated with social media, coping with the anxiety of algorithms, always chasing the next post and content block. Finally, we asked experts what they see trending in the future of influencing.

A KID'S DREAM

YouTuber and influencer are becoming new dream jobs for kids. A survey of children from the United Kingdom, China, and the United States notes that eight- to twelve-year-olds are three times more likely to aspire to be a YouTuber (29 percent) than an astronaut (11 percent).[3]

As the prevalence and success of influencers increases, the dream is turning into reality. Nothing says this more than the University of Nebraska athletic department's program, Ready Now, which was designed to help its student athletes become better influencers. In partnership with Opendorse, a company specializing in athlete influencer marketing, the Nebraska Huskers are learning to "perform to the peak of its ability on social media," including an evaluation of their current brand, as well as content that could have a negative impact on their brand in the digital world.[4] Fred Hoiberg, the men's basketball coach, says in the same press release, "The earlier we can help our young men and women understand the value of their personal brand, the better positioned they will be for whatever professional path they choose."

For younger generations, an education in influencing is becoming the new liberal arts. But what is the social and psychological impact of being the brand?

WHO ARE THE INFLUENCERS?

Through the relationship they have with their followers on social media platforms, influencers shape perceptions, set trends, and affect purchasing decisions. They engage with their audience for many reasons. Often it's a career path with the goal of earning a living through sponsorship deals or direct monetization.

When it comes to the business side of things, influencers promote products, services, campaigns, their personal brand, and their content. For instance, Juliette Porter, who through her sexy posts engages with her audience about the MTV reality show *Siesta Key,* on which she co-stars, promotes her swim wear line, JMP the Label, and brands such as FabFitFun. For other influencers, it's all about content they want to get noticed in categories like music, comedy, and gaming.

Others choose to exert their influence to share news and information, as well as educate and promote social causes. For example, Autumn Peltier is an Anishinaabe Indigenous rights activist using her platform to advocate for clean drinking water in First Nations communities and across the globe. More and more, influencers are blending their careers with taking a stance on social media, like Chella Man, an actor, model, artist, and activist, who is known for sharing his experiences as a deaf, queer, transgender, Chinese, Jewish person.

The significance of influencers and their disseminating of information came to the forefront in one instance as the White House briefed thirty influencers from platforms including TikTok, YouTube, and Twitter during the beginning of Russia's war with Ukraine in 2022. Officials said that they wanted to arm the influencers with factual information because their content about the war was reaching millions of viewers, many of whom were younger. Officials were also interested in counteracting pro-Kremlin propaganda that the Russian government was paying a group of TikTok influencers to produce.[5]

CREATOR VERSUS INFLUENCER

At the start of it all, the term "influencer" didn't exist. It was around 2011 that the YouTube-tied term "creator" took hold to refer to its stars and eventually was adopted by other platforms like Tumblr.

"Creator" is an all-encompassing word that takes into account more than being an internet personality; it's an umbrella term for writing, editing, producing, entrepreneurship, and so on. However, as users began to flood Instagram, they moved toward the term "influencer," which is more generic across platforms.[6]

For some, there's a stigma tied to the word "influencer" because they think it evokes the idea of endorsements and -isms like materialism and consumerism rather than art, entertainment, and creativity. Self-termed creators think of themselves as videographers, photographers, writers, artists, entertainers, and editors first.

Indeed, the distinction between "creator" and "influencer" is fuzzy. YouTube juggling sensation Josh Horton addresses this problem in one of his YouTube videos during the Black Lives Matter protests in 2020: "I've never loved the term 'influencer' for what I do for a living. I've always said content creator, video creator, YouTuber. But at the end of the day, I am an influencer. I have a large platform, a lot of followers, which I'm able to influence. I think I'd be doing you a disservice if I didn't talk about what's happening in the country right now, in the world right now."[7] Horton recognizes the importance of his influence along with his creativity. In the zeitgeist, the two terms are still battling it out.

WHY ARE WE GLUED?

More than half the world now uses social media. The reasons for it are multifaceted. Tristan Harris, a technology ethicist, is one of many who discusses the manipulative and sometimes nefarious ways that apps get eyeballs on screens with addictive qualities built into the system.

But millions of users aren't coming to social media as zombies either. Laura Vogel, digital media producer and owner of Winged Pup Productions, says, "When we open a social media app, we're looking for something. We are lonely or bored, or tired, or overwhelmed, or intellectually hungry, or any of those things. . . . Creating content gives people something, whether it is connection, or a distraction, or making them feel less alone."

Everyone has their different social media habits and go-tos. For example, when asked how much time he personally spent on social media each day and how the time was spent, billionaire entrepreneur Mark Cuban responds, "Probably an hour, two at most. It depends, if I have time to kill or with my kids, I'm on TikTok, maybe Instagram. If I'm looking for information, I'm on Twitter." Like a lot of people, that's a decent amount of scrolling. In fact, as of 2022, internet users worldwide averaged 147 minutes per day on social media.[8]

FOUR TYPES OF INFLUENCERS

Marketers have broken down influencers into four categories: mega, macro, micro, and nano.

Megainfluencers: 1M+ Followers

A-listers, icons, celebrities, star athletes, high-profile politicians, and standout social media stars equal megainfluencers. They have social reach (the amount of people who see their content) into the stratosphere. For instance, as of mid-2022, Portuguese soccer star Cristiano Ronaldo had nearly 500 million followers on Instagram, while musical artist Beyoncé had about 275 million. Other megainfluencers include cosmetics giant and reality TV star Kylie Jenner, social media personality MrBeast, musical artist Drake, sports comedy group Dude Perfect, and musical artist Ariana Grande.

If a brand wants to reach a mass audience and be a global success, it will likely reach out to a megainfluencer—but it comes at a price. It's not unusual for top-tier megainfluencers to get $1 million for a single sponsored post.

Megabrands like megainfluencers, such as the collab between extreme sport YouTuber Devin Graham and automaker Subaru. In their #MeetAnOwner campaign, Subaru used influencers to promote the Impreza through various videos, including Graham's, which featured him and his friends speeding down a slip-and-slide and parachuting off a cliff.

Interestingly though, biggest doesn't always mean best. Influencer marketing platform Markerly found that "as an influencer's follower total rises, the rate of engagement with followers decreases."[9] It seems the bigger the celebrity, the more impersonal things can get, leading to a weaker connection with their followers.

Macroinfluencers: 100K–1M Followers

Many macroinfluencers achieve fame and celebrity from social media, as opposed to having already achieved celebrity in the real world. They gain prominence through blogging, vlogging, going viral, or simply having entertaining, beautiful, funny, or inspiring content.

Their audience tends to put a lot of trust in their expertise and view them as highly knowledgeable about their specialty or specific niche. Whether it's fashion, comedy, gaming, sports, or any of a host of other specialties, macroinfluencers know how to capitalize on their perceived authenticity and connection with their audience.

Microinfluencers: 10K–100K Followers

Microinfluencers are regular people who generally have specific areas of expertise and are laser focused on a topic, be it nail art, henna tattoos, drone photography, or model airplanes. These specialists and industry professionals are viewed by followers as authorities in their fields.

As opposed to celebrities or social media stars, microinfluencers tend to have a highly specific, uniform audience of people interested in a niche topic.[10] Because people view microinfluencers as experts who know what they're talking about, followers are inclined to trust them and engage with them.

Even though microinfluencers have smaller reach, they shouldn't be discounted by marketers. One study showed that 82 percent of consumers surveyed said they were highly likely to follow a recommendation made by microinfluencers.[11]

Nanoinfluencers: 1K–10K Followers

Nanoinfluencers have a strong online voice in their community. They may be local politicians, religious leaders, or community leaders—or they may not be a leader at all. They might simply be a neighbor who is a topic specialist and has influence with friends and family. Because nanoinfluencers personally know a lot of their followers, levels of online engagement and loyalty are off the charts. With this upside comes the downside of much less social reach.

Jolie Jankowitz, an influencer marketing consultant and former senior director of influencer marketing and talent partnerships at FabFitFun, sees value in each tier and partners with influencers at each level, although super nanos, who have around 1,000 followers, are lowest on the list. The general rule that most brands stick to is 10,000+ followers. However, Jankowitz indicates that there are always exceptions for amazing people with cool stories.

Mae Karwowski, CEO/founder of the influencer marketing agency Obviously, says that in terms of the tiers, there are different strategies for different objectives, but she tends to favor a blended approach. She also has an interesting and perhaps counterintuitive take on working with macroinfluencers: "One thing we found works really well is if you have one or two macros, a handful of midtier influencers and then a few hundred microinfluencers. It really creates a great circle. The micros are excited to be working with this brand and working on something with these macroinfluencers. And then, you're getting brand awareness from the macro and excitement around that.

And then you're getting really authentic stories from these smaller influencers who are really excited to participate."

Karwowski is also a proponent of working with large groups of microinfluencers and believes that's the future. She says, "If you can work with 100 or 200 or 500 microinfluencers at a time, it's the same thing as launching 500 pieces of creative via Instagram ads and seeing what performs best. You're really gonna learn so much about what your potential customer responds to and what they don't respond to."

In general, the difference in pay and lifestyle among the different tiers of influencers is vast. Megainfluencers have staff to help them do things, whereas micro- and nanoinfluencers do it on their own. Throughout the book, we include a variety of influencers and creators in order to get a colorful and complete image of the industry.

RISE OF THE
DIGITAL INFLUENCER

In the beginning there were content creators, but the idea of monetizing content wasn't even a twinkle in their eyes. The people who were in it at the time describe a creative renaissance powered by young talent. These were the first digital influencers.

SHOW ME THE WHAT?

Naomi Lennon, president/founder of Lennon Management, who was one of the first to the party managing YouTubers around 2008, says, "I don't think that a lot of them had a big ambition to make a lot of money or to become super famous. I think that they were just creative kids and needed an outlet." She describes a group of young people with a common story. They were the outcasts, the freaks, and the bullied, who didn't fit into football and cheer culture. But these kids without a group "found their audience, and then engagement, which became like a family for them." It was something purely intrinsic and maybe something of a psychological necessity for a group of innovative outsiders.

With money far from their minds, Lennon says there was a backlash from content creators when YouTube announced its Partner Program, which put ads on the platform and monetized videos. She remembers some of the talent in the room raising their hands and asking if they could turn their ads off—or at least if they could give the audience one week to watch their videos without an ad. They felt bad, like they were selling out. "That's how passionate and how connected they were. Of course, when the money started to flow, perspectives change," she says.

THE NEW PUNK ROCKERS

Punk rock spit in the eye of the music establishment in the 1970s, just the way the first creators spit in the eye of the entertainment establishment in the 2000s. Punk rockers like the Ramones, Patti Smith, and the Sex Pistols exploded on stage, donning spikes, safety pins, and leather and belting out rebellious antiauthority songs, which many of them produced and distributed themselves through independent record labels.

YouTube royalty Sarah Penna, currently senior manager of creator launch at Patreon and former chief creative officer/cofounder of management, media, and marketing company Big Frame, says that the first content creators were much like punk rockers by giving the middle finger to the media industry. She describes a time when the excitement was palpable because all of them knew they were building something special. The big picture was a feeling that these digital revolutionaries were democratizing media.

Industry heavy hitter Dan Weinstein, currently partner/cofounder at Underscore Talent and former president/cofounder of the global multichannel network Studio71, says it became clear early on to people involved that a new creator class was emerging, one that was on the precipice of an entirely new form of entertainment. "Hollywood hadn't been disrupted in [ages]," Weinstein says, "and here came the disruptors, a new breed of talent, a new breed of celebrity and a new form of entertainment."

Penna also talks about the other side of it—a more incisive side. "We had a chip on our shoulder because of how the media would cover YouTube stars at that time like, these are kids in their mom's basement in their pajamas making millions of dollars." That condescending narrative helped fuel creators; it drew them closer and further established their self-made group identity as hardworking, misunderstood talent. However, the biggest middle finger to the mainstream was that they were making significant money without bosses.

A COTTAGE INDUSTRY: WHERE THE COTTAGE TURNS INTO A MANSION

In 2008, Sarah Penna left her home in San Francisco and headed to LA, just like many YouTube stars from around the country did at the time. LA was the place to be for all things digital, and the well-known MCN Maker Studios launched in California in 2009. (Multichannel networks, or MCNs, were organizations launched to help YouTube channels grow and monetize.)

As the people flowed in, so did the money. A fancy car here and a mansion there started to pop up in the tight-knit community, where everyone knew everyone. Penna remembers seeing creators starting to drive fancy cars and buying houses, like Danny Zappin, aka Danny Diamond, CEO and cofounder of Maker Studios, who bought a house in Venice, California, the site of big parties with the biggest YouTubers.

Penna's crew at the time were mainly her clients, some of whom included DeStorm Power, Philip DeFranco, Jenna Marbles, Colleen Ballinger aka Miranda Sings, Ingrid Nilsen, Tyler Oakley, and Jimmy Tatro. Penna also met, managed, and married popular YouTuber turned filmmaker Joe Penna, aka MysteryGuitarMan. These were the first generation of YouTube stars.

THE VIDCON CONNECTION

VidCon, now a famous annual digital media convention, served as a major force in bringing the emerging digital community together, as well as connecting the community with their fan base. Founded by YouTube creators Hank and John Green (Vlogbrothers), the first VidCon, held in the basement ballroom of the Hyatt in Century City, drew about 1,400 video stars, industry insiders, and fans. The convention was acquired by ViacomCBS in 2018; it's now held at the Anaheim Convention Center. In 2019, they celebrated their tenth anniversary with 75,000 attendees and more than 120 brand exhibitors.[1]

Penna describes a very different then-versus-now vibe, including fainting fans then who were able to meet their favorite YouTube stars without being impeded by bodyguards like they are today. Fans and talent shared the same elevators back then. "It was very sweet," Penna says.

She also recalls how interesting it was seeing a lot of personalities who were clearly more comfortable behind their cameras interact with rabid fans. She cites her husband MysteryGuitarMan as a prime example: his videos show him as extroverted and bubbly, but his personality in person is chill and mellow. It was a dynamic both fans and famous had to come to grips with.

Famed YouTube star and comedian GloZell Green says that back in the day, she was isolated in her room uploading vlogs, not collaborating with anyone or really knowing much of anybody at first. That all changed when she attended VidCon and met up with the YouTubers whose videos she had been sharing and who had in turn had been sharing hers. "We were the weirdos. We were the odd ones. No one knew what we were doing, and you just had your own little following. And we were just having fun."

Everyone winged it as they went along. Weinstein recalls being on a panel, talking about this new form of entertainment, but then breaks into a laugh, saying, "The other fun part was nobody knew what they were talking about at the time. We're literally making stuff up. And the more you said it, the more it became true. . . . It just became real."

It became very real. Epiphanies happened at VidCon. Naomi Lennon attended the first VidCon as she began to get more immersed in the digital space. VidCon solidified it. "These kids, they had come with gifts and letters, and they were crying for these YouTube stars that no one was giving any attention to. And as soon as I saw that, I was like, 'OK, this is where it is,' and never looked back."

They say that if you want to follow the trends, you should follow the teens. Lennon did just that, signing YouTubers like Brittani Louise Taylor, who was one of the first women to get to 1 million subscribers.

AN INDUSTRY DISRESPECTED

Naomi Lennon was originally a stand-up comedy manager who worked for various management companies, including well-known Brillstein Entertainment Partners. Tired of the late nights at comedy clubs and personally interested in YouTube at the time, she explored signing online talent but was met with pushback. They told her it was going to ruin her career and that YouTube was "just a phase." She recalls somebody rhetorically asking her, "Why would I care about the Fine Brothers when we have John Stamos?"

There was, and remains today, a definite snobbishness about online content. Lennon laments that the powers that be just didn't get it. "I remember sharing the content with them and it went over their heads. They were like, 'What is this? This is absolute garbage. It's so lowbrow.' They really didn't understand it. But I understood it."

While the people on the inside and a few keen observers from the outside had a sense for the changing culture and thought they were onto something big, outsiders and the mainstream looked down on it. While some things have changed today, some things haven't.

Today, the biggest entertainment players are scouring social media for ideas, story lines, music, models, comedians, and just plain talent. Two standout examples are Issa Rae and Lilly Singh. Rae is the creator and star of the award-winning "The Misadventures of Awkward Black Girl" on YouTube, which landed her a deal for the HBO series *Insecure*. Singh, a successful Canadian YouTube star, became the first person of Indian heritage to host a major US broadcast network late-night talk show—*A Little Late with Lilly Singh* on NBC—for a couple of seasons. The way industry insiders and society in general are looking at online content is shifting at a rapid pace. It's bringing diversity with it.

However, online content and the influencers and creators responsible for it still get a lot of flack. Raina Penchansky, CEO/cofounder of influencer marketing agency Digital Brand Architects, which was acquired by industry giant United Talent Agency in 2019, says we need to be more broad-minded in the way we think of influencers/content creators. She frequently gets asked, "Aren't there enough influencers?" To Penchansky, that's like saying, "Aren't there enough artists and musicians or actors?" She adds that there will always be new forms of art, but every new art form for centuries has been criticized.

In the 1800s, the Impressionism art movement drew criticism and scorn from critics because painters like Manet didn't follow the imposed rules of what mainstream art was supposed to be at the time. These artists' departure from the norm branded them as radicals. When TV came along, it was dubbed the boob tube, and many feared it would turn us into mindless, TV-controlled zombies. Newton Minnow, known as the crusading FCC chairman, delivered a notorious speech in 1961 in which he called television a "vast wasteland."[2] And when Elvis came on the scene in the 1950s, there was a significant portion of the population that thought his hip gyrations were a pathway to hell for civilization.

Of course, not everything is Elvis or a Manet. Some influencers are making sophomoric, low-quality art and entertainment, and some don't fit into the art and entertainment category at all. But the social media content creation revolution is bigger than a group of junky photos and videos. "Influencing" in its broadest definition, encompassing all its disparate content, is a radical new movement in art and entertainment.

Not only did the traditional Hollywood players at the time not understand the new form of art and entertainment, but they also didn't understand the new artists. Lennon says that influencers "had so much control over their own destiny—of their own art, and over their own businesses that it just took awhile for real Hollywood to figure out how to actually work with them." Influencers value their freedom, and at the beginning in particular, they coveted that freedom more than, say, a traditional actor, who needed the backing of a Hollywood machine to be successful.

The entertainment business isn't about letting artists run amok; it's about controlling the product. But influencers didn't need or want to give over control to the powers that be. They had the brands directly coming to them. They posted directly without needing to pay for distribution. They created without notes from middle management. They had their own vision for what they wanted to put out. How do you work with someone like that under the old model?

Lennon speculates that jealousy also played a role in the awkward and undefined relationship between Hollywood and influencers at the time. Executives turned up their noses at the influencers' content and then would turn around and "invest so much money into their content, and they wouldn't get any following. Some of my clients could spend very little and get 100 million [views]."

STANDING ON A PLATFORM

Social media in its essence is sharing of information, using websites and apps to facilitate communication, networking, content exchange and community building online. Influencers are the ones who, through the mastery of this space, stand out and shine among the millions of social media users. They do it through blogs and vlogs. They do it on social networking platforms like Facebook and LinkedIn; microblogging platforms like Twitter and Tumblr; photo-sharing platforms like Instagram, Snapchat, and Pinterest; video-sharing platforms like YouTube, Instagram Reels, TikTok, and Vimeo; and messaging platforms like WhatsApp and Discord.

From Friendster and MySpace to Facebook

A lot of people probably wouldn't recognize the name of what is considered to be the first social media site. Founded in 1997 by Andrew Weinrich, the platform SixDegrees allowed people to create profiles and friend each other. The site was perhaps too far ahead of its time and had trouble expanding; not too many people were on the internet yet. Youthstream Media Networks acquired SixDegrees for $125 million in 1999. However, the site only survived a few more years before it was closed by Youthstream Media Networks amid reported financial troubles at the parent company.

In the early days of social media, there were many newcomers that looked to build on what others had done. In the wake of the shutting down of SixDegrees, the next wave of social networking companies kicked off with the launch of Friendster in 2002, followed closely by MySpace in 2003 and Facebook in 2004. Friendster and MySpace had varying degrees of early success, but it was Facebook that ballooned into the giant it is today.

Started by Mark Zuckerberg and some of his friends while students at Harvard University, Facebook quickly grew into a household name and stomped out all competition. The site topped 2 billion monthly users and eventually went public with a stock offering that valued the company at just over $100 billion. In summer 2021, Facebook topped $1 trillion in market capitalization.

The cofounders of Facebook became billionaires many times over, and were the youngest billionaires on the Forbes rankings of the wealthiest people. But as can be expected, with massive success comes a torrent of criticism and attacks from all sides, causing its valuation to slide from its high. Facebook has been accused of being a monopoly and sued by the US government, and just about every state in the Union is claiming that the social networking giant has violated antitrust laws and should be broken up. The site also has often been hit with privacy complaints and was well known for routinely changing its settings, sometimes making users' posts public rather than private, as some thought.

More recent attacks have focused on Facebook's not regulating political messaging and permitting ads that some say include false information, with both Republicans and Democrats lambasting the site and grilling Zuckerberg during congressional hearings. Despite all this, Facebook is a mountain, with everyone else looking up at it in terms of size and scope. That doesn't mean it will stay that way. In fact, polling data suggest that the demographics of Facebook users is aging, with many younger users favoring other social networking services such as Instagram, Snapchat, and TikTok.

Blog Mania and an OG Influencer

The early 2000s saw the rise of blogs. Evan Williams and Meg Hourihan started the platform Blogger in 1999, and once Google acquired it in 2003, the floodgates opened. The free service is credited with helping to bring blogging into the mainstream. A lot of big-name blogs that are recognizable today popped up during this time, like Dooce, Gawker, and the Huffington Post.

Mario Armando Lavandeira Jr., aka Perez Hilton, the controversial celebrity gossip blogger who openly admits to hurting people with some of his bad behavior early in his career, isn't shy about saying he was a pioneer. "I really am the first influencer," he says. In 2004, he started on Blogger, which eventually evolved into the searing, sparkly, very pink site PerezHilton.com. "I've been so successful, and blessed, and done so many wild and amazing, unprecedented things. . . . I opened Britney Spears Circus tour—that video montage. I was in Rihanna's S&M music video. I've been name-checked in so many songs and written about in so many books."

Hilton muses that the favorite part of his journey so far was when he was able to hire his mom and his sister to work for him: "I realized—wow, my little hobby that turned into my job is now even bigger than me. It's enabling me to support my family!"

Blogs allowed writers to escape gatekeepers by giving them a direct platform for their voice. The 2008 economic collapse left Lorraine Ladish, a writer originally from Spain, without work, without money, without a marriage—without anything. She ended up on welfare trying to take care of her small children in Sarasota, Florida. Then she stumbled into blogging. "I realized, I don't have to look for a job and I don't have to switch careers. I just have to take it online." In the beginning, she made "peanuts," but she persisted in growing her online presence. Today, Ladish makes her living as CEO/founder of Viva Fifty, a bilingual online community for women fifty and older.

So-called mommy bloggers—which today seems like a dismissively diminutive name for what they do—are real women talking about real issues pertaining to the psychological, economic, and cultural issues surrounding parenting. They have made a breakthrough in terms of blogs and subsequently on other platforms like Instagram. Brands love mommy bloggers.

Before Shanicia Boswell started Black Mom's Blog in 2015, she was a single new mom on welfare living in Atlanta, Georgia. She wanted to create a better life for herself and to carve out a niche "to show a positive representation of Black motherhood," which was missing at the time. After several months, when her number of followers rose to around 30,000, Boswell created a media kit and started pitching to thirty or forty brands per week. Her first client contacted her, offering $500 for her to post a baby carrier. After about six months of monetizing, she had made $16,000. Today, Boswell earns her living as an influencer; her many hats include speaker and writer.

Fashion is another topic that lent itself to blogging and took off. Raina Penchansky watched it happen while she was at Coach before Digital Brand Architects. There was a shift in terms of who the consumer was gravitating toward, who they were inspired by, and what their purchasing intent was. "It was really becoming less of the traditional magazines and more of, at the time, what you would consider street style bloggers."

That shift happened in every niche, in every vertical out there. From book bloggers to travel bloggers, influencing took hold in the blogosphere and fanned out to other platforms. Food bloggers started getting their own shows on traditional TV cable networks, and cookbook offers came in. Networks started turning to them as new talent.

But with another swing of the pendulum, blogging became less fashionable. Stephanie McNeal, a senior culture reporter at BuzzFeed who covers influencers and internet culture, says that when Instagram became lucrative, many influencers dropped their longer-form content. Currently, though, she is seeing people who started out as bloggers missing it and choosing to go back to their roots, where they have control over the platform. Also, she says, "A lot of journalists going to Substack has shown bloggers that they can do similar things." Substack is a platform that enables writers to get paid for newsletters via a subscription model.

Microsizing the Blog

In 2006, social media gave birth to the tweet. Jack Dorsey, Noah Glass, Biz Stone, and Evan Williams are responsible for the unique microblogging and social network site. When Twitter went public in 2013, it had around 200 million users and has since been an ongoing cultural phenomenon. Originally, users had 140 characters to express their thoughts, beliefs, opinions, and jokes—anything and everything that you would say in a blog, only microsized. Twitter increased the character restriction to 280 in 2017, giving users more space to vent. As a gold standard original, Twitter skews a bit older now.

Michael Schweiger is CEO of influencer marketing agency Central Entertainment Group (CEG), a go-to agency for reality TV stars and pop culture icons. He says his agency was among the first talent agencies to dip into the influencing industry; it started early, with platforms like MySpace and Twitter. Smaller brands came to CEG interested in making sure celebrities were mentioning their products on Twitter. Schweiger says they started off by doing casual postings on these celeb accounts—things like, "I love your brand; I use it every day." It was pretty much bare bones at the time; there was no call to action, no swipe ups. They based the pricing model on the number of followers because that was before engagement was easily measured.

Now, Schweiger says that brands have moved away from Twitter because it's more for "musings and politics." Twitter was always the digital spot to share news, discuss social issues, and get political; however, the forty-fifth president of the United States, Donald Trump, solidified Twitter as the place for politics.

Lorraine Ladish also has moved away from Twitter in favor of sites like Instagram. She remembers a few years ago hosting "Twitter parties" or "Twitter chats," which were hour-long discussions revolving around a specific topic such as parenting or a social issue, and people would use a hashtag and follow it. There was usually a host/moderator and attendees, who were often incentivized to join by sponsored giveaways. Ladish made anywhere from $1,000 to $2,000 per party. Brands measured success by how many people their hashtag reached. However, she says trends change, and brands are looking for other ways to showcase themselves now.

Instagram: It's the Photo, Stupid

There's a new king of the social networking space when it comes to a platform for brands. Instagram, a mash-up of the words "instant camera" and "telegram," was the brainchild of Kevin Systrom and Mike Krieger. The first evolution of Instagram was Burbn, an homage to Systrom's love of good whiskey and bourbon. Eventually the app got whittled down to its bare bones—photos, as well as likes and comments with sharing capability. It became Instagram, which launched in 2010 and was acquired by Facebook in 2012 for $1 billion in cash and stock. Instagram reached the milestone of 1 billion users in June 2018 and 2 billion users in December 2021.

At this time, Instagram is an influencer's paradise and is a standard go-to for brands. Brittani Louise Taylor, who got her start on YouTube, is loving Insta now. She believes that it's become "the whole beast"—an influential platform that advertisers love because they get the same return on investment, but it's a lot quicker, causing jobs to veer from YouTube to Instagram. For example, she says if someone needs to promote a product like a TV show quickly and they only have a week, it's hard to turn out an involved video on that deadline. Posting a photo or a simple video on Instagram Stories gets it done and yields the same results.

In the beginning, Instagram was simply posting a photo in a few clicks. Then in 2016, they launched the Stories feature, which allows users to share photos and videos that disappear in twenty-four hours and use fun filters just like Snapchat. They added live video that same year. In 2020, Instagram announced Reels to compete with TikTok's short video format.

Before becoming an influencer, Joey Zauzig worked in the fashion industry. He ended his nine-to-five career as a manager of the men's fashion department at Tommy Hilfiger, where he noticed a lot of the marketing budget shifting to digital. Among the first people to start using Instagram when it was new, Zauzig posted random pictures of food and friends until, using hashtags for the first time in 2016, and posting a selfie wearing a pair of round blue sunglasses. When it blew up, he figured he had a new career.

He notices that content has evolved in the platform's short history. It's not just about pretty pictures anymore. Users are demanding authenticity from their influencers. Zauzig says he went from posting daily outfits to reaching out to the LGBTQIA+ community and sharing experiences like being bullied or having skin-care problems, showing the humanity behind the picture.

Video Killed the Radio Star but Gave Influencers a Superpower

Three former PayPal employees—Chad Hurley, Steve Chen, and Jawed Karim—launched YouTube in 2005. Google bought it for $1.65 billion in 2006.

Former Groundling and OG YouTuber GloZell Green quickly tired of the late nights at comedy clubs (much like talent manager Naomi Lennon) and stumbled into blogging and then vlogging on YouTube with no idea that people were actually paying attention. She describes it this way: "The outside world had no clue what the internet was. So you have this subculture—this little group that loved you, and you're kind of famous in your own little world. But other people are like, what are you doing? And how are you making a living? What are you doing in your room talking to yourself all the time? . . . It was this bizarre, underground world to people."

She clearly remembers the first $10 she made on YouTube. She was used to getting a tangible check in her hand from other jobs, but here, all she had to do was click. "I'm not sure about this. I'm not trying to get arrested for something that's shady. I don't understand what's going on," she thought. But when $10 started coming in every day and no one came to arrest her, she figured it was all OK. Not only was it OK—it launched her into a new world, one where she had a much higher profile, with millions of people knowing who she was, including some pretty powerful ones.

In 2012, Green gulped down a ladle of cinnamon as part of a challenge, then blew up with over 58 million views—something bittersweet, as she still has medical issues from accepting that challenge. But it was in 2015 that Green did her famous interview with Barack Obama. Green credits that interview with helping her become legitimate in her community.

YouTube's content has gone through many different phases over the years. Sarah Penna discusses how it first started out as vlogs and talking heads; then people started innovating and getting creative with the content comedically, musically, in every way. At one point there was a British invasion, where a lot of the top YouTube talent were "cute boys from England." Then came the gurus, and of course the video gamers took over.

The rise of video game playthroughs can be at least partially attributed to a YouTube algorithm shift in 2012 to watch time, which favored longer videos. The longer eyeballs were on the screen, the higher the algorithm pushed your video, which resulted in more recommendations and views. Penna says it was frustrating and disheartening to many YouTubers she knew at the time. She said that a lot of YouTubers had the attitude that, "'It takes me three days to make a two-minute video. And I'm being punished for being super creative.' So there was a lot of disillusionment that happened at that time."

Enter Vine. Founded in 2012 by Dom Hofmann, Rus Yusupov, and Colin Kroll, the app was acquired that same year by Twitter for a reported $30 million. As opposed to YouTube's longer videos, Vine allowed users to share short six-second, looping videos. Penna believes that it came in at a pivotal moment because people who were disheartened with YouTube quickly rebuilt an audience at Vine, monetized it, and engaged with it.

Ray Ligaya, head of talent at influencer marketing agency Viral Nation, along with many others, insists that Vine changed social media. Users got even more creative with it than expected. The short time frame turned into a challenge rather than a negative. Users experimented with things like parody songs, physical comedy, song covers, stop-motion animation, dance moves like twerking, and clips pulled from movies and news, all of which contributed to the meme-ification of cultural moments. Vine also played an integral role in getting underrepresented voices heard, as many of the most active and popular Viners were from the Black community.

A whole crop of stars like Cameron Dallas, Lele Pons, DeStorm, Shawn Mendes, King Bach, and Amanda Cerny used Vine to the fullest, before the platform's demise in 2016. It's speculated that Vine's downfall was because brands did not see it as a viable option; in addition, the company proved unable to keep up with features put forward on other platforms, which caused its biggest stars to jump ship.

In swoops TikTok, which ByteDance, known as the Chinese Facebook, released in 2016. TikTok videos started at up to fifteen seconds but have grown to a limit of ten minutes in length over the years. Penna believes that TikTok has had a "renewing" effect on the digital community. TikTok took the world by storm, but then it got caught in the eye. It has faced accusations of security and privacy issues; it has also been the target of political conspiracy theorists, according to news reports.[3] Other than the security issues, Naomi Lennon believes that TikTok is not monetizing as efficiently as it should: "They've got a big following, but then they're not making the money that they could be making." She thinks that's why some TikTokers aspire to be YouTubers.

An interesting and almost full-circle dynamic has erupted between the TikTok and YouTube communities. TikTok star Isabella Avila says, "YouTubers tend to look down on TikTokers just because we're newer, but they don't realize that mainstream media looked down on YouTube in the exact same way just a couple years ago." YouTube is part of the mainstream now.

Some of the rivalry seems to come from the fact that more money and more time go into YouTube videos than TikTok videos. TikToker Kyle Hernandez says, "I have a lot of respect for YouTube creators because I know what goes into it—hours and hours of editing, hours and hours of video creation just for one video in comparison to TikTok where you pull out your phone for five minutes and you've already got brand new videos. It's two totally different areas. I respect the hustle on both ends."

One thing is certain, it's now cool in many circles to be a You-Tuber or TikToker or an influencer in general, unlike back in the day, when it was considered a geeky activity. Penna likens it to comic books back when only geeks and nerds liked them. People made fun of them for giving that stuff any attention at all. Then came the era of smash hit movies based on comics, and suddenly it was the on-trend thing to do.

"That brings a different sort of personality to the table," Penna says. Today, in the influencing world, there is a mix of character types. The cool kids are hanging out with the artists and the nerds, and video is propelling it all.

Livestreaming, with platforms like Twitch, founded in 2011, and Instagram Live, started taking off before Covid-19 hit, but it seems like the isolation during the pandemic solidified and hastened live-streaming's big present and future.

Just Audio

Clubhouse has proved that some people may not want to be seen but do want to be heard. Developed by Paul Davison and Rohan Seth, the voice-only app was reportedly valued at around $100 million in 2020. The Clubhouse experience has users enter virtual chat rooms to talk with others about anything—politics, entertainment, everyday issues—with the cameras off.

New Apps on the Block

There's a whole new generation of apps allowing influencers to gain control of their own destiny through subscription-style payment models and other forms of direct payment such as Patreon and Kajabi. In the future, there will be a continuous flow of new ways to connect and monetize, with advertisers and without, on social media. The key is pivoting as quickly as the platforms do.

Currently, platform diversification is the trend in influencing, especially with Gen Z. Stephanie McNeal says, "The newer influencers are very adapted to cross-platform stuff. So, going from TikTok, to Instagram, to Substack, to YouTube, and being able to do it all as one brand."

RISE OF THE REALITY INFLUENCER

TV reality stars are ordinary people coated in the fairy dust of fame, which gives them a certain glow and captures attention. With one foot in stardom and the other foot in the everyday world, they are making a significant impact as influencers.

Kim Kardashian and the Kar-Jenner clan are the epitome of the reality-to-influencer phenomenon. As *Keeping Up with the Kardashians'* twenty-season stint on the E! Network came to a close in 2021 before starting a new show on Hulu in 2022, the TV show aspect almost became an addendum to their massive online presence. In a 2020 interview on the Netflix series *My Guest Needs No Introduction with David Letterman,* Kim Kardashian revealed in a roundabout way that she could make more money posting something on social media than she made doing a whole season of KUWTK. The most common figure bandied about in the media is that she commands around $1,000,000 per post.

It's no surprise, then, that she told Steve Forbes at the 2017 Forbes Women's Summit that social media is "the most amazing tool that's been invented to help brands." Kim, as well as her sisters Khloé, Kourtney, Kendall, and, most of all, Kylie, are a study in influencer ingenuity and digital marketing genius. They show how reality TV stars can translate their TV audience into digital influence.

Michael Schweiger and CEG have been involved with representing the talent from a huge slate of reality TV shows, from Bachelor Nation to the Housewives franchise. He says that when talent started seeing the Kardashians making so much money and then people coming out of nowhere, going viral and getting rich, their antennas went up for influencing.

Paul Desisto, founder of Paul Desisto Talent Management, was there at the beginning as the reality revolution moved online. Just out of college, Desisto was a popular DJ performing in Las Vegas, Atlantic City, and Miami, and playing on stage with popular electronic dance music DJs at the time like Avicii and Steve Aoki. He credits this with helping him learn the entertainment business at a young age.

Around 2011–12, top DJs charged up to six figures for a couple of hours at a nightclub or a concert, which caused a lot of venues to start looking for other ways to pack in their target audience: millennial women. Desisto says, "A lot of times in business, you want to work with the nonobvious choice. At the time, everyone was going after one solution when you had to be creative."

Using Facebook and Instagram keyed him into the YouTubers and reality stars people were posting and talking about. This in turn led him to CEG, which at the time specialized in reality star/pop icon personal appearances. Desisto identifies 2014 as the time the business model shifted as Instagram's popularity grew and the direct-to-consumer model came on aggressively. To get the word out, the small to midsize direct-to-consumer brands had to do something different. They had to veer.

Managers and agents started to recognize that the fan base for reality TV stars and pop culture icons is made up of great customers with incredible purchasing power. They're usually affluent women aged twenty-five to thirty-five—an audience that brands want. Desisto collaborated with a group of entrepreneurs, many on the Forbes "30 Under 30" list, who were his friends and business associates, to capitalize on the reality TV money machine. He worked with brands like Pura Vida, HelloFresh, and SmileDirectClub, and he did one of the first paid post activations on Instagram for FabFitFun. The combo of direct-to-consumer and well-known influencers seemed to blow up overnight. Desisto estimates that he's done between $100 million to $200 million worth of influencer deals.

Now in his thirties, Desisto acknowledges the importance of what he learned at twenty-two. He says that the music industry/entertainment business is a closed political circle: "It's a small group of people that control so much power and what becomes popular. It's really hard for independent people to break into that political world. And it's the same thing with direct-to-consumer brands. You have to know and work with the right people. . . . We all sit together, and they share trade secrets, because they're not competitive companies. They tend to use a lot of the same parties for their marketing and strategies, so to speak, because they're friends too."

However, today, it is harder to mimic that particular level of success. Desisto believes that the barrier to entry is significantly tougher because Instagram is a lot busier now than a few years ago, when there were far fewer companies using it. But even though the boom of the nascent stage has waned, the industry still thrives, particularly as traditional brands continue to enter the space.

A NEW ECONOMY

Sarah Penna smiles in full self-awareness that she's waxing nostalgic as she looks back: "It was so much more innocent and [now you have] all these kids running around like Jake and Logan Paul causing problems and being gross. It makes me sad."

For those wildly popular YouTubers, innocent days are long gone, with both brothers caught up in controversy. Older brother Logan posted the body of a man who hanged himself from a tree in the "Japanese Suicide Forest," while Jake Paul was accused of looting during social justice protests and using age-inappropriate material as clickbait.

Along with the sweet times at the beginning, Penna also acknowledges the bitter dramas and rivalries that inevitably existed, like the one she cites Phil DeFranco as having with Maker Studios. However, she qualifies it by saying, "It wasn't like the scandals that we see today in the YouTube and TikTok space."

Undoubtedly the kids running around during that time not only changed the arts and entertainment industry but also changed the cultural landscape nationally and internationally. Every day, the industry is changing the life of individual influencers. Of course, there are the superstars—the Kylie Jenners of the world, or athletes like Cristiano Ronaldo, with hundreds of millions of followers, which in turn helps them command millions of dollars. But then there are the everyday influencers.

Mae Karwowski says that the industry "created an economy for people who are creative and didn't really have an outlet or access to anyone who could get them on a TV show or something like a mainstream channel." She wonders what some people would be doing now if it weren't for influencing. As an example, she mentions an influencer who was a server at a chain restaurant and is now making $3 million a year doing DIY videos. The influencing industry has become a major force in the economy that benefits independent-minded creatives.

3

RISE OF AN INDUSTRY

At the beginning of her influencing career, fashion influencer Kristina Zias was content to negotiate her own rates with brands, and she was good at it. "I would hear certain rates and numbers that other friends were getting in deals, but I was securing bigger ones for myself," she says. But then Zias realized that time is money, and that there was value in having help through outsourcing. After making the decision to grow her team, hiring a manager was the first step.

With the proliferation of influencers and the brands that want to work with them, a need was created. There has been an explosion of influencer marketing agencies to meet that need. In this chapter, we look at the role of agencies, agents/managers, and PR professionals and their relationships with influencers and brands.

WHO ARE THE PLAYERS?

Jacques Bastien, cofounder of Shade, an influencer marketing agency that represents Black and Brown influencers, says there are many different players in influencer marketing, but the top three are influencer marketing platforms, management/talent agencies, and influencer marketing agencies.

Influencer marketing platforms offer a more automated approach that allows brands to manage a small campaign on their own in house. The software used by influencer marketing platforms helps brands find influencers for their campaigns. Bastien says it's a model that focuses more on quantity than quality.

Then there are talent managers and talent agencies. The distinction between manager and agent is that a manager provides career guidance for their clients and tends to be more personally involved with them, whereas agents tend to do the bulk of legal negotiations and contracts for clients. Because of the higher level of involvement required, managers tend to take on fewer clients than agents. Bastien says that agents and managers are the people you go to for quality, not quantity; their goal is to get their talent as much money as possible.

The third player is the influencer marketing agency, which is a blend of the previous two. Agencies merge software and technology with a personal touch, and they want high-quality influencers.

In addition to these three, Bastien identifies other folks who also join the party, like PR agencies and advertising agencies that use influencers as part of their outreach for campaigns.

IT STARTED WITH MCNS

Multichannel networks, or MCNs, offer influencers and creators help with things like programming, audience development, sales, and promotion. Sarah Penna defines an MCN as a "network of YouTube channels that are under one centrally controlled company with the idea that that company will be able to grow and monetize the channels better than if they were just individually managing it on their own."

Dan Weinstein is a pioneer in the industry and cofounder of MCN Studio71 in 2007, which was sold to German broadcast company ProSieben in 2015 as part of a larger $83 million deal. Currently Weinstein is a partner/cofounder at Underscore Talent, formed in 2021, a management company focused on helping talent leverage the "attention economy" to its fullest, including a gaming and esports division.

Before Weinstein moved into the digital space, he started out as a traditional manager. The transition away from the traditional occurred when he noted that representing creators/influencers was more nuanced than representing actors or comedians. He describes his observations about the creator/influencer class at the time and how the MCN came to be:

> You needed to provide them value in other ways. You needed to help them understand their audience. You needed to help them grow their reach and their audience. You needed to help them monetize their audience through other means, advertising being the primary one—brands and sponsors and all that sort of stuff. You needed to get their content in other places, so that they continue to grow the breadth of their audience and their ubiquity of content. And that required a lot of infrastructure to do that appropriately, and an infrastructure that wasn't necessarily revenue generating. It was all in service of the talent. And so, at the same time, YouTube was starting to roll out this concept of an MCN, an entity that was given the rights to communicate to YouTube on behalf of the talent, and somebody that was helping this creator class better execute on YouTube, which they were not capable of doing themselves at that time. And so we were sort of told to become an MCN. This is around the time when the Partner Program was launching, and creators could start to share in the ad revenue of the platform. Maker [Studios] and Fullscreen were just starting to get up and going, and there was a lot of momentum in the VC tech world around YouTube in general, but around content creation, social video, and this concept of an MCN. And so we pivoted our business at the time, from being purely a management company to being an MCN. . . . That business was called Collective Digital Studio when we first became an MCN.

Later, the company got out of the traditional management business and focused on Collective Digital Studio, which became Studio71. Weinstein thinks that one of the reasons they were able to survive so long is that they were "a little smarter about it" than other MCNs. He says they never tried to grow as big as some of the others, adding, "We tried to remain focused and representing the tip of the spear of the talent and being a little bit more thoughtful about the deals that we were making. . . . We never got too far ahead of our skis."

Today, for the most part, industry professionals agree that the MCN model is a thing of the past. Penna says, "The aggregating tens of thousands of channels together model is gone. . . . I think everyone recognized the value of actually managing people and bringing them actual opportunities and growth. I think the hypothesis was correct, but it just never came to fruition." Penna adds that MCNs, in general, were not able to turn the large collection of channels into more money for influencers than they could get on their own from YouTube, and it was hard for the MCNs to focus on so many influencer channels in a way that helped them all maximize their revenue potential. "Let's say you're an AwesomenessTV and you have 90,000 channels; you've got fifteen that you're really paying attention to and monetizing. . . . I felt bad for the creators who signed into MCNs thinking they were gonna make more money, and they didn't."

In 2014, Big Frame was acquired by AwesomenessTV, the digital media arm of DreamWorks Animation, for $15 million. To put that into perspective, around the same time, Disney acquired Maker Studios in a $500 million–plus deal.

Naomi Lennon, who started out as a traditional manager, believes there's an inherent conflict of interest built into the MCN model. She says, "I've come from talent management, where the whole point of being a manager is to represent the interests of my clients. The issue was that MCNs were saying that they were managing them. However, they were really looking at the profits of the company, whereas I was at odds with them, because I looked at the bottom line for each of my clients. So there [were] a lot of instances where I would go head-to-head with them. And there was a lot of conflict. It was highly competitive."

COMING TO THE PARTY

Lennon saw the big agencies like Creative Artists Agency (CAA), United Talent Agency, and WME starting to look at digital talent in the beginning. But the giants wade in slowly when it comes to changing a business model. Lennon says it wasn't easy for them: "I remember when they first started to get into it, they also were quite shocked, because they were trying to sign a lot of my clients and weren't able to take them and get the foothold that they thought that they were going to have. . . . It was definitely very different than anything that was happening in Hollywood in many ways. It started to break down the fabric of all of those [top talent agencies]."

Lennon recalls hearing conversations among CEOs and other higher-ups downplaying the significance of YouTube, saying things like, "At the end of the day, they all want to go to TV and movies, so when they are ready to transition, they're just going to automatically come to us." It took awhile for traditional agencies to figure out how to work within a new framework where the clients had a strong vision and more control over their own destiny.

Sarah Penna believes that the large agencies were smart to look before leaping. She says that while CAA took their time getting in, it was one of the first talent agencies to do so:

I think they were right in taking their time and jumping into it because the revenue streams are (A) much more complicated and (B), frankly, lower than if you rep a top actor, and complicated because by the time you're ready to sign with an agency, you're a big YouTube channel. You've probably grown mostly by yourself

... and your biggest revenue stream was probably your AdSense [Google's program for sharing ad revenue with influencers]. So as an agency, you have to say, "Are we going to go and take a percentage of that AdSense revenue?" Frankly, we didn't have anything to do with it and it was existing before we came onto the scene, or are we going to take a flyer on that and hope that we can monetize them in other ways? So it is a little complicated.

When they eventually did get into it, there was reportedly friction because clear roles weren't yet established. Penna says, "They were out there trying to sell brand deals, but that's our bread and butter. That's how we keep the lights on. So there was a time when we had to get into some hard conversations with agencies about what we wanted them to do."

Now all the big players have jumped in, with thriving digital agencies that are able to offer things like podcasts and merchandising. Not only are they full-service agencies, but they also have separate production entities like Endeavor Content, one of the oldest and largest agency-affiliated studios.

A CLOSER LOOK AT AN INFLUENCER MARKETING AGENCY

As of 2020, there were 1,360 influencer marketing agencies and platforms around the globe.[1] Here's a closer look at what it means to be a successful influencer marketing agency.

The idea for Viral Nation began to take shape as former university classmates Joe Gagliese and Mat Micheli got into the athlete influencer space, signing a couple of NHL players and a few other athletes. Then they ran into a roadblock. Athletes made too much money for where the social media market was at the time. Gagliese, co-CEO of Viral Nation, says, "Even if we could get an athlete a social deal, it wasn't enticing enough to get them to dedicate their time to it." That's when they started looking at noncelebrity, everyday influencers, who at the time weren't nearly as big a deal as they are today. Gagliese and Micheli are just one example of the historical move from repping expensive and hard-to-obtain athletes and celebrities to everyday influencers. At that time, it was radical positioning, something way out of the norm.

They recognized that these everyday, regular people had the ability to persuade their own audiences, and they believed that if brands were so heavily invested in traditional places where audiences live, like TV, magazines, and billboards, why wouldn't they be interested in large audience opportunities like influencer marketing? It turns out that Forbes "30 Under 30" winners Gagliese and Micheli were spot on, and in founding Viral Nation in 2014, they hit a "gold mine in terms of an industry and have been building on it ever since."

So what does a modern, global influencer marketing agency look like? Viral Nation, which is headquartered in Toronto, Canada, runs influencer campaigns across North America and everywhere from South America to Dubai to China. At the time of the interview, they had successfully run campaigns in the $6 million to $10 million range. They also have breadth, using influencers from the macro to nano levels, reaching across verticals like gaming and beauty, and reaching across platforms. They've run campaigns for brands as diverse as Match.com and Disney, with about 110 employees around the globe.

Something else that's changed from the earliest days of influencer marketing is the tech. Every influencer marketing agency out there is trying to find a way to put out the best numbers. At today's scale, it's not enough to tell brands that the post got a lot of views. Gagliese says that new tech and partnerships with social platforms "enable us to deliver analytics and reporting to companies at a standard at which they're used to for their other forms of marketing." For example, Viral Nation has licenses with platforms to deliver their back-end data, which means a platform like YouTube gives Viral Nation all the data on an influencer's video so the influencer doesn't have to. The data go deep—deeper than views, likes, and shares. The information includes analytics like where viewers watched it, what sort of device they used for viewing, and how long they watched. Gagliese believes that this is the way you "increase trust and eventually budgets since some brands are still in the discovery phase" of this type of marketing.

Several years ago, looking toward the future, Gagliese and Micheli wanted to position Viral Nation as the "new modern full-service agency." Now they have a content production company, which allows them to do everything from TV commercials to social content. They also have developed a "full media division out of San Francisco that can run all forms of paid media performance marketing. We have a head of strategy and strategists who were able to build brands." They have a department that specializes in brands wanting to connect with businesses rather than consumers; this department is able to handle all aspects of the campaign, from hiring influencers to the creative aspects. Viral Nation also owns Viral Nation Talent, which represents hundreds of influencers.

Gagliese believes that one of the biggest differentiators of influencer marketing from other forms of marketing is managing the personalities of so many people involved in each campaign: "Unlike other forms of marketing, it's truly people management at scale." Some of their campaigns have up to 1,500 influencers who need to be corralled and directed.

Looking at the rise of influencer marketing companies that coincides with the rise of influencers, there's a sort of chicken-and-egg scenario; the more influencers flood the field, the more agencies pop up, and the more agencies pop up, the more they drive the industry.

PR AT A NEW LEVEL

In 2008, Liza Anderson founded Anderson Group Public Relations, a thriving celebrity and entertainment PR agency. A few years into it, she noticed a shift. She remembers one particular incident that solidified the status of social media in her mind. A manager came to Anderson wanting to mainstream a couple he represented. The couple was Alexis Ren and Jay Alvarrez (who have since broken up), a stunning pair who posted photos of themselves on Instagram doing things like jumping out of airplanes and hot air ballooning in exotic places around the world. They were a social media sensation followed by millions, but they weren't googleable. This meant that the only things that came up on Google searches of their names were their social media, like their LinkedIn profiles.

Anderson and her team worked with the pair to increase their visibility by finding opportunities in mainstream print media and on talk shows. She says, "One thing set off the other. The PR set off the social media; the social media fed off the PR, and I was like, 'Oh, we're onto something.' I mean, they already knew they were onto something, jetting around the world, getting everything paid for, living a beautiful lifestyle. This brings PR to a whole new level. . . . And from there it just exploded."

Today, as a representative, there's a much bigger talent pool to choose from. Anderson calls influencers today's modern movie stars because they have a bigger audience than most people do on TV, and they have bigger box office draw than a lot of movies coming out, with the exception of blockbusters based on properties owned by Marvel and DC Comics.

Anderson enjoys working with both influencers and actors, but she recognizes that they're coming at it from different angles, with influencers more often approaching things from a business point of view and seeing opportunities to monetize, whereas actors "have people to do that for them."

When it comes to PR, influencers have flipped the entire script, not just changed a line or two. Anderson uses the examples of Jessica Alba and Gwyneth Paltrow. Both were already famous when they started, respectively, the Honest Company (a natural baby and beauty company) and Goop (a wellness and lifestyle brand). In contrast, influencers usually start their companies first; then publicists come in and help them get famous.

Still, some influencers approach PR with reluctance. Anderson says that there may be a certain element of, "'I don't necessarily need the fame and the paparazzi and the red carpets.' I think young influencers today are very focused on their following and having loyal followers and followers that are engaged in parts of their lives, so the excess or the outside doesn't necessarily make a difference, which I think is what a lot of their reps are saying." Press and social media work well together, but it depends on the ambitions and goals of the influencer as to whether or not they choose to take advantage of PR.

DIGITAL MARKETING AND PRODUCTION

Laura Vogel, founder of Winged Pup Productions, is a digital marketer and producer. She describes her job as being in the middle of a spectrum, with advertising on one side and PR on the other. The advertising side is "buy this thing," whereas the PR side is "I'm gonna come on this television show and talk about this thing that I'm doing. And if you want to buy it, here it is." Digital marketing meets in the middle. It's direct to fans, so there is no filter for the marketing. When PR people pitch a story, they have to go through the press; they don't control the story, because the morning show or the magazine tells it. With digital marketing, people get to tell whatever story they want, but it's not solely sales related, like advertising is.

Vogel gives the example of well-known fashion designer Isaac Mizrahi: "I produce his YouTube channel, and every single week we post a new video, and very often those videos are just entertaining, and the idea is to build his brand as an entertainer over time because he was in fashion for so long. But his real passion is entertaining in terms of comedy, song, storytelling. He is an incredibly gifted musician and singer. And that's what he wants to focus on now. So telling that story and showing people that he has those skills. Now, sometimes that also means selling tickets to a show and talking about his book that came out. But it's much more like, let's build a brand and let's create content over a long period of time."

Vogel works on long-term strategies to help clients reach their goals, as well as day-to-day strategies regarding what should be posted and where. For example, she chooses different topic umbrellas and decides whether long- or short-form video is the best fit. Her first step is helping the influencer answer the questions "who am I?" and "what is my brand?" A concrete brand book, including things like preferred colors and a logo, is useful when it comes to articulating concepts on a website. Then enter platforms like Instagram, Facebook, and Twitter. Vogel comes up with a strategy for each platform and creates posting-schedule guidelines. She also produces content, so she runs photos and video shoots, creates graphics packages, and writes copy.

Vogel says, "I help the influencer or celebrity put out what they want to say and what they need to say in the best way possible. But I'm not creating them. I'm not creating a false person. They are who they are, and then I'm going to help them articulate that online. So ghostwriting doesn't really work because the whole reason why social media works is because it's authentic. That doesn't mean it's not considered or managed."

For instance, Vogel works alongside powerhouse PR person Jill Fritzo and has helped run social media for Bethenny Frankel, entrepreneur and former star of *The Real Housewives of New York City*. Vogel says, "I can help a celebrity or an influencer or whoever it might be, make content that they're passionate about for an audience that is interested and content that is positive, constructive, informative, and useful, and that contributes something rather than is narcissistic or selfish, and takes something away. So, for example, if somebody else posts a selfie and it's like, 'just me today,' that's not useful, interesting, [or] engaging, and it achieves nothing. But if I'm Bethenny Frankel, and I'm posting a no-makeup selfie, and I'm talking about how this is me just as much as it's me when I have a bunch of makeup on and how it's important to me to show my daughter that it's OK to be confident in any iteration of who you are, that's really positive. And that's valuable."

IS MANAGEMENT A MUST?

Many of the influencers we talked with for the book told us that doing it on your own is still a viable option; they like the fact that they are in an industry where this kind of independence is possible. However, as influencers build their business, bringing on a team seems inevitable.

For every influencer, weeding out the unscrupulous and settling on the legitimate is a challenge—the most prolific stories being about unethical industry professionals who misrepresent fees, skim off the top, and in general exploit their clients and take more than their fair share. Running into unethical practices can happen at every stage of an influencer's career, but they are an even greater threat when someone is willing to risk it all for the promise of growth. Vigilance and due diligence are a must when bringing together the best team possible.

4

BEING THE BRAND AND THE
HOTNESS OF AUTHENTICITY

In influencing, authenticity is everything. Raina Penchansky is adamant about it in terms of the success of a post. "If you can see the strings and it feels forced, generally, it pretty much fails, no matter what," she emphasizes.

For most successful influencers and creators, the word "authenticity" is always on the tip of their tongues. They know it's what brands want—and what fans want. TikTok superstar Charli D'Amelio, who at age sixteen surpassed 100 million followers, said in a 2021 *Tonight Show Starring Jimmy Fallon* interview on NBC, "You have to be as authentic as you can be 'cause people can tell when you are not being as authentic, and they don't resonate with that as much."

As influencers work toward building themselves as a brand, how does authenticity fit in? This chapter is about the process influencers go through to develop their brand—and the psychologically healthy and unhealthy ways of doing it.

WHAT'S MY BRAND?

In the world of athlete influencing, developing a brand is often an explicit focus, so we want to begin by delving into that world as we explore personal branding.

At spring training in Arizona with the Major League Baseball Players Association, Blake Lawrence, CEO/cofounder of Opendorse, which specializes in athlete influencer marketing, spoke to a room of players about what it means to be a brand. One of the players in the room was Trevor Bauer, who is highly followed on social media, but also a highly polarizing player. Lawrence posed a question to the room: "If you went to Trevor Bauer's Instagram channel right now, what would you see?"

A player in the room answered: "He's gonna be saying something controversial about the Major League Baseball commissioner. He's gonna have a video talking about how the Houston Astros are cheaters. He's gonna have a video breaking down the science of pitching."

The answer that player gave defines Bauer's brand. Lawrence says, "A brand is a promise, and it's what somebody expects to see the minute that they're interacting with that athlete. . . . The first three things you think about that person, that's their brand." The promise goes deep. Daniel A. Rascher, professor and director of academic programs for the sport management program at the University of San Francisco, underscores the affective part of branding. He says it's also the "emotions that somebody feels inside when they see you" that defines your brand. It's an all-encompassing experience. When it comes to a brand, the audience wants to know it and feel it.

T. Bettina Cornwell, Philip H. Knight chair holder and head of the department of marketing in the Lundquist College of Business at the University of Oregon and coauthor of *Influencer: The Science Behind Swaying Others,* says, "Some people can manage two or three topics they regularly are involved with, but most people can't skip across fifty and develop a following."

If you go to an influencer's social media platform and it feels scattered or completely counterintuitive to what people know about them, it's failed personal branding. In contrast, a platform that tells you who that person is right away, shows content revolving around a clear message, and focuses on one to three story lines has the elements of an effective personal brand.

WHAT'S MY BRAND VALUE?

Brand value is the financial worth of an influencer's personal brand. It's basically the monetary value of the influencer. For Lawrence, determining brand value is all in the numbers. It can be calculated blindfolded, without knowing who the athlete influencer is, as long as you have the right data set. He gives the example of "a football player with 100,000 followers on his channel. Their average engagement rate is 4.6 percent. Their impression to follower ratio is 82.2 percent, and the performance score when they share branded content is negative 1.12. And so, based on all these factors, we know, on looking at the last ten years of data, that this person should command around $1,218 for one tweet."

He argues that even with premium players, the social media data tell the story, and their brand value will be reflected in it. "If LeBron James says the same thing as Anthony Davis, they're both superstars, but LeBron is going to have a more impactful impression to reach ratio, or engagement rate, or total engagements, and therefore you don't even need to know if it's LeBron or Anthony Davis; you can see it in the data—this person matters to their audience at a higher degree than this person."

As adept influencers develop their brands, they pay close attention to their social media data to understand their brand value.

IS BEING THE BRAND BAD FOR MENTAL HEALTH?

Influencers are in the unique position of being the brand. It's intertwined with who they are as a person. As the prevalence and success of influencing increases, people are seeing themselves as a brand at younger and younger ages. Is developing as a brand while you're developing as a person detrimental? Not necessarily. The pros and cons have a lot to do with how someone goes about it.

Erin A. Vogel, a social psychologist and senior research associate at the University of Southern California Keck School of Medicine, says identity formation is a natural part of growing up. Much of what teenagers struggle with is how to define themselves. She brings up the interesting point that brand loyalty has always played a role in younger people's evaluations of themselves. For example, she notes, "Having a certain brand of clothing as part of their personal style can be a really important part of how they view themselves and how they want other people to view them."

For influencers, it's a similar idea, but it gets taken to the next level because social media shines a spotlight on the process. "They really are kind of seeing themselves as synonymous with that brand. And they're building their own personal brands too—how they see themselves and how they want to portray themselves. So I think that developmentally that's a normal process, but social media makes it really explicit. People are consciously thinking about their own personal brand and their relationship with existing brands."

In this normal process, here heightened by social media, Vogel sees positives and negatives. On the positive side, if social media helps younger people in their identity formation, it can be a normal, healthy thing. She qualifies this by adding, "As long as they're still able to be open to exploring different sides of themselves and different interests." For her, the trouble starts when people look solely to social media for validation of their personal brand in the form of likes and comments. If they don't get likes and comments are negative, which inevitably some will be, it can be distressing.

Again, this process isn't entirely different from how people developed before social media. Young people have always experimented with portraying themselves in different ways, looked at their peers for feedback, and sought approval. But as Vogel highlights, "social media puts numbers on that approval in a way that can be really compelling, and a driving force for a lot of people searching for that approval in the form of getting likes and comments."

Social media, influencing, and branding clearly up the stakes in terms of identity formation; in some ways, it may even accelerate it. However, by approaching the process in the right way, its damaging aspects may be mitigated and the benefits emphasized.

CREATING A PERSONAL BRAND

For Jeff Chilcoat, founder of Sterling Sports Management, helping athletes develop their brand starts with the simple process of sitting down and getting to know them. He says it's necessary to "learn about what makes them tick. Learn what's important both on and off the field or course. We want to figure out: What do you enjoy? What's important to you from a charitable standpoint? What do you want your legacy to be? And then try to figure out where you're going."

Chilcoat gives the example of one of his clients, pro golfer Stacy Lewis, who has been number one in the world twice in her sport. When Chilcoat and his team initially talked with Lewis, they found that it was important for her to leave golf in a better place for women and to elevate women's platforms, so that's the way they approached her personal brand. Chilcoat says, "We tried to put her with brands that understood that about her and would help her in that goal. So that's what we try to learn and then go out and pull that off. . . . And sometimes you can. Sometimes that athlete's profile is not large enough, or what they're really about is the same as twelve other people, and it's hard to get traction there." Then there are some that don't really want a brand; "they just want to go do their business and go home," he says.

Blake Lawrence also believes that an initial candid talk is an integral part of uncovering a person's brand identity. He advises that people envision their life as a thirty-minute documentary. Then, each week on their social channel, they should shed a little light on what they think would be a main chapter in their book. "If you had a hard upbringing, and you're thankful for your hometown community, tell people that. And if you struggled through injury in college, tell people that. If you're excited about an upcoming vacation because you never experienced that as a kid or you always had that experience as a kid, tell people that."

In essence, the influencer becomes a storyteller online. The key for many is to make sure that it's a true story.

AUTHENTICITY: THE TRUE STORY

The mantra for influencers and industry insiders is authenticity. In doing interviews for this book, we found that "authentic" wins for the word most used. But how authentic can an influencer be on social media—and is there a cost?

First and foremost, it's important to acknowledge that social media isn't the only place people try to put their best foot forward. People do it every day: at their jobs, at school, at parties, on dates. How many times has someone asked, "How are you?" and you feel like answering "Life sucks!" but find "Great!" coming out of your mouth instead. Psychiatrist Carl Jung developed a concept around this phenomenon: persona. A persona is the mask people wear in public situations in order to fit into society. It's a compromise between the true self and societal expectations, rules, and norms. Problems occur when people lose touch with their authentic selves and become all persona. Someone who morphs into their mask will be obsessed about what everyone else thinks, developing a weak, conformist personality without a true core. This is a danger for influencers whose persona is their brand.

Lisa Filipelli, partner at Select Management Group, says, "The persona that you put on the internet is so different from who you are in real life. It's curated. It's filtered. It's edited. And I think that it's hard to live an unfiltered life when your career is a picture-perfect version of who you're trying to be." When asked if she thought that anyone could be truly authentic, she replies, "No. I don't think that you can on the internet. I think that you absolutely can in real life. But I think anything that goes through a filter, or a process before posting is curated. I think you can do your best to present who you want to be. But ultimately any public presentation of you will be whatever version you want it to be."

Influencers identify their true selves with their brands to varying degrees. Some who consider themselves performers have a complete separation between themselves and the characters they play on social media. For example, Australian comedy influencer Tim Montgomery says, "The moment my social media changed from a personal experience to me playing a character, many of the cares, worries, and insecurities associated with social media disappeared."

However, for many influencers, there is a genuine, deep desire to put their authentic selves out there for the world to see. Some experts like Filipelli push back, arguing that there are limits to how authentic you can be in an online public space. The very nature of responding to feedback—changing content according to what the audience prefers—is acquiescing to what the outside world wants, not what the true self wants. This places limits on authenticity. The monetization of content, in general, places limits on authenticity.

The rub is that it is difficult to know what grabs people's interest. The marketing industry is built around making researched, educated hypotheses about what the consumer wants, but in the end, it's still a guessing game. Colin Wayne Leach, professor of psychology and Africana studies at Barnard College, Columbia University, says that people may feel pressured or pushed to do or reveal things in order to supply content that attracts attention. This in itself amps up the process and could lead influencers toward doing more and more extreme things. Then it increasingly becomes a guessing game about what will resonate with the audience, rather than about an initially honest form of self-expression that someone hopes will resonate. This can move an influencer away from authenticity and toward the "business of supplying authenticity that is by definition not authentic anymore," causing self-alienation. Leach cautions that this is a risk for anyone who is "psychologically or financially dependent on the clicks."

Does this mean that influencers are fake, or that they should forget about trying to be authentic with their audiences? Absolutely not. Blake Lawrence says that in developing a brand, ideally, "your social channels become a reflection of who you are, more than a reflection of who you think people think you should be." It can be beneficial for both marketing and personal reasons to develop a brand that is a close approximation of self.

For instance, nineteen-year-old Rave Vanias, TikToker and member of the Vault collab house, says that she is a slightly downscaled version of her brand. "I'm being a lot more extra for the camera. A lot of people have a lot more energy and are a lot more extra for the camera." Her friends, however, often tell her that she seems like the same person on and off camera.

A way of conceptualizing online authenticity is to look at it as a version of an individual's true self. Cornwell describes the personal branding process as "communicating about yourself to others. . . . Then, it's about deciding the part of you that will be the communicated part, and how close will that be to the real you?" She calls it putting up "guardrails" around the communication with followers, so that the influencer can choose their emphasis and focus of the message. How raw and real they get is up to each individual influencer.

THE COST OF FULL-FRONTAL AUTHENTICITY

Artists like Frida Kahlo, musicians like Adele, writers like Toni Morrison, and actors like Marlon Brando have always had the burden and privilege of baring their soul to their audience. They show their torment in paintings, share their stories in books, and reveal heartbreak in songs. Actors delve into their own subconscious pool of experience and emotions so that they can bring authenticity to their characters. Sometimes they put themselves at physical risk by doing dangerous stunts or gaining and losing a large amount of weight to keep things as real as possible. In some ways, it's how creatives earn their stripes. Authenticity gives credibility to artists and entertainers.

At a deeper level, however, authenticity allows artists and entertainers to capture what it means to be human and to foster a sense of connectedness among individuals. They want people to be able to relate to their art, and perhaps see a part of themselves in it. Authenticity adds meaning to art and entertainment, and gives the audience and the creative something more than a superficial experience. But the price is high. When artists and entertainers bare their soul, they open themselves up to be consumed as entertainment. Their hurt, joy, triumphs, and tragedy are laid out for people to judge. Some people view vulnerability as a weakness and pounce when they see it. Others think it is just a spectacle, something to consume and toss aside when finished.

The phenomenon of influencing inflates this cost to potentially toxic levels because the buffers have been taken away. Metaphors come between writers and their truth, and characters come between actors and their truth, but for many influencers, who put their life out there, it's a stark version of their raw truth on the screen. This has tangible consequences. Some influencers report that sharing special experiences during the day with their romantic partners isn't as meaningful for them or their partners after they've already tweeted it, vlogged it, and/or posted an image of it. Intimacy involves openness, vulnerability, and privacy. Sharing so much with the world can take away from the closeness of friends and partners.

Another major issue with the lack of a buffer is that judgment from followers cuts deep. They're not attacking and ridiculing a fake character; they're attacking you—your lifestyle, your personality, your essence. It's a game with high psychological stakes.

CHOOSING WHAT TO SHARE

For influencers, deciding how much of themselves to put out there can be a struggle. Vulnerability and openness are often rewarded with high audience engagement but can push influencers to go further with divulging their personal life. Often when an influencer is young or just starting out, the choice of what to put out there is less of a deliberate, conscious one and more of a feels-right-at-the-moment decision.

Aysha Harun is a twentysomething Ethiopian Canadian and Muslim influencer living in LA. Her brand encompasses beauty, lifestyle, fashion, and modesty. In 2011, when she started her YouTube channel, she was sixteen years old. A few years ago, Harun went through a public divorce—public because her audience got to know her ex through her channel. She says, "Trying to figure out how much I was going to say and how much I wanted to keep private was a challenge. It's opened my eyes to how much I truly have shared over the years and whether or not I want to scale back on that because I share, probably 70 percent of my life on the internet, so there's very little that people don't know about me, which is a good and bad thing."

Harun feels conflicted and stuck in a paradox about how much of herself she wants to share. She credits being on social media with making her more open and vulnerable; she's happy with those changes. Sharing successes, failures, and struggles connects her with her community. "It's almost like a friendship at this point. I see the same people that have been commenting for five plus years and I think of them as my friends, and I'm sure they think of me as someone they know in their personal life too even though in the end, we are strangers, but I think that's the beautiful thing about the internet."

She also thinks that going through the divorce publicly was a big part of her healing process. The audience sensed this. "Sharing that so publicly and allowing people to relate to my content in such an intimate way, I think really helped build an even stronger community. . . . And that means a lot to me as a creator because I'm always looking for new ways to just connect with my audience and build on my content and make it better and better." During her divorce, many of her followers commented that this was some of the best content they'd seen from her in years.

Even with all this positive reinforcement, Harun is thinking about keeping intimate relationships to herself in the future; she mulls over the possibility of pulling back a little. "It's important to have a strong boundary between your personal life and your public life. And I think I'm learning that and I'm growing into that. . . . Moving forward as I get older, there's obviously going to be a lot more that I go through, and it probably would be best to just keep that to myself, but I don't know, honestly. I kind of just go with whatever feels right in the moment, so I could be saying this now and then feel a completely different way another time."

For some, like Bachelor Nation's Ashley Iaconetti Haibon, aka Ashley I, the boundaries are more delineated. She will not post about sex with husband, Jared Haibon, also from Bachelor Nation. "I don't really talk about our sex life. I'm not really open about that—even on my podcast where we talk about stuff like that. I'll be way more vague in those kinds of conversations. That doesn't mean that I won't talk fertility and trying to get pregnant and female issues. . . . As far as relationship issues, I'm pretty open about that, too. But that's probably because we don't really have any!"

In terms of setting boundaries about what gets posted and what doesn't, Iaconetti Haibon and her husband have less of an agreement about what to share and more case-by-case conversations. "If there's anything that I'm going to post that is maybe like a little bit risqué or edgy, I just say, 'what do you think about this?'"

Influencer and activist Kim Guerra also checks with her partner about posting, but that doesn't mean the boundaries don't get violated once in a while. She recalls an incident when she filmed a pillow fight for TikTok with her girlfriend, who wasn't happy to have it subsequently posted. Her girlfriend thought it was too intimate to be shared. Each person has their own comfort level, and this situation helped Guerra learn more about her girlfriend's red lines.

Because Guerra has a master's degree in marriage and family therapy, she has expertise in setting boundaries with her audience. She says, "There are times where people do ask very personal questions or want to know a little more than I'm willing to share. And in those moments, I tell them 'you can ask me whatever you want, but I can also refuse to answer whatever I want.' It's a tone around, I'm inviting you to share some of my life, but also, I will hold off if I feel it's not appropriate, or if I'm not ready, or with something that I'm still working through."

Guerra invites her followers into her life in one of her poetic earlier posts: "I'm going to share little bits of writing here and there—little puzzle pieces of myself floating like messages and glass bottles on this ocean of social media. Feel free to pass them along."

KEEPING THEM HONEST

If influencers get too wrapped up in their persona or brand, external checks and balances help counter it. Followers, family members, and teammates all play a role in helping influencers keep it real—as long as the influencer chooses to see the signs.

Signs from Followers

When asked how she defines her brand, Mary Fitzgerald, a star of the Netflix reality TV series *Selling Sunset,* says she thinks of herself as a Realtor, but because of the show she adds "girl next door" to her definition. Thinking further about her brand, she notes, "It is grounded. Just simple. I don't really do anything over the top or flashy. I'm not too glamorous—I mean, I'm middle-aged."

The type of social media posts that do well for her are most often the ones with her handsome French husband and castmate Romain Bonnet; the ones with her other castmates from the show like Amanza Smith and Chrishell Stause; and anything where she is being authentic, just showing what she does in her everyday life. "If I do anything too staged, my fans don't seem to like it. I actually had a phone call with my team the other day, and it's so weird, because what works for some people doesn't work for me. People don't want to see me just straight promoting a product. They don't want to see me doing something very staged. They want to see me in my natural environment in my life, just being authentic, almost as if they're still watching the show," she says.

Insiders have told her that the difference between actors and reality stars is that people feel like they actually know reality stars. They seem more approachable. Also, fans are "more likely to actually get mad at you if they see you post something where they don't feel like that is who they know. They almost get hurt or mad," Fitzgerald says.

Fitzgerald paid attention to the signs and changed the way she promotes brands because of it. Now she needs to see the details and approve the campaign before she agrees to anything, and it has to be more than just reading stale lines. "I'm not gonna read a script because it's not going to do well. No one's gonna like it. It's not going to sell. That's just not me. That's not what my viewers want to see, so they're just going to swipe right past it."

By refusing to do inauthentic promotions, Fitzgerald avoids the type of comments that included people asking her why she would do something like that because it's staged and obviously paid or faked. She says, "I don't want to do that to the people that are following me for liking me."

Fitzgerald has learned a lot by trial and error; she now asks people what they would like to see from her. Stuff about the show? Her daily life? Homes? Products? She also found a way to tap into the market more organically. She says her followers are always asking her about products she uses to make her skin glow and what kind of lip color she wears. "Certain things like that, they want to know and they buy it," she says. This helps inform her content-creation choices.

Signs from Family

As the creator of Badass x Bonita, Kim Guerra brings forth a brand and movement centered around the Latinx community, which includes apparel emblazoned with empowering messages. She brings up the degree to which family and friends are conscious of an influencer's brand. During conversations, loved ones will point out "'That's on brand,' 'That's off brand,' or 'That could be a shirt!'" Guerra says. "Even your friends and your circle are aware of your brand and how that is part of your life, and personhood, and livelihood." However, her family also helps make sure she doesn't get lost in her brand—her brother in particular. At a premiere's after-party, fans came up to Guerra and her brother saying how much they loved her and how cool she was. In true brother form, he said, "Oh my gosh, she is not cool! She's one of the most annoying people in real life!"

Guerra, who struggles with the perfect image some followers have of her, actually embraced what her brother told her fans. She says, "If people knew me or met me in real life, they would not think I was as cool. I'm pretty dorky and clumsy, and as my brother said, annoying, and people don't always get to experience that. . . . I challenge myself when I do lives or when I am in person at events to be extra intentional about trying to burst their bubbles." Guerra doesn't want to be idealized or put on a pedestal, and she consistently reminds her audience of that.

Signs from Teammates

Blake Lawrence argues that athlete influencers are in a great position to stick close to the truth because teammates provide checks and balances. He says the following situation will happen a lot: "A guy will post something standing in the locker room hallway, and then he walks in the locker room and half the team already has their phones out. They see it and immediately start giving them shit because that's what you do. Let's say that you get dunked on in a game, but you still win the game. After the game, the entire locker room is like, 'Dude you got dunked on,' and they just razz each other. So there's even more need to be authentic as an athlete because you have an immediate audience that's critical that you have to literally see every day."

Whether the influencer is an athlete or from another category, the key is to make sure they're not living in a bubble and allow family, friends, followers, and teammates to provide them with a little context, so they don't move further and further from the truth of who they are.

EVOLUTION OF A PERSONAL BRAND

For influencers, developing a brand isn't a static process. As they evolve, their brand evolves. An influencer who starts out as a teenager and continues into adulthood is going to mature, become interested in new things, and pass through different milestones that change their perspective. The following are stories of two influencers who have gone through in-depth changes over time that are reflected in their brands.

Brand Story: Kevin from *Bling Empire*

Kevin Kreider stars in the Netflix reality TV series *Bling Empire*, created by Jeff Jenkins, a producer of *Keeping Up with the Kardashians* on the E! Network. The show gives the audience a voyeuristic look at a tight-knit group of wealthy Asian American friends. Kreider is the handsome, middle-class model who acts as the anchoring center around which swirls the trappings of affluence.

When Kreider was three years old, a Pennsylvania couple adopted him from Seoul, Korea. "I grew up in a white family, in a white setting, and always just sticking out whether I wanted to or not. I was very much made fun of. I knew I was different because people told me I was. . . . Even my own teammates were racist toward me. And the coaches didn't really see it as racism. . . . It affected my emotional health for a long time growing up, because I always felt like I was never good enough, even if I succeeded and became whatever it is that I wanted to become. And I always felt like I had to try harder—be more than others."

In college, things improved somewhat because there was more diversity on campus. Since he hadn't really dated before, romantic relationships were new to him. "I had to learn dating skills and social skills. I didn't know what to do with girls. You can only read so much about sex and dating without actually being in it!" Kreider thinks that his insecurities led him to overcompensate with lifting and fitness. He immersed himself in it.

For a while, Kreider thought that his brand on social media revolved around health and fitness. But with some perspective, he came to realize something different. Now, he sees his brand as the "Asian American journey." He goes on to explain, "It's representing and advocating for Asian American stories. And if I want to get down level to it, it's probably the Korean adoption story, because that's who I am. So I think that's my brand. And everything that I do is toward that. . . . My agencies that I'm about to sign with were attracted to me because of my message and my purpose. . . . I've never strayed from it. I don't want to compromise it either or sell out, per se. Everything I do is towards that brand."

Brand Story: Chloe from *Siesta Key*

On the MTV reality series *Siesta Key,* Chloe Long is a center for drama and controversy among the attractive young men and women whose lives the show follows. *Siesta Key* first aired in 2017 when she was twenty-one years old. Long has always wanted to capitalize on her platform. Every season the show airs, her following grows; she sees it can be "a tool that you can use to make money and advertise for things." She debated what she should do for a long time. She thought perhaps a boutique, but she really had no idea and put it aside.

However, some clarity and focus came to her during the pandemic. "I've always struggled with anxiety. And I just saw how my anxiety was getting worse—my mental state was getting worse. And I know I can't be the only one." It made her realize she wanted to create a brand around herself and use her platform to help people, as well as benefit financially. She came up with the idea of a lifestyle blog, focusing on both mental and physical health, which she calls Concept by Chloe. It launched in August 2020, but she started to "push people to follow Concept way before it was in action."

One of the biggest tools that boosted Concept was a promotional video she did with a videographer who helped capture what Concept is all about in a video. "I posted it on my personal Instagram—I have 400,000 followers or whatever—and thankfully, I have the cast who, we are actually all very good friends, posted it on theirs as well, which combined, I believe we have close to 3 million followers," she says. Chloe defines her brand now as "powerful, meaningful, and spreading love and light."

Because Long is still growing as a person, it affects her content. She wants her audience to follow along with her journey. If Long has a bad day or a rough week, her content will reflect it. Even though she wants to deliver a positive message, it's important for her to be realistic about it. "I'm not gonna fake it. That's my strategy with my following. . . . I want to be as real and authentic as possible. . . . I think the more honest you are, the more of a connection you make with your following and the more likely they are to really stick around and stay faithful," she says.

During the pandemic, Long has also learned some lessons about authenticity in advertising. "You really have to be careful about what you're advertising about. You may be getting a check, but is that thing that you're advertising true to yourself? So I think you can see that I've made a transition in the last four or five months, where I've stopped advertising for certain things."

GIVING THE BRAND PERSONALITY

Joey Zauzig has a big brand personality. Charismatic and uplifting, with plenty of sex appeal, he adds his own unique take on men's fashion, fitness, and skin care. For him, giving a brand personality means being truly yourself, and if you don't mesh the two, you're not going to be successful in the long term, period. "Some people think they can keep it separate, but you can't. It's your brand. If you want it to be long term, it's all in," he argues. Zauzig isn't alone. Many influencers feel the same way.

However, although most people in the industry advocate authenticity, they also advise tapping the brakes sometimes. Particularly for younger influencers, managers like Naomi Lennon advise clients to pause before they leap. "I do think about how they're going to feel about things in a few years. They're putting so much of themselves out there, and they don't even know who they are yet. And they're being put down. They're online making content and having people judge them."

Lennon coaches her clients to make a plan rather than being purely instinctual and going moment by moment. "I talk to them about the future as adults. And what that means and try to put things into perspective for them. Because obviously when you're younger, it's not even possible for you to imagine yourself five years older. So I'm always trying to help them. When you're twenty-five, when you're thirty, who do you want to be? Where do you want to be? . . . They're all very free. They're all spending a lot of time with each other. And I don't know if they always have the best people around them. So I do what I can do to be there. And listen, I always tell them my honest opinion—sometimes they don't want to hear it."

THE FIGHT FOR RELEVANCE
AND SECRETS TO SUCCESS

The word "relevant" flows like water when you're around influencers because it's the way they sustain life online. During Whitney Cummings's podcast *Good for You* in 2020, star YouTuber and former Viner Amanda Cerny warns, "the faster you climb, the faster you could lose your relevancy," urging influencers to work hard and use going viral as a stepping-stone rather than a destination. Without developing a solid connection with followers, an influencer's career can be short-lived; it can spiral out of control without warning if the signs are ignored.

The anxiety of keeping current and staying culturally significant is unique to the influencing profession in a way that differs from other careers. Accountants, pilots, teachers, and firefighters don't need to stay in the thick of the zeitgeist to do their jobs. Relevance isn't a prerequisite for most fields. Although relevance is at the center of influencing, it doesn't guarantee a career in influencing. Lots of influencers have a good following but don't know how to monetize. Tim Karsliyev, founder of one of Instagram's first and biggest motivational accounts, Daily Dose, says, "There's a lot of young people in the industry who have millions of followers and can't even make $1." He encourages new influencers to have a plan and be proactive. "If they [brands] are not choosing you—you gotta go out there and try to get them. You gotta have some strategy. You gotta be smarter. You gotta look better."

In this chapter, we'll explore ways influencers achieve success, overcome competition, and maintain that all-important relevance.

STATUS IS THE BLUE CHECK

Twitter introduced the verification badge, also known as the blue check mark, in 2009, and it has been a status symbol ever since. The blue check means that the influencer or organization has been checked out by the platform and that they are who they say they are. Many other platforms soon followed, also adopting a check system. It helps weed out imposters and parody accounts, but as a side effect, it became a symbol of legitimacy, celebrity, influence, and success.

Chloe Long gets the blue check question often. Before Long was married, she went on a few dates with people who didn't know that she was on a TV show. She says, "I've had guys be like, 'Oh, you have a blue check?!' and then all of a sudden, they're way more interested in me. . . . I think the blue check is the first step of like, you're in the elite level of humans, which is a fucking problem."

She goes on to say that she understands the concept behind it. Long admits, "It makes me feel upset because I am totally one of those people that's like, 'I have a blue check!' And I remember the day Amanda got it. It was a congratulations thing. Literally, it was like, 'Oh my God, this is so exciting! Congratulations!' because she was one of the last ones of our cast to get it. . . . But with that being said, once you get that blue check, I do think it also helps promote when you want to promote things on Instagram to make money. . . . People will take you more seriously."

Kevin Kreider uses the blue check mark as a sorting system. He says, "With the thousands of DMs and messages I get every day, a blue checkmark will catch my eye and I'll open it because it's a valid stamp of approval of like, this person has a little bit more influence than the normal person. And so that, to me, is important to have when you get bombarded with messages." He also reiterates the status element of being verified: "It's important because it puts a stamp of approval—you're sought after. And I know it shouldn't, but it's almost like having a degree from Harvard."

To maintain exclusivity, the process for applying for the blue check is stringent, including submitting press clippings. There are media reports of illegitimate, underground, pay-to-play verification processes.[1] An influencer we interviewed told a story in line with these reports, saying they were aware of DMs sent to influencers promising verification for a fee, usually in the thousands, and that allegedly some of the people behind those DMs are working with a person on the inside.

THE COMPETITION

In any profession, chasing success leads to competition. Whether it takes the form of healthy competition or not is another question. The follower numbers are publicly displayed so influencers can see how they compare to others. Reality TV influencers know this well. Chloe Long says jealousy of people with more followers is a real thing, adding of her *Siesta Key* costar Juliette Porter's following: "Juliette, who the show is kind of centered around, has 700-plus-thousand followers. Would I, a year ago—would I be more envious of that? Yes. And that's such a problem that we care about that type of stuff."

When asked about influencing competition on the set of *Selling Sunset,* Mary Fitzgerald says, "There is a competitive nature to it. . . . I don't think that I've heard full conversations, but I have overheard, 'How many followers do you have? How many have you gained? How many does she have? I wonder why she's getting more than me?' . . . I know when Amanza first came on, she was way behind the rest of us. And she's kind of like I am, where she doesn't really care that much; besides, the more followers you have, the better your engagement, the more opportunities you get. So that's definitely a reason for her wanting to build hers. But some of the girls just want it because it shows they're the best and that they're most popular." Fitzgerald makes the distinction between career competition, which is more about trying to move ahead in the field, and competition that is spurred by unhealthy psychological characteristics.

Bachelor Nation's Ashley Iaconetti Haibon acknowledges that, just like with every industry, there is "competition and jealousy" in the influencing industry, but there is also a unique fight for relevance. She says, "Every time there's a new season [of ABC's *The Bachelor/Bachelorette*] you get worried about who's going to hit the million, or now, as social media is even more intense, 2 million. Now you're a Bachelor success if you've hit 2 million. And I think that a lot of people are like, 'OK, well, if they're going to get to that number, then why would the brands give me the deal? They're new. They're fresh. They're exciting. They're relevant. So now they're going to take my brand deals.' I think that everybody's a little worried when they see the numbers going up on new contestants."

If someone was a fly on the wall, what conversations would they hear among reality TV show influencers? If it's Ashley I and her husband, Jared Haibon, they would probably be talking about influencing with their best friends in the franchise, Jade Roper Tolbert and Tanner Tolbert. Iaconetti Haibon says, "We could talk to them about that lifestyle for hours and hours. I think you talk about what works and what doesn't. What gets the clicks? The struggle to figure out what to post when you have nothing interesting going on—like those droughts of time. How to keep the engagement up. . . . You talk a little about the competition, like who's doing well and why the heck they're doing so well? Sometimes you'll be like, 'Oh my God, that person posted boring content, and yet they're still getting so many clicks because they're so relevant.' . . . I don't like to deny jealousy. Of course there's gonna be."

Because the Haibons are established now, the competition doesn't get to them as much. However, Iaconetti Haibon admits, "I think what really stresses us out is, how long is this going to last? Can we buy a house? Can we take on that business venture? When we talk to our financial advisor, he's like, 'How long do you project this?' We think we can safely say we'll be making this kind of money for the next three years, but after that, we're totally blind. So that's stressful."

To combat this, the Haibons are always looking for ways to diversify and find other career options that they can lean on after this is over. Her master's degree in broadcasting meant that Iaconetti Haibon was able to navigate her way into being the "unofficial Bachelor reporter." Both Iaconetti Haibon and Jared Haibon also have podcasts, which keep them at the forefront. She says, "People thinking of me as a go-to source for Bachelor news has kept me more relevant than a lot of other people."

For some, money is a way to try to buy relevance and help to sustain life online. They pay for out-of-this-world photography, couture, hair and makeup, and locations—in general, a social media team. Kevin Kreider says, "For everybody I know, at least, social media is the most important thing, and they'll spend thousands and thousands of dollars on their social media. I spend like nothing. . . . I don't want to pay thousands of dollars to attract it. I want them to return for who I am because it's sustainable." Anything to get an edge on the competition!

DOES MAINSTREAM EXIST ANYMORE, AND IF SO, DO PEOPLE STILL WANT IN?

As influencers have entered the picture, the look of what is or isn't mainstream keeps changing. Traditionally, mainstream is thought of as any place that uses gatekeepers, like network TV, major film studios, popular streaming services, newspapers, magazines, and book publishing houses.

Some OG influencers like Perez Hilton swear by mainstream attention as a road to success and longevity. He says, "From the very beginning, I got mainstream media recognition and approval. If it was not for that cosign, I would have faded away. . . . I think it's fair to say the one thing that has been missing for me is a consistent and regular home on television."

Hilton believes that even with a huge number of followers on the hottest apps, if no one knows your name outside of that app, you're "doomed." He gives examples of influencers who have harnessed the power of mainstream successfully, like Charli D'Amelio:

> She will most likely have a very long career for a very long time because she has been able to get mainstream media attention in a way so that no other person on TikTok before her was able to. Before that, this other girl named Loren Gray was the most followed person on TikTok, but she never got the mainstream attention that Charli D'Amelio has, so that mainstream attention is what's going to ensure Charli's sustained success. Same with Logan Paul and Jake Paul. They've transcended YouTube and have become mainstream celebrities, whether you like them or not—and most likely you don't like them, at least Jake Paul. Logan Paul has kind of been able to mature a bit and somewhat improve his public perception. But he and his brother will most likely always be successful because they're not just YouTubers that are just popular on YouTube, or on YouTube and Instagram. They have mainstream press talk about them. And that's really the key to life.

Hilton cites his own TV appearances, books, references in popular media, and general googleability as part of the foundation that sustains his career. But as the landscape is changing, does coveting the mainstream provide the stability that influencers seek?

Looking at the direction that Dan Weinstein is taking now versus the past says a lot. Weinstein has a great sense for the influencers and content that translates into the mainstream. He talks about the early days, when the goal was to transition people off of YouTube into traditional entertainment, likening YouTube to an A&R platform. A&R, which stands for artists and repertoire, is a music industry term referring to scouting and developing talent. The thought process, according to Weinstein, was, "let's leverage the audience to make better deals or traditional" deals. So Weinstein and his team did the Breadwinners movies for Nickelodeon and the *Annoying Orange* TV show for the Cartoon Network.

Even though Weinstein ended up with a lot of wins in this area, many didn't. He attributes his success to understanding that audiences are different, and the viewing experience is different on various platforms. You can't take something from one platform and stick it on another platform without thought. He says, "The way that you would succeed is figure out what was the connective tissue? What was resonating with the audience? And then create something wholly new that leaned into the medium that you were actually playing with, not create a web show on television, create a TV show for television, but leveraging what was resonant about this over here."

Another ingredient in his secret sauce was to look for content that had a point of view, not just a personality that connects with the audience. For example, Freddie Wong created *Video Game High School,* which was a unique piece of IP that fit in with his audience and required long-form storytelling.

Nowadays, however, Weinstein's thinking has shifted. He says, "It used to be the goal was to get people off YouTube and put them on television or film. I don't think that's smart anymore—even if you can do it and do it successfully." He credits a meeting with popular YouTube host Ray William Johnson with opening his eyes. Weinstein says,

He was doing hundreds of millions of views a month. He owned it. He made it on his dime. And he was making millions of dollars. I took him into E! Networks as a piece of talent and said, "We should translate this show to television. He should be your next *Talk Soup* person—Joel McHale."

We went down that road. They liked the idea, and I got the deal back, which I would say is egregious, but it was their normal talent deal, which was, "We own the show. You get paid $20,000 a week or $25,000 a week. We get 15 percent or 20 percent of all your other business activities and . . . and . . . and . . . and."

Ray looked at me and goes, "Why would I do this? My audience isn't on E! television. I'm making four times the amount of money on YouTube. I'm my own boss. I'm creating my own content. How do we make that bigger versus going onto E! television?"

I was like, "you know, that's pretty smart."

Weinstein had a similar change of heart with Rhett James McLaughlin and Charles Lincoln "Link" Neal III, aka Rhett & Link, who created the YouTube series *Good Mythical Morning,* a talk/variety show that Weinstein thought would have a great home on someplace like MTV as a late-night show. "For years, I was like, how do we put this on television? And after a certain amount of time, I'm like, this doesn't belong on television. Why would we give this to MTV? It makes a lot of money on YouTube. We are in full control of it. We can experiment. We can do whatever we need to do with it. There are other businesses that we can build off of it. And now it's its own media company. . . . Now, that doesn't mean that Rhett and Link can't go do a TV project that makes sense for their brands, but it's got to be the right project and the right deal. And it's got to fall into a more cohesive strategy about what you, the creator, are trying to do. So to me, the goal is not, 'let's get on television.'"

Over the course of her career, Sarah Penna has seen the transition to mainstream work to varying degrees of success. She gives Philip

DeFranco, known as the Jon Stewart of YouTube, as an example of someone who knows how to stay relevant through different generations. "To me, this is a person who nailed it. He never tried to take his show to traditional media. He kept his fan base. He leveraged it for merchandise, for other shows, for podcasting, and really has maintained the core of what he did but reinvented himself many times over to great success each time," she says.

Penna has seen other examples of digital talent achieving success by leveraging their influence to launch merch like clothing and makeup lines, as opposed to diving into the mainstream pool. She argues, "These are the things to me that are much more of a long-term success marker because you still own your audience, and your revenue is recurring. . . . That's always the direction that we try to push them in. And then you can, of course, do film and TV on top of that, unless you're somebody like my husband, who was willing to say, 'End of YouTube career. End of MysteryGuitarMan. I'm willing to start from the bottom as Joe Penna, writer/director and this is my second career.' And [we] built it up from there, because his movies have very, very little resemblance to what his YouTube channel was."

Subsequently, Joe Penna has had directorial accomplishments with films like Netflix's *Stowaway* in 2021, which he also cowrote. Sarah Penna attributes some of his success to always knowing that he wanted to be a director and having a specific goal for his post-YouTube days. He didn't always know what kind of movies he would make or how exactly his career would manifest, but he had something to work toward. He started by directing commercials and music videos; sometimes he did them pro bono to get where he wanted to go.

However, for some talent, finding a place after YouTube, mainstream or otherwise, isn't easy, especially when the videos showcase their personality. Penna poses the question, "Where do you go from there? A lot of them didn't finish college. They dropped out because their YouTube channel was so successful. A lot of them were very smart and saved money, and some of them weren't. It's kind of the celebrity thing and they have to reinvent themselves. I know a lot of them have done well and gone and gotten social media jobs and have been able to phase out of the public space in a graceful way. We also have some talent that spectacularly exploded and broke down and deleted their entire YouTube channel and I never heard from them again, and I hope that they're OK."

It runs the gamut from total collapse to stardom. Penna points out talent who have crushed it over the years, including DeStorm, Hank Green, and Zach King. "I think it's a willingness to reinvent yourself and change with the times—and a desire to stomach the grind," she says.

Max Levine, cofounder of Amp Studios, attributes part of Brent Rivera's phenomenal success to keeping his brand and content close and not going too far mainstream. Levine says, "He's doubled down on his content, while everyone else is like, 'Oh, you have to get into traditional entertainment—this, that, and the other.' He has done stuff on Nickelodeon or been on a Hulu show. And funny enough, we just turned down something on Paramount+ yesterday. I'm not saying we're not going to do those things; you just have to be careful. And, I think they have to complement very well." Rivera executive produces and cohosts the Nickelodeon nighttime talk show *Group Chat* and starred in Hulu's *Light as a Feather,* a teen horror series.

Levine reiterates, "I'm not saying 'don't do that.' I'm saying . . . 'it's great if you can do that stuff, but you also have to balance it.' When we were doing this Nickelodeon show in the summer, it got to a point where we couldn't keep up our content capabilities—where we had to make sure we're hitting on our weekly YouTube video and our Instagrams and our TikToks and everything else. And we have our media company that we had to look over and the creators in it, and Brent kind of got pulled away—then everything is really affected. He owns and operates that versus being a talent on a show where you're a hired gun, in a sense. So again, you have to be careful."

Levine advises homing in on your craft and doubling down on it, but not to the exclusion of shows and other linear type of opportunities. This can be easier said than done. He warns, "You have to be careful, because when you ignore what got you there, you lose your main audience or core audience, and then it slips away after. And, if you really make it like that (1) you have, like, a 2 percent chance to make it, and (2) it has to be like, you're the star of Netflix's biggest show for it to really get to the next level, because if not, you're in danger of losing what you've worked incredibly hard to build and what is growing. . . . You're giving up what you have that is extremely valuable for the chance at something less, equal, or potentially a little bit higher, in my opinion." Still, there are agencies out there that push their successful influencers into auditioning for shows and getting into the music industry, to their detriment.

The discussion, however, still begs the question: Is there a pinpointable mainstream anymore? The answer seems to be, it's all relative. What's mainstream to one generation may not be mainstream to another. Mainstream to Gen X and baby boomers might be more linear content, while to some millennials, Gen Z, and Gen Alpha, apps are mainstream.

Weinstein thinks it's all converging, with influencers like Charli D'Amelio as relevant as celebs like Scarlett Johansson to certain demographics. And really, are the Kardashians TV stars or influencers? Is Netflix TV or digital? (He argues TV, but still.) Then there's Disney+ getting into short form. He says, "It's all getting blurred, and idea of digital versus traditional—I don't think exists anymore."

Even from a PR perspective, where the focus is mainstream media attention, the lines are blurry. PR guru Liza Anderson says, "I think if you're an influencer on TikTok and you've got 10 million followers, that's pretty mainstream, but that doesn't mean that you could google them and they've got three pages of googleable feature stories and interviews. It's a different definition of mainstream. I think that they're both right." She uses the Kardashians as an example. The reason they're so big is that they've got millions upon millions of followers, but they also appear regularly on talk shows and in magazines. Particularly if an influencer has a product to be sold, "mainstream" press can add credibility.

Ray Ligaya, a musical artist known as Mansuki in addition to his work as part of Viral Nation, calls mainstream press an extra push, noting, "It's good to have it. It's bigger, more traditional companies supporting what you do online. . . . I was talking with our PR team and we're looking to find more [mainstream] interviews. For instance, I did a CNN interview two meetings ago and they're looking to have our talent get interviewed too, and I'm like, this is great PR. This is great for our talent, and this is, to me, comparable to a brand deal. This is a big deal, to be a part of such a big network. It's very, very important. It's important because this gets you verified—having these types of traditional PR articles with these major networks will get you verified."

Influencers' relationship with the mainstream is a complicated one that is continuously morphing as the definition of mainstream shifts. Even as the target moves, influencers still covet what it has to offer.

A DASH OR TWO OF DRAMA

In summer 2021, drama surrounded the Battle of the Platforms boxing event as YouTuber Faze Jarvis accused TikToker Michael Le of trying to start a "fake beef" to promote the fight, which in the end seemed to turn into a real beef. Whether real or not, beef slinging and drama dredging feed relevance. Ligaya acknowledges, "Drama is a huge thing in this space."

Because it's not a hard road to online infamy via controversy, it's become a commodity. Lisa Filipelli says, "For some people, that controversy and chaos is a purely acceptable career path on the internet." Even though fans sometimes claim that they don't like the drama surrounding their online faves, influencers know otherwise. More than watching scandalous shows via streaming, the internet provides the audience with a way to insert themselves into some seemingly harmless controversy at a time when their own real life may seem lackluster. Unfortunately, all too often, it's not harmless.

Rave Vanias of the Vault collab house says of fans, "They love drama. That's what they feed off of. Literally, there's TikTok pages that just post things about our drama and have millions of followers and get so many likes, because people like drama. . . . So I think some people, to get more relevant or to get some sort of temporary spotlight kind of thing—you know, five minutes of fame—they start things for drama."

Nobody knows this better than Perez Hilton. He argues, "Shocking people and scandal—that's tried, true, and tested. It works so well. . . . I love stirring the pot, and you can stir the pot and not be nasty or evil or rude or mean." One way he stirred the pot was by starting a beef several years ago with Charli D'Amelio in which he commented on one of her TikTok dance videos, writing, "Anyone else think it's inappropriate for a fifteen-year-old to dance to this?" D'Amelio replied with, "i'm sorry i'm just trying to have fun! :)."[2] In the video, she dances in a bikini to a remix of "Sugar" by Brockhampton, a sexually charged song. D'Amelio's fans immediately responded with outrage for what they viewed as Hilton's public shaming of a teen girl.

However, Hilton was not just unremorseful about starting the feud—he relished it. He says, "What really set it off was the fact that she saw my comment and responded to my comment. And even though my comment wasn't bad and even though her response to my comment wasn't bad either, her fans are overwhelmingly, incredibly young on that platform and very protective of her. . . . I was instantly the enemy for her fans. And it went bonkers. But I'm so thankful that their attempts at canceling me only helped me. I got so much press out of it. . . . If you google 'Perez Hilton, Charli D'Amelio,' so many people were writing about that. And there was even a petition with over 200,000 signatures, and all of that only helped drive traffic and awareness to my TikTok. It only helped me grow, and at a much faster rate than I had been growing before. So it was just a win for me. So to all of them, I say thank you."

Rey Rahimi, best known for dishing gossip on her YouTube channel Hot Tea, is also candid about the success she garnered from drama. She says unabashedly, "I gained, like, 10,000 subscribers from beef with a bigger channel. A lot of people, in order to stay relevant, they kind of need to create some sort of drama around themselves." Rahimi isn't unaware of the fact that some of the calculated controversies and hype that influencers manufacture can be unethical, as is the case when people make up stories, propagate rumors, and bully, shame, degrade, or just put others though hell for attention.

Then there's another kind of spectacle: thirst traps, which are sexually charged images posted to get attention. Hype House member Vinnie Hacker is an example of someone who got a huge boost in followers because of thirst traps; he became known pretty much for his shirtless posts. Hot, however, fades over time. To maintain relevance, there needs to be a strong foundation underneath the pretty.

LOW-KEY WAYS OF STAYING RELEVANT

The road to relevance for influencers doesn't only consist of drama and making the biggest splash. There are the things they plug away at—things that make up the daily grind. Some of those things include consistency, quality content, engagement, and diversification.

A majority of influencers and influencer marketing professionals we interviewed talked about the importance of consistency as basically a prerequisite to longevity in the industry. Underlying that kind of commitment to posting is a strong work ethic. Mae Karwowski says, "It's really hard work to be that consistent and to consistently create content and publish it and interact with your audience. . . . These influencers are posting across multiple channels, easily twenty, twenty-five times a week. If you're on TikTok, the average for an influencer is like, ten to fifteen TikToks a day. The creativity and the ability to do that work and edit that video—it's so much more than I think people really give it credit for. And then to keep that up. It's one thing to do it if you're having a great day. It's another thing if you're having a terrible day."

However, as every industry professional acknowledges, lots of posts without captivating content is a road to nowhere. From the beginning, luxury lifestyle influencer Aditi Oberoi Malhotra strategized to dependably create quality content, which got her noticed by the brands. Her pinch-me moment came when she was called in for a meeting at the offices of LVMH Moët Hennessy Louis Vuitton. Malhotra says, "In my experience, putting out good quality content and consistency is the key. It's very important to post every day so that people remember you. People look forward to looking at your content. . . . I don't want to push content just for the hell of it. I want to put out content that adds value to someone's life, even if it's one person."

Malhotra found that if she got too caught up in the numbers, like how many people followed her, it became a detriment, making it easy to lose creative control. Instead, she moved to focusing on creating trending yet original content, developing new concepts and networking with brands, peers, and followers. It's important to remember that with influencers, a post isn't just a post; it's an interaction. Posting consistently doesn't mean that you stick something up and it's done. Influencers check their comments and react to and interact with their followers.

Malhotra tries to reply back to as many comments as possible, particularly if someone asks her a question, such as a product inquiry.

She notes, "We should really appreciate that someone is taking time out to comment on our pictures. . . . Of course, when the day goes on you get busy, but at night I do read all of them and in fact, I go back and like their comments too. I also ask questions. What do you like about this picture the most? I posted five images of my outfits and I asked them, 'Which one do you see yourself wearing?' I am very interactive with my audience, even on stories I do polls all the time and ask them what kind of content they want to see because you are getting live feedback. That's the best part about this whole thing—the way it's been created—you can ask people what kind of things they want to see and what do you love the most." The point is to make the audience feel special.

Aysha Harun, also in the fashion, lifestyle, and beauty space, has a similar approach to Malhotra's. "One of the best ways to build a stronger community and a loyal following is actually replying to DMs, replying to comments on YouTube, on Instagram, and just sharing that you're also just as invested in your audience as they are in you. I think a mistake that a lot of creators make is they just stop replying to comments and stop engaging with their audience, and that's when people drop off and they don't feel as connected to your content." When Harun first posts a photo or video, she tries to take the first thirty minutes or an hour to reply to comments and DMs. Throughout the day, she does a few more, adding up to about thirty to fifty replies a day.

As influencers get more successful, responding can become rote. It can get overwhelming. BuzzFeed reporter Stephanie McNeal says, "Just responding to DMs could take five hours a day. I've interviewed someone who pays someone to work thirty hours a week for her, and her only job is responding to DMs. . . . Most big influencers will get 1,000, 2,000, 5,000 DMs a day and just going through and figuring out who to respond to—that just takes time."

When an influencer gets bigger and the hate comments grow, it can become more and more distasteful to deal with the comments, leading them to ignore their followers. Perez Hilton argues that this is a huge mistake, but one that happens fairly often. He says, "The top tier of influencers on TikTok—for the most part—a lot of them don't even engage with their audience. How dumb is that? You need to be responding to comments. You need to be liking the comments. It's your job!" He attributes the lack of response to thinking they're famous, young, and invincible, as well as trying to avoid toxic comments. For Perez, who's an OG, it's a different story—a cynical but true story. He says, "I'm a seasoned professional, and those comments don't get to me. I respond to the hate comments because I'm smart enough to know that engaging with engagement just gets you even more engagement. And sometimes engaging with hate is even smarter than engaging with a positive comment. Because engaging with a negative comment, not only will get you more hate, but then it gets your supporters supporting you as well."

Something to remember is that most influencers aren't just engaging with followers from one platform. Staying relevant means being on as many platforms as possible without spreading yourself too thin. It becomes especially important when a platform like Vine crashes and burns. The survivors are the ones who can read another platform well and know how to make the transition. Every influencer is always looking for the next big app. They are either jumping into it, or feeling like they should jump into it.

For a while, Harun was solely focusing on YouTube, but then Instagram caught everyone's attention. It became a whole other income stream for her. Now she wants to get more into TikTok. She says, "When people really enjoy a personality, they like to focus, and they like to follow them on all the different socials. So I think it's a part of staying relevant, unfortunately, but that's kind of what the internet's about. You have to stay relevant or else you might drop out of people's minds."

Tip	Rationale
Do "eye-catching" stuff in the first three seconds	When people want to see what happens next, they're more willing to watch the video.
Have a high-quality camera	Suarez believes that the algorithms favor images from high-quality phones.
Have good lighting	Suarez swears by high-quality lighting, which enhances the look of every performance.
Post frequently and consistently	In the beginning, Suarez posted five to ten times a day on TikTok and saw it start to pay off. He says, "Even though I wasn't getting as many views as I wanted, something I noticed was, I was being on people's 'For You' page very often very frequently, which was helping me to get brand deals, even at small numbers." However, as he started to figure out what does well on the algorithm, he remained consistent, but tapered off on the frequency.
Project high energy	Being high energy, or "extra," is a way Suarez and many influencers grab attention. "I was very loud and I'm also a very energized kid. I look like I'm on like five cups of caffeine every time I'm filming."

Table 1. TikTok star and influencer Joshua Suarez's tips for getting attention

THE BASICS OF GETTING ATTENTION

For TikTok star Joshua Suarez, known for comedy and prank-related videos, success online means getting back to basics. He learned a lot simply by trial and error. "I figured out how to get people's attention," he says. Table 1 lists a few things Suarez says have worked for him that are along the lines of what many other successful influencers practice.

INFLUENCER FRAUD

Bots and fake accounts are a huge issue for the business of influencing. They can derail digital marketing efforts. Influencers' buying fake followers, likes, comments, and story views has plagued influencing since its inception. Other examples of influencers distorting their metrics include following and unfollowing people automatically through apps, and using comment pods, which are groups of users who agree to systematically follow, like, and comment on each other's posts to increase engagement for everyone. In fact, 55 percent of Instagram influencers were part of some kind of social media "fraud and fakery" in 2020, which was an 8 percent decrease from 2019.[3]

If you were to audit a random person's followers, 5 to 30 percent could be bots, spam accounts, fake accounts, or inactive users; however, it doesn't necessarily mean that the user bought those followers or intended to deceive their audience.[4] It's common for social media users to be spammed, and inactive user accounts are ubiquitous.

Still, some influencers are haunted by fraud in the industry. Johnny Jet, dubbed "the original travel influencer" by *Forbes,* wonders whether his failure to play the "fake" game by purchasing followers affected his career in the beginning. "I think I hurt my career. At times, I feel like I should have done it. But in the long run, it's better [not to have done it]. It's kind of like, I'm the turtle and the other ones are the hare. I'm just slowly going." Even though Jet doesn't have the numbers that some have, he has high loyalty among his followers and has had a long career as a travel influencer. For many influencers, fakery seems like a quick fix, especially when it seems like they're lagging behind their peers. Experts advise that in the long run, an authentic influencer with an authentic audience is the legitimate path to success.

What's being done about this type of online fraud? In 2019, the New York state attorney general announced a landmark settlement with sellers of fake likes and followers on social media.[5] Attorney General

Letitia James stated, "Bots and other fake accounts have been running rampant on social media platforms, often stealing real people's identities to carry out fraud. . . . With this settlement, we are sending a clear message that anyone profiting off of deception and impersonation is breaking the law and will be held accountable." Platforms are also cracking down on fake engagement by locking users out of their accounts when they recognize fraudulent activity. Sometimes they even take legal action, such as sending cease-and-desist letters, against sellers. Jet believes, "It's definitely getting better. But it's still that way."

MONEY: THE MEASURE OF SUCCESS

The amount of money that influencers earn is like a bouncing rubber ball; it fluctuates wildly. In pop culture, people often think of influencers as being rich. For example, the average cost per post for a celebrity influencer like Dwayne "The Rock" Johnson is over $1.5 million.[6] Influencers can rake in millions. In his YouTube video, "21 YouTuber Secrets You Never Know . . . ft. Unspeakable," gamer and YouTube star Preston Blaine Arsement, aka Preston Playz, reveals that the estimated revenue for his Preston channel in July 2021 was $268,429.44. But such high figures are only valid for the top tier of influencers, which together comprise a drop in a vast, open sea.

Factors that go into determining influencer pricing include the influencer's metrics, the type of content (videos cost more than photos), and how the brand is going to use the content (How long is the campaign? Are images going to be used as ads on their websites?). Even though it's hard to pinpoint what an influencer makes because of a lack of standardization and because it's dependent on quite a few factors, in Table 2, we round up the average influencer earnings per post on a few different platforms according to Influencer Marketing Hub, which includes a "midtier" influencer category with the core four of nano, micro, macro, and mega.[7]

Platform	Influencer level	Income per post
Instagram	Nano	$10–$100
	Micro	$100–$500
	Midtier	$500–$5,000
	Macro	$5,000–$10,000
	Mega	$10,000+
YouTube	Nano	$20–$200
	Micro	$200–$1,000
	Midtier	$1,000–$10,000
	Macro	$10,000–$20,000
	Mega	$20,000+
TikTok	Nano	$5–$25
	Micro	$25–$125
	Midtier	$125–$1,250
	Macro	$1,250–$2,500
	Mega	$2,500+
Twitter	Nano	$2–$20
	Micro	$20–$100
	Midtier	$100–$1,000
	Macro	$1,000–$2,000
	Mega	$2,000+
Facebook	Nano	$25–$250
	Micro	$250–$1,250
	Midtier	$1,250–$12,500
	Macro	$12,500–$25,000
	Mega	$25,000+

Table 2. Average influencer earnings per post according to Influencer Marketing Hub

Jessy Grossman, influencer talent manager, consultant, and president/founder of Women in Influencer Marketing, says that when negotiating, a few things to factor in are payment terms, exclusivity, and usage. Many influencers forget to factor in the fact that they frequently get paid ninety days out—and sometimes the net ninety starts when the campaign is over, not necessarily when the contract is closed. It's thus important that influencers be educated about running their businesses more efficiently and accounting for that fee schedule. Influencers can run into problems when they've outlaid money for the campaign by hiring photographers or makeup artists and the like.

Exclusivity is also a huge issue in influencing, particularly with larger deals. Grossman has this to say about exclusivity: "A $100,000 deal or a half-a-million-dollar deal might sound shiny and great from the onset, just looking at a number like that. If there's exclusivity—let's say it's a beauty influencer and it's exclusivity against all makeup for the entirety of the campaign, you hope that covers more than what you made last year. . . . I'm not opposed to exclusivity. In fact, I would love to just have this category be exclusive to one brand. I never wanted my clients to be working for two competing brands. It's not a good look for anybody if they're talking about Walmart one day and Target the next day—who in a lot of people's eyes are considered competitors. But if my client is not going to be working with Target, who pays pretty well, or vice versa with Walmart, I need the other companies to be able to compensate for that. It's not just paying for that partnership. There's exclusivity involved. It's about paying and compensating for the missed work that you're going to inevitably have to turn down as well."

Usage is another important piece of the puzzle. If the content is being reused on the brand's social media, that's a given, but if it's being boosted beyond what would be organic on social media, Grossman says there's value in that, because the influencer's likeness is being used and so many eyes are seeing it. Influencers should get monetary compensation for those additional people.

Of course, all of this doesn't come until later. For most, it takes a while to be able to earn a living at influencing. Aysha Harun says, "I don't think I started making money until probably five years into it." When influencers do start making money, many don't realize that they have to reinvest in order to scale. Harun says, "I feel like I've gotten as far as I have now because I was able to invest in certain areas. For a while on YouTube I was obviously creating all of my content, but I was also editing all of my content. What I realized is, I wasn't able to post as much as I wanted to and as much as YouTube suggested, so I invested in getting an editor and all of that kind of stuff. And I thought at first it would kind of rub my audience the wrong way, but they actually really appreciate that because they get more content now. . . . I think what people aren't realizing now is how YouTube and social media and the influencing world has become its own industry, and there's thousands and thousands of people who create their own little businesses. So I think learning how to scale out and not being afraid to invest in certain aspects of your content is so important for growth and just being able to create a larger community in the future."

How much an influencer invests in creating content also fluctuates wildly. When it's a megainfluencer, like Preston Blaine Arsement, the price tag goes way up. In the same YouTuber secrets video, Arsement estimates that he spends an average of $6,000 per video.

When brands pay an influencer, they are essentially paying for services like editing, writing, styling, makeup and hair, photography, videography, set designing, modeling, performing, and so on. Many influencers think that they're not getting paid adequately for the multiple tasks they perform or hire out, especially when they're offered freebies instead of cash as payment. Curve model and fashion influencer Kristina Zias would like to see changes in the industry with regard to influencers' taking jobs for no money. She says, "I think that influencers just need to value themselves better. . . . Influencers, especially smaller ones, can really get taken advantage of when they don't know their value." Zias has learned to say no to opportunities along the way that are not advantageous, but she admits that even now, if she deems it a good opportunity, she'll take it for low pay.

Product isn't the only thing brands substitute for pay. The also use exposure as a type of compensation. Self-styled "extremely queer and incredibly trans" writer, speaker, and organizer Eli Erlick says, "I remember right after moving to New York, one of my first gigs here was with a very big makeup retailer. I think that's also the least I've ever been paid. Especially because the people they used, who were all trans, had an online presence, they felt more inclined to say that this was about exposure. I see that a lot with influencers—that we can be paid with exposure while photographers, models, or editors can't."

Saying no to a chance to work with a big brand for little or no pay is easier said than done. Many influencers are caught between the need to support themselves versus taking what they can get and maybe advancing their career.

LACHLAN ROSS POWER: A GAMING SUCCESS STORY

Esports personality Lachlan Ross Power was the first Australian gamer on YouTube to reach 10 million subscribers back in 2019. That same year, he won a Nickelodeon Kids Choice Award for best content creator from Australia/New Zealand. In 2020, the Lachlan Skin, an Icon Series Fortnite outfit, was released, which is a top-of-the-mountain honor for *Fortnite* players. Power's following and brand keeps growing globally, with viewership predominately from the United States. As of mid-2022, he had over 5 billion views and was closing in on 15 million subscribers.

Born in 1995, Power had a passion for gaming during his high school days, watching things like *Call of Duty* videos in the infancy of gaming on YouTube. In his first year of university, he started posting

Minecraft videos. He recalls, "When I was in high school, I realized after what seemed like a lot of these *Call of Duty* YouTube channels, they would openly talk about their monetization. And that was a very new thing on YouTube, especially for the gaming space to be able to monetize your content. So I knew that was possible getting into it, but I didn't really expect it to actually take off in a way that it did. And I was able to very early on kind of monetize through Minecraft servers as well. Building this very small community on my *Minecraft* experiences, and pretty much making a game within *Minecraft* and having people pay for access to stuff very early on in my career, really allowed me to grow revenue from a very small community. I think the saying out there is if you have a Twitch community or streaming community of like 100 people—100 dedicated people—you can do very well in the space. It doesn't take a lot."

But he didn't stop there. He founded the lifestyle brand and gaming organization PWR. It's a combination of competitive gaming, street wear, and entertainment. He says, "PWR did start out as an apparel line. It was originally called Power by Lachlan. And then we transformed that brand into PWR the organization back in 2020. And so that's kind of its own separate brand focusing on collaborations with certain brands, certain content creators, certain athletes."

As of 2022, the organization has about ten people on the staff side focusing on apparel, content, and creative, and about twenty professional gamers and content creators. They're constantly trialing and hiring people in new roles. What draws people to Power's content? He believes it's a combination of displaying good game play and the excitement he creates. Viewers message him saying they like his energetic personality. Power also attributes healthy viewership to quality content. He says,

> What we're doing there is we're really trying to revolutionize what group form content looks like. From a content creator perspective, obviously, on my channel, you're going to see me sometimes with

one or two other people. On the Power channel you're going to
see ten of our players, plus a few other players. Our editor has a
hard time working on these videos, because they're working with
ten to fifteen perspectives, but they come out really well because
there's just all these story lines we've woven together in a game
of *Fortnite,* and it always ends up with one winner, and they're
always a really great spectacle for the *Fortnite* scene. So those are
a little bit different. And they just supply this real unique type of
content that really isn't out there on the space, for *Fortnite* at least.

Engaging his audience as much as possible is also a priority. Power
says, "One of our focal strategies right now is specifically through
Discord. It's really this digital community that we're building—real
time digital community. The chat is real time. And we have voice chat
channels and all that stuff. But I definitely try my best to engage the
community, and the extended Fortnite community and the extended
gaming community wherever possible."

Power is optimistic about the endless possibilities in front of him
and his organization. He won't rule anything out for the future. He
wants PWR to "try and adapt" and take opportunities where they
can.

SCALING THE MOUNTAIN

The career span of an influencer sees many different milestones:
the ability to earn a living at it, or perhaps one day creating a line
of merch. Only a small percentage of influencers reach the top of
this profession, and an even smaller percentage manages to hang
on to the top. It's not easy to scale. Mae Karwowski says, "It's hard
to become a really big influencer. You have to be really smart. And
you have to have a team that's really smart. And a lot of people don't
make that transition or can't do it. They can't figure it out." When

asked if she thought most influencers last around three to five years, she responds, "I think a lot of people, they might last three to five years, but I feel like we're also minting new TikTok and Instagram celebrities every five minutes."

Max Levine shares his concerns about longevity in influencing. He says, "My whole philosophy is 95 percent, or even maybe higher, of content creators don't really last after a few years, and there's, I think, different layers of this creator economy that are bubbling up. But it's hard, and a lot of times people are doing it by themselves, or maybe they get some type of traction on their own, but they can't really sustain it, or namely, they start making money, but it burns them out." He credits being passionate about the craft, adapting, and innovating to his long-term success.

LaToya Shambo, CEO/founder of digital marketing and influencer agency Black Girl Digital, relates longevity to being strategic about delivering content and growing a brand. For her, this means paying attention to metrics and learning what the audience wants, but it also means being original, consistent, and engaging. "People want to know that you exist beyond your post," she says.

In the end, for those who want to shift from brand to business, influencing can't just be about hustle; it also has to be about planning for growth, which according to Shambo looks like getting an agent, having a plan for averaging X amount of brand deals per month, and pursuing other growth opportunities. But again, it boils down to hard work and commitment. She says, "There's nothing easy about being a great influencer. There's something easy about being a mediocre one. But if you strive for excellence, there's nothing easy about it. When I look at some people's profiles, I'm like, how are you so amazing? They're just so consistent. The quality is clean."

Whether mediocre or excellent, how long can an influencer really last? When asked, Raina Penchansky wouldn't put a number on it. She thinks about longevity from a different angle, making a distinction between using the generic term "influencer" and talking about influencers as content creators with a point of view. She asserts that it's not possible to put a "shelf life" on the latter.

NOT GETTING "LOST IN THE SAUCE"

Disability lifestyle influencer and actor Lauren "Lolo" Spencer sums up influencer longevity well by saying people make the success they want to see and boiling it down to the basics. Spencer says, "If you don't pay attention to the algorithms, if you're not paying attention to hashtags and quality of content, or even have a real purpose behind just wanting to create cute videos and cute pictures, you're going to get lost in the sauce. And acting is oversaturated, but the influencer market is ten times more oversaturated. And there's the false narrative of all you have to do is post content and you'll become successful and make money on social media. No, it's way more involved. There's a lot more work involved, and people get it misconstrued, so everyone's fighting to be successful in a way that they think is easy. But influencer culture is not easy at all."

BRANDS THAT GOT IT RIGHT

Defining Wins in Influencer Marketing

Influencer marketing is here to stay. Close to 68 percent of US marketers from companies with 100-plus employees will use it in 2021.[1] Moreover, it will represent 20 percent of US digital ad budgets in the same year, according to Business Insider. But which companies are all in, and if they are, who's doing it right? In this chapter, we'll look at the ones that got it right in terms of influencer marking, including Chipotle and FabFitFun, together with brand success secrets in the digital arena.

DIGITAL DISRUPTOR BRANDS

Even though it's not a shiny new object anymore, influencer marketing is continuing to evolve—but it hasn't necessarily been the big companies that have been defining it. In a 2020 interview, Joe Gagliese says, "It's still in the discovery phase for a lot of brands, although some have really adopted it. . . . Generally, it's just like everything, right? The big, big, big organizations are usually the last to the table and that's because they not only have the layers of that group within the organization, it's their general instinct to avoid risk. All these companies go out and figure out if this stuff's good stuff, and if it's good stuff, will it come in with a lot of money?"

Gagliese and his team talk about the brands that are willing to take the leap. They are "digital disruptor brands—brands that come out of nowhere, whether it be Uber or these very millennial-style successful brands. You know, the mattress-in-the-box companies and all these cool disruptive brands who have come out over the last five years have really been the ones who have said, 'I'm making this a channel and I'm going with it.' They are the type that define the market, generally."

The process of push and education with larger businesses can take between two and three years to get to a point where they're fully engaging. Gagliese has become familiar with the process from the point where they say "let's try this" and initiate a $20,000 campaign toward growing to millions a year. For Gagliese, it's about building trust as they get their feet wet and start out small. But there's enormous protentional for growth. "To a Procter & Gamble or to a Coca-Cola, $50,000, $100,000, $200,000 in marketing budget is what they pay in fees for one afternoon of other things that they do," Gagliese laughs.

Mae Karwowski emphasizes the fact that the pitch is much different now than it was when she started Obviously. At that time, it ended up being primarily educational. "I would spend a majority of the meeting explaining what we do, explaining what an influencer was. It was not uncommon for—I'm not kidding you—thirty people to show up to a meeting, all bringing their lunch and asking a bunch of questions, and it became like a brown bag lunch session. . . . There's so much growth in terms of brands that really haven't ever done anything with influencers. There are a lot of brands who haven't even come online yet. But then, brands who are on the cutting edge, who are in the Fortune 500, they'll have influencer teams. They'll have an influencer marketing manager that we'll work with, whereas before they were like, we don't know who you should talk to."

Now she sees a lot of industries that are really winning that weren't previously, some of which began after the Covid-19 pandemic hit. For example, Obviously began working with insurance companies after the pandemic began. She also cites financial companies, telehealth companies, and health care companies as part of the growth. "Now, you're seeing that adoption has really gone over that bell curve, and those slow adopters are like, 'Oh, I should figure this out too. This really does make sense for me,' which is exciting because there's just so much opportunity in those industries that had previously said, 'I don't need to do this.'"

Raina Penchansky believes brands, both large and small, often don't use influencer marketing to its fullest potential. She says, "Brands sometimes make the mistake of looking at influencer marketing as a check in the box, as opposed to a genuine element of a more robust marketing strategy. . . . There's so many incredible ways to work with influencers that can really create a meaningful impact for a brand. . . . I think it's a matter of reframing where it fits inside of a marketing budget. And the reality is, if you're thinking about any marketing budget today, it's like, where are the eyeballs? They're all on social, so the majority of the money should be there. I think the other big mistake is that people aren't putting enough money into it."

FABFITFUN

Early on, many direct-to-consumer brands saw the potential of influencer marketing, learned their way around the new space, and propelled themselves to growth. FabFitFun is one of those brands, founded in 2010 by co-CEOs Daniel and Michael Broukhim and editor-in-chief Katie Echevarria Rosen Kitchens. The FabFitFun box, which is delivered to consumers each season, includes full-size products across beauty, fashion, fitness, wellness, home, and tech. It's a lifestyle membership model that also offers year-round options, such as FabFitFunTV, a streaming video service providing on-demand wellness content. Their target audience is women from twenty-five to fifty years old, but they have a wide age range of members, from teenagers to ninety-plus.

Jolie Jankowitz, an influencer marketing consultant and former senior director of influencer marketing and talent partnerships at FabFitFun, took notice several years ago when the industry began to shift, with influencers becoming more valued than celebrities in terms of their ability to sell product. She says, "That's when I came to FabFitFun to launch the program, and honestly, after the first season or two, we very quickly realized the impact that these creators, these influencers, had on our business in terms of revenue. As soon as you see those sales numbers, you know it's a no-brainer to scale."

She launched the program in spring 2014 and quickly grew it. They gifted product to YouTubers, making sure it resonated in communities on that platform, and worked with all types of influencers across the board and across every social channel, including bloggers and fitness influencers. Reality TV stars also played an important part in the beginning. Jankowitz says, "We worked with a handful of reality stars because we realized that there was something super authentic and relatable about them and everyone was already so invested in their journeys. They just felt like they could be your best friend—your neighbor. They're just like us, and they were really good at showcasing the good and the bad. They weren't just these people with perfectly curated feeds."

At the heart of Jankowitz's influencer marketing strategy is authenticity, and she takes it farther than a lot of marketing professionals. "Of course, we look at following and engagement and likes, shares or comments. . . . We look at that, but we look at that way less than any other brand, because again, it's truly just about who that person is. The number one question I get asked from other brands who are launching influencer marketing programs of their own is, what's the equation for pricing out an influencer or for knowing if they're a good fit? There is no equation because you just know in your gut if they're going to make sense for your brand," she says, acknowledging the controversial nature of putting a good fit and authenticity above metrics.

One of Jankowitz's favorite influencers along these lines is Tiffany Jenkins, a comedian, speaker, podcast host, and author of the best-selling book *High Achiever: The Incredible Story of One Addict's Double Life*. Her remarkable story, along with her humor and openness, about mental health issues on Facebook Live caught Jankowitz's eye. "We approached her and we're like, 'You're so authentic. You would totally resonate with our member base. Can we partner with you?,' and she was like, 'I've never done this before. I don't even know how to price myself or what to say.' Women like that are the people we try to partner with, but I think there's definitely an interesting story there. She was a receptionist in Sarasota, Florida, years ago and now she's thriving off of this career as an influencer—but a true, genuine influencer. She actually has influence over her audience."

At the time, Jenkins had a few hundred thousand followers, but remember, Jankowitz isn't solely hung up on the numbers. "There could be a microinfluencer who sells more boxes or sells more product for any of these other brands than a macro with 3 million followers just because they're a better brand fit and they're more authentic. I've seen influencers with a million plus followers who have sold nothing and then micros who have sold many units of something," she says.

Because of the focus on who the person is as opposed to the number attached to them, a more open and dynamic relationship develops between brand and influencer. For FabFitFun, it's not just a money exchange. They take their influencers out to lunch. Jankowitz told us that during the time she was with FabFitFun, she found that "the best influencer marketing is relationship and collaboration based versus transactional. And with FabFitFun, we really, really, really value the relationships that we have with influencers, which is why we have so many long-term partnerships. Part of valuing your relationship is trusting the influencer to say what they want to say—let them say what they like about the FabFitFun box or FabFitFun as a company or the specific products. We don't want to feed them lines. They know their audience best, and we lean on them. And again, that's what's going to perform the best as well."

Part of the collaboration process at FabFitFun is appreciating the influencer for all the hard work that goes into one piece of content. Merchandizing their box beautifully, getting the right angles, editing the photos—all of that takes effort. Jankowitz says, "A lot of them take pride and have a lot of integrity in their work. It takes time to make that content, and it's important to us to actually appreciate them for who they are."

Toward the goal of achieving a tight collaboration, Jankowitz prefers longer-term partnerships that span a year or two, although they have a variety of deal structures. For the long term, she says, "The deliverables are a little bit more extensive, whether they're in our TV commercials or creating more content for us outside of just social and things like that. It really ranges per influencer, but we prefer the longer-term partnerships because they feel a little bit more meaningful, and we like when the influencers are truly invested in the brand and we want them to be genuine brand advocates, and we only partner with people who are genuine brand advocates."

As of 2021, FabFitFun has partnered with over 40,000 influencers and continues growing their number of partnerships with influencers. They tend to have an open approach, as opposed to other sales-oriented, performance-driven brands, and they do knowledge shares to help each other out.

CHIPOTLE

Chipotle Mexican Grill Inc., aka Chipotle, is a fast casual restaurant chain well known for burritos, which are made to order in front of the customer. Their food is particularly big with Gen Z and millennials, so the company is future-forward in its thinking about influencers as part of a marketing strategy.

Before social media was a thing, Chipotle worked with influencers like Ozzy Osbourne, who had an open passion for the brand on the reality TV hit *The Osbournes*. When they recognized the opportunity in 2003, they gave Osbourne the very first Chipotle celebrity card, guaranteeing him free burritos for life, in order to keep him close and build that relationship. Over the years, they've expanded the celebrity card program to digital influencers.

Tressie Lieberman, vice president of digital marketing and off-premise for Chipotle, says, "Depending who that person is, we go over the top to deliver extraordinary experiences to them just to let them know how much we care about them." She cites their past partnership with superstar internet personality David Dobrik as an example: he had a huge following and a genuine love for Chipotle before receiving any compensation. They delivered to him in a fun way in order to get him talking about Chipotle with his millions of followers, like presenting his first celeb card with a mariachi band in tow.

Because they wanted to create a big cultural moment, the first campaign they did with Dobrik was around National Burrito Day. Lieberman and her team noticed two things. First, people love Dobrik's merch. Second, Dobrik ordered the exact same thing at Chipotle all the time. They put these two things together and developed the concept of selling Dobrik's burrito on National Burrito Day, giving his fans a chance to buy "his merch," in the form of a Chipotle burrito. Putting products online that people could easily order allowed Chipotle to create buzz and join the conversation, but it also allowed them to measure the direct sales of that particular product.

Other times, they've worked with Dobrik for campaigns like Cinco de Mayo, where it's about creating engagement. In this case, they had him as the talent showcasing the Chipotle lid flip. This is a cool technique that they had noticed in a restaurant: a team member would take the covered bowl, then hit it in such a way as to flip the lid over. Dobrik showed his audience how it works on TikTok, which kicked off the ad campaign and created a movement of people wanting to try the lid flip. In that case, it wasn't about sales from any product related to Dobrik; it was about his being the star of their content to drive engagement.

In terms of the creative process, Lieberman prefers having one-on-ones with influencers, as opposed to conversations filtered through agents and managers. She says, "We've been very hands-on with David. I've been on many calls with him, and he's told us he has hated ideas and come up with new ideas. And that's been awesome—a very raw collaborative, transparent relationship. Other times you're going through other people, and work isn't as strong when that happens. . . . The more you can just get on the phone or on a call and talking directly, it makes things work so much better. And the idea is so much stronger. I would love to see more of that direct collaboration."

Ironically, not long after our interview with Lieberman, on September 17, 2020, Chipotle cut ties with Dobrik as a result of a series of controversies and allegations against his content creation group, the Vlog Squad, including sexual assault, bullying, and creating a hostile environment (see chapter 12). A March 2021 Yahoo! News article reported that Chipotle took the allegations very seriously and did not have any future collabs planned.[2]

Before this incident, we asked Lieberman about something Mark Cuban says about the potential downsides for companies partnering with influencers, which is that "you take on ownership of everything that influencer does."

In essence, Lieberman agrees that it's one of the inherent risks of influencer marketing. "It depends on the level of the endorsement and the relationship, right? But if you are synonymous with that person, and they are the biggest advocate, and you've been very vocal about that relationship, and they do something, certainly the brands can get tied into that conversation. And I do think that's part of influencer marketing. . . . You want to have some level of trust that they're going to do the right thing, but everybody's human, so there's a risk associated with doing any type of influencer marketing."

In order to combat that, they focus on an up-front screening process, trying to pick people who are going to properly represent the brand, but obviously that's not infallible. She adds, "Where you see this happen more, and maybe Mark is talking about celebrity endorsements, when you have big paid advertising campaigns running versus just somebody who loves the brand, and that we're giving a celeb card to. It's really when you have a big television ad running, right? And you've got a pro sports person running product and they're completely tied to your product. That's where people have to move quickly, and you turn off advertising and all that and break partnerships."

In terms of Cuban's comments about brands taking ownership of everything an influencer does, Blake Lawrence notes that it's "an interesting concept that is to be debated," then uses the hypothetical example of advertising in traditional sports media like the magazine *Sports Illustrated* to make his point. "The article on the left page and the advertisement on the right are there next to each other. But the advertiser's decision to advertise in that moment is not their endorsement of the content on the left. It is aligning with an audience. So if you can start to decouple advertising from just general content shared on social channels, it makes it easier to understand that a brand aligning with an influencer or an athlete doesn't necessarily have to say, 'we're all in.'" He believes influencer marketing doesn't need to be a 100 percent endorsement of whatever the influencer says or does throughout their life.

Because sometimes the rewards seem to outweigh the risks, brands like Chipotle push forward with influencers and platforms that lead culture. For example, Lieberman admires and likes to collab with director and artist Pablo Rochat because he has a brilliant mind and comes up with new ways to tell stories within a platform by taking existing tools and hacking the platform. She says, "It's all about the creativity. . . . How do we get that conversation rolling and keep innovating and keep trying new things?" For her team, it's crucial to constantly be testing, learning, and experimenting. However, doing things that haven't been done before comes at a price. "There are going to be some unknowns in the process," she says.

Part of innovating—getting a feel for the culture and keeping Chipotle on people's radar—is taking new and different platforms into account. TikTok has been a particularly standout platform for Chipotle because it gives the company "the opportunity to drive, in some cases, billions of views around topics because of the algorithm of TikTok where we can really see things take off in a big way. For Lieberman, "going viral" is a dated term, but she says viral videos are essentially what you get on TikTok with insane metrics, like a piece of content showing how to make their white rice getting 8.4 million views and over a million likes. Lieberman says, "We continue to be where our customers are and engage with them and show up and listen to comments. And we obviously stay close to what's happening in the news, but we are really about being where our customers are."

What has Lieberman learned from her experiences working on each of these campaigns over the years? It's vital to put in the investment on paid advertising to help amplify the content so it gets as much visibility as possible. She says, "It's worth investing in the talent and investing in the idea to make sure that it succeeds." She uses the example of a TikTok time-out campaign that Chipotle did and ended up licensing a song from Justin Bieber—a costly endeavor. She says, "That's a big decision as a brand. It's an investment. And ultimately, we thought, hey, this is Super Bowl level, right? We want to have a big name and TikTok is a platform that thrives on music. And, he just had a song 'Yummy' come out, and we thought, wouldn't it be great to have that song associated with our food, so we

Reason	Remarks
Cultural relevance	"Kids love Chipotle, and it's very culturally relevant. When you have a very culturally relevant brand, like a Chipotle, Starbucks, or Chick-Fil-A, it makes your job 99 percent easier."
Innovation	"They really do push the envelope on collaborations because they're like, OK, interesting, but we've heard of that before; do you have anything else?"
Collaboration	"They're not just like, hey, here's a bunch of money and here's a script—go create it. I think they want it to be a little bit more thought out and have input from the creator."
Experiential	They're "not just paying people to read off talking points. For instance, Brent got a burrito card, and he was so excited about his burrito card. He's like, 'When's the burrito card coming? I can't wait to get it.' And it's not like he eats Chipotle every day, but it's kind of a status thing where he can go into Chipotle and get a free meal or whatever. . . . They do a really good job at just creating experiences versus, hey, here's money. Go, hit these talking points and create this content."

Table 3. Reasons Max Levine, cofounder of Amp Studios, likes working with Chipotle

made the investment. And what was really cool about it—not only did it help get the campaign to take off on TikTok, but Justin himself tweeted about it, and covered it in his Instagram story, which wasn't even in our contract. He was just genuinely excited. He's a big fan of Chipotle and he was excited that we were using his song, and he talked about it with over 100 million followers. So you get what you pay for sometimes, and sometimes you're lucky and things exceed expectations. But you have to engineer things to give it the best shot to take off."

From the other side of it, Amp Studios, home of YouTube mega-stars including cofounder Brent Rivera, has influencers who have developed successful partnerships with Chipotle. Table 3 lists a few things that Max Levine says work for Chipotle.

BRAND/INFLUENCER FIT

There's both an art and a science to matching an influencer with a brand. Some agencies lean more toward AI to foster partnerships; others prefer the personal touch, while many meet somewhere in the middle. Michael Schweiger prefers the personal touch; he attributes a large part of CEG's success to understanding the people they represent. He says, "We kind of pride ourselves on that we're not an AI-based company; we're HI. We're human intelligence. Our agents have an understanding of our clients and where they want to be and where they want to go. Do they want to do a podcast? Are they a good blogger? What sort of brands are genuinely connected with their lifestyle? We wouldn't take one of our influencers and put a brand with them which is against their lifestyle. We wouldn't put alcohol with a fitness brand. We wouldn't do a fast-food brand with a chef-style foodie—someone who likes to create different foods. We wouldn't put a cheesy household product with a decorator. . . . There's a juggling act of finding the right brand category that goes with the right influencer category."

He argues that it's the personal relationship between the agent and influencer that fosters great fits. "We pick the phone up and talk to them and know it's their birthday next week and know that they drive a horrible, old car and would like to get a new one. We'll know that they're doing home renovations and they just bought a sofa. . . . We know what's going on in their lives, so we know what brands would fit a particular lifestyle."

They're an agency that likes to develop long-term partnerships between brands and influencers that may take the form of a twenty-four-month-long campaign. They're not averse to taking on small brands, but a lot of research and selectivity go into making sure that, first, it's something the influencer will be honestly excited about, and second, it's a quality product with well-established supply lines. Their setup as of the interview is ten teams, with each team headed by a brand manager/agent and three to five brand talent coordinators. On a weekly basis, a team may be handling ten to fifteen brands and fifty to a hundred posts.

Bad matches are frustrating to both influencer and brand. TikToker Kyle Hernandez talks about an experience he had with a high-end sunglasses brand that went awry. He posted a video featuring their product that got 600,000 views, but the views didn't translate into sales. Out of 1,500 people who came to their website after watching the post, not one person bought the $200 pair of sunglasses. It frustrated Hernandez because he felt like they were blaming him for things going wrong. Both parties were unhappy because of a lack of understanding about the influencer, his audience, and brand compatibility.

BEYOND ONE AND DONE

Lorraine Ladish, a full-time influencer who addresses aging, health, and wellness, has around thirty brand deals a year. Some of them are ambassadorships that last six months, a year, or longer, and some are one and done, meaning that the influencer does something like a single Instagram post or one Facebook Live, and that's it. If the partnership is successful, then the brand might come back later for another hit.

Ladish and most influencers tend to prefer long-term relationships with a brand. She says, "Not only are you doing something over time, but you also develop a relationship with a product—with a story line.

And of course, money's coming in so that's nice." Ladish has ambassadorships with brands including Consumer Reports and Procter & Gamble's Hair Biology, which is a line of hair products for women over forty-five. Negotiating exclusivity is always a big part of it. Generally with ambassadorships they are prohibited from working with a competitive product. Short-term deals tend to pay less money if they don't want exclusivity, but Ladish says, "It's a bit silly," because no other brand is going to work with you anyway if you just posted about a different one, so an influencer has to take that into consideration.

Influencer Kristina Zias also likes long-term relationships, arguing that brand recognition and repetition by using a product over and over again make a big difference. She says, "Brands sometimes expect there to be one and done—huge sales. And that's just not realistic. That's not how people shop."

Influencer talent manager Jessy Grossman agrees. "It's so rare in influencer marketing that it's first touch, which means an influencer posts one post and immediately a customer purchases a product. It's usually second or third touch, in which they see that influencer post a few times and then they're moved to buy product. So it's sort of analyzing the data of what's coming in—the amount of impressions, the amount of swipe ups to purchase, but it's also comparing it against the realities and the trends of influencer marketing. . . . If somebody puts a bunch of money into a first round of content production and they're quote, 'disappointed' that they didn't immediately sell X amount of units, it's worth looking into, of course, of why that is, but I would argue that the sweet spot is really on the second or third rounds of additional brand recognition."

WALKING THROUGH THE PROCESS

What does the campaign process look like from beginning to end? Raina Penchansky sums up what the journey looks like when a brand comes to them. First, they narrow things down by asking the questions, "What are you trying to achieve?," "What are the goals?," and "What are the KPIs?" KPI stands for key performance indicator; it provides a quantifiable way to evaluate the success of an organization's goals and objectives over time.

Then they move on to the next step, which Penchansky says is "understanding how we're going to make sure that there is the right representation within that campaign—that we're being cognizant of making sure the campaign is diverse in the right way, not just in a way of checking the boxes."

Penchansky points out that for some brands, this is their first foray into influencer marketing, so there have to be conversations around expectations. She believes that it is incredibly important for brands to have an understanding of what the end product is going to be and managing that expectation. Then they can shift focus to the granular, like what the content looks like and the parameters around it. Penchansky's suggestion is that they let the content creator run with it. The brand should give them a sense of what it wants, but then let the influencer define what the content looks like, because influencers "know their audience best and they know what's going to be most well received. . . . Brands really should look at influencers as creative directors in a sense that you're working with a creative agency—they have distribution, they're the talent, they're the concepts—and sort of let go of control."

Then it becomes about avoiding that age-old clash between the corporate and the creative. Mae Karwowski talks about expectations and the chasm that can exist between brand and influencer:

> There's really kind of a gulf between what a brand marketer wants and assumes of an influencer and what an influencer and content creator wants and assumes, in terms of their participation in a campaign with the brand. I think a big thing is that these people are really creative and they're content creators and they live and

breathe this, so they care about their audience. . . . And they're really tuned in to what's going to perform well and what's not. I think sometimes on the brand side, even of marketers who are treating it more like a commercial or treating it more like a Facebook ad . . . they're just so overly prescriptive, that even if it's totally what the brand wants to get out there into the world and it's the right message, it's gonna ring really hollow if the influencer actually does that.

That's why the team at Obviously coaches brands to give the influencer parameters, but then let them do their thing: they are more likely to know what's going to be a hit on their channel.

THE BUSINESS OF
LIKES AND HATE

Combating Bullies and Trolls

An influencer's ride on the roller coaster of likes, no likes, hateful comments, and positive affirmation is much more intense than a casual social media user because it's their livelihood. Influencers can't just shut it down, turn it off, or walk away. It's a hazard of the profession. In influencing, there's no HR department to visit after you've been harassed.

Raina Penchansky believes that because influencers are putting themselves out there and monetizing their platforms, they have a responsibility to listen to the audience who supports them and makes purchases. "You do have an obligation to listen if they want to say something to you. We don't have an obligation to listen to hateful comments." Penchansky makes the distinction between genuine, productive criticism versus hateful, malicious nonsense, like comments calling her clients' children ugly.

Stephanie McNeal notes, "If you put yourself in the public eye, you have to expect a level of scrutiny, but I think it's a shame that it goes so far, like if you're an influencer and you have a miscarriage, and you get hundreds of DMs telling you that they're glad your baby died, which happens all the time. I don't really think anyone deserves that. But I do think, at this point, it's something that people just have to expect."

Like many, when asked, McNeal seems to grasp at a solution to something preposterously hard to solve. She acknowledges the role of the platforms, but at the same time she thinks that the platforms can only do so much. She says, "The hate is coming from people, and I think for a lot of people, for whatever reason, attacking people makes them feel good, and so that seems to be the bigger societal problem to me. . . . I think the platforms could do more. . . . Instagram has tried a couple of things, like flag if you see somebody saying something nasty to someone. I don't know how you [change] thousands of people who just enjoy sending death threats to people." McNeal acknowledges there's not one all-encompassing solution. The approach has to be multifaceted.

Throughout the rest of the chapter, we'll touch on how likes and hate affect influencers and the different ways they handle the onslaught of negativity, as well as the flip side: when it's the influencer generating the hate.

All of us are evolutionarily hardwired, chemically predisposed, and in general made to react in a certain way to likes and hate that can have some really bad consequences. Industry insiders and psychologists weigh in with practical, doable solutions, but they each emphasize the sizable challenge of changing the way influencers react to likes and hate. It's an uphill battle they have to face every day.

WHY DO WE CARE SO MUCH?

We care what people think about us because it's part of who we are—part of our evolution, chemistry, and psyche. The likes and hate hit influencers where they live. Mike Brooks, licensed psychologist and coauthor of *Tech Generation: Raising Balanced Kids in a Hyper-connected World*, expresses it plainly: "We want to be liked at a basic psychological level. We feel good when we're liked." People are social creatures who strive for connectedness. It's a fundamental human need.

According to psychologist Abraham Maslow, people have a hierarchy of five need levels. Once we meet the first basic physiological and safety needs of food, shelter, financial security, and health, we move on to the need for love and connection, then to the need for esteem, respect, and appreciation from others. Only at that point can we move toward being self-actualized, which is working at being the best selves we can be.

Online, it's that need for love and respect that can really trip up influencers. Not only can it prevent them from becoming self-actualized, it can also lead to a host of issues, like anxiety and depression. But it's not only the hateful comments that get to influencers. It's also the absence of likes. The number of likes an influencer gets can be the difference in whether they pay their mortgage or not—basic needs, but it also cuts at a deeper level. The saying "it's not personal, it's business" doesn't apply to influencing.

Chemical Cocktail

Larry Rosen, expert in the psychology of technology and author or coauthor of numerous books including *The Distracted Mind: Ancient Brains in a High-Tech World,* says that the concept of likes is straight Skinnerian reinforcement. "Something becomes a positive reinforcement when you do an activity, and it makes you want to do it again. That's exactly what happens with likes. When you get a like, it makes you want more likes—need more likes." It's all about trying to feel good. On the flip side, if you don't get the requisite number of likes, it's punishment, the same as if someone sticks their hand in a plug and gets shocked. Punishment gives a consequence, such as a shock, that makes people not want to do the behavior again. Rosen explains that if you don't get a lot of likes, then you're going to question it and not want it to happen again, leading to a dilemma of

"What did I do wrong? Why is this happening?," which is an internal punishment of the self—a slap to the self-esteem.

During the ups and downs of reinforcement and punishment, a biochemical cocktail gets shaken up. With likes, Rosen says that influencers are getting a hit of feel-good chemicals like dopamine and serotonin. Frenetic usage, obsession, and addictive behavior can result as the influencer becomes dissatisfied with the current level of likes and adulation, needing more. One study found that when teens saw their own photos or other's photos with a large number of likes, their brains reacted the same as if they were eating chocolate or winning money.[1] The primitive part of our brain wants more of the good stuff, not less.

When there's a negative hit of no likes, the chemicals of depression and anxiety get pushed to the top. In a study published by *Child Development,* students who received fewer likes reported more negative emotions, including rejection, than those who received more likes.[2] It's no surprise that adolescents who had already experienced bullying were the most vulnerable.

The consequences of this up-and-down cycle are major for influencers because it's their business to stay in it. They can't choose to get off the ride for too long.

Negativity Bias: When the Bad Stuff Sticks

Why is it an influencer can get ninety-nine positive comments, but it's the one negative comment they obsess over? Bad feedback has staying power that can follow someone for hours, days, weeks—or indefinitely. The reason: negativity bias, which is the idea that negative things tend to stand out more than the positive ones, causing a greater impact on a person's psychological state. Not only do people notice negative events more, but they also tend to dwell on them more.

Brooks says this focus on negativity has evolutionary roots. Fifty thousand years ago, if we missed the negative news that there were lions at the watering hole, we could die. But if we missed the good news that there is a tree bearing ripe fruit nearby, we'll still live another day. The problem is that today, there's no immediate death by tweet or slaughter by lack of "like," so we experience an evolutionary asymmetry. There's a mismatch between the way we're wired and the way society and technology have evolved. Detrimental psychological consequences for influencers live in the space of that mismatch.

ARE INFLUENCERS DIFFERENT FROM ANY OTHER ARTIST OR ENTERTAINER?

When the Melissa McCarthy/Jason Bateman movie *Identity Thief* came out in 2013, McCarthy had to put up with well-known film critic Rex Reed's body shaming in his critique of the movie. In the review, Reed referred to her as a "female hippo" and "tractor-sized." McCarthy responded by saying Reed must be "in a really bad spot" and "swimming in so much hate," while also acknowledging that those type of body-shaming comments might have "crushed" her when she was younger.[3]

Artists and entertainers have long been subject to scathing criticism of their work, as well as vile personal attacks. Why is this kind of criticism different than the hate influencers encounter? In a discussion about Vincent van Gogh, the tortured artist who went unappreciated in his day, Brooks quips, "Yeah, he didn't get a lot of likes." But there's a big difference between what creatives have experienced historically and what creators are on the receiving end of today. Brooks says there used to be a longer timeline between creating the work, making the work available, and then creating the next piece. There's a high frequency of content being produced today with immediate feedback, leaving barely any time for the influencer to take a breath and reflect. It's a bullet train of post, feedback, post, feedback.

Rosen says, "Imagine van Gogh putting up a picture on Facebook or Instagram and having a million people go, 'What is this thing with dots here?' 'This doesn't make any sense.' 'This is stupid.' 'This is not art.' 'This is bullshit!' It probably would have hastened van Gogh's depression because he was subject to depressive bouts."

The number of people who are piling on has an impact. It's the difference between getting hate from a few versus hate from a few million.

TRENDING HATE

Nechelle Vanias, cofounder of the influencer marketing and talent agency Six Degrees of Influence and mother of influencer Rave Vanias, noticed a significant pattern online. Poring over the negative comments received by her influencers, she saw that they were repetitive in nature. If it was about accusing somebody of cheating, there would be the same comments, such as "You're a cheater. You don't deserve your platform. Go kill yourself," over and over again.

As a sociology major, Vanias attributed this phenomenon to the herd mentality, which refers to the tendency people have to follow and copy whatever the crowd is doing at the time. When you add the negativity bias on top of it, the path gets really dark. Brooks says, "It's easy for hate, outrage, judgment, anger, and fear to trend—they're very primal emotions."

The anonymity of the digital space makes it easier. It exacerbates the piling on because people view their comments as having no consequences. When two known influencers have a beef with each other, it's not just one-on-one; it's anonymous fan base against anonymous fan base. Rave, a TikToker, says that influencers "will target each other and then you have fan bases behind it, so you're now [it's like you're] in high school, but with a whole gang behind you. And so they're going to notify that influencer and then their people are going to go fight back to that other influencer's people."

A particular kind of trending hate on TikTok are "fairy comments." Filled with sweet-looking emojis in between mean words, passive-aggressive fairy comments start out benign and end with a cruel twist, like "Love yourself, cuz we don't" or "I wish you were a flower, so I could step on you." They're meant to be used on "enemies," or videos that people don't like.

Rosen says if you watch any TikTok, Facebook, or Instagram fights, "you'll see that once somebody makes a negative comment, then others feel justifiably right to jump in and agree." The negative comments then start multiplying and generating likes for the people posting them. Vanias also notices that followers seem to post exact or similar comments in hopes they would get attention and likes. In essence, followers are reinforced to be negative.

Wanting to protect her influencers, Vanias intervened. She figured a way to cut through it might be to interrupt the hate train, because it's too hard for ten-, twelve-, and sixteen-year-olds to go against the grain by saying something different. So Vanias descended into the conversation with her "street team" and battled the negative words with positive words. Each time, she noticed the direction of the comments shift from negative to positive.

Another telling anecdotal confirmation of her hypothesis came after they turned the tables on a conversation and a negative commenter said, "Sheesh, I was just posting a spam comment." It became unpleasant for this person when they stopped getting likes for their negative comments and started getting criticism because the tide had turned. Vanias believes this method is most effective if you cut the negativity immediately and also limit some key negative trending words.

Using positive comments to combat the negative ones is a solution that is getting more attention now. For instance, CivilRights.org recommends increasing positive messages of tolerance.[4] They say, "Part of modeling what we don't want to see is modeling what we do want to see."

A strategy some insiders advocate is keeping direct messages open to the public even when posts are getting a lot of hate. The logic is that it's better to have negative comments hidden in a DM rather than posted for everyone to see, since hate begets hate. If it's in a DM, the influencer is the only one who sees it and others can't pile on. The downside is that the hate still finds its way to the influencer.

Some influencers try not to read the comments after the first hour they post because at that point, if the video becomes big, it gets to other people's pages who may not be fans. Among their followers, hate isn't as much of an issue. Once posts reach beyond those followers, the problems start, and if a post goes viral, it's all up for grabs.

Because influencers are never going to be fully able to exert control over trending hate, Vanias wants her clients to develop the skills they need to cope. "We recommend a lot of therapy. . . . I happen to be a big proponent of therapy. . . . Someone has to help these kids navigate something that's unimaginable."

A DOUBLE DOSE OF HATE FOR REALITY TV STARS

Reality TV stars live with a conundrum. Fans feel like they know them, but because that relationship is through a screen, they don't always see them as flesh-and-blood people with feelings. It's like the way kids view their teachers in elementary school; they can't picture them with a life outside the classroom. However scripted, or not, reality TV cast members have real feelings, and they have real reactions to hate. In some ways, this phenomenon spills over to all influencers who also experience that contradictory close yet distant relationship with their followers.

Chloe Long of *Siesta Key* says, "I know I'm on this platform, so I've put myself in a position where people feel like they have the right to comment about anything they want, because they see me on a television screen. It's almost as if I'm not a real person." This sense of familiarity, combined with the belief that there's some kind of relationship there, can give fans a sense of entitlement—like they have a right to say anything and everything.

Mary Fitzgerald of *Selling Sunset* echoes Long's sentiment. She's grateful for the platform, which allows her to give voice to things that are important to her, but at the same time, she has to deal with the downside. She laments that some people "want to criticize and try to drag you down . . . but I don't think I get that as much as some of the other girls do."

Long emphasizes that the most controversial cast members on the show get the most hate. While Fitzgerald isn't one of the most controversial on her show, Long is at the center of scandal. "The more you have an opinion, the more drama you start, the more people come for you," she says, adding, "Girls get it worse." She says underscoring the kind of hate women can get is an important part of the discussion. Sexual harassment, rape threats, body insults, slut-shaming, and general misogyny plague women online. In addition to being hurt by this type of hate, people may also feel anxious, scared, hypervigilant, and intimidated.

Here's more on how Mary Fitzgerald, Chloe Long, and Ashley Iaconetti Haibon handle the hate.

Mary: *Selling Sunset*

Like many influencers, Fitzgerald's response online has evolved over the years. Around season 1 of *Selling Sunset,* when the surge of followers on Instagram was new, she felt compelled to respond to the hate a few times. Her trigger: when the comments targeted her now husband, Romain Bonnet. "I'm very protective of him," she says, voice filled with emotion. Today, however, Fitzgerald rarely responds to any negativity, preferring to ignore it. When there is a response, "I kill them with kindness, and it's worked." She'd rather not do it in an open post, choosing DM instead because she doesn't want to shame people.

In one instance of hate, Fitzgerald found she was getting a lot of comments such as, "You're ugly," "You look like you're going bald," and "You look old." At first she didn't know they were connected. However, when she went back though her posts, she realized that the same woman had been verbally assaulting her nonstop for eight months.

Choosing not to ignore it anymore, Fitzgerald responded to her though a DM saying, in essence, the following: "I see that you have been trying to get my attention for going on a year now. So I'm gonna go ahead and give you my response. I don't know you. You don't know me. But I'm sorry that you have all these negative feelings towards me. I'm not sure what I've done, but if I'm honest, I think you're probably dealing with something yourself and projecting it on me. I feel bad and I wish you nothing but the best and emotional healing going forward. I don't think we should ever be mean to one another. There's nothing good that comes from it. But I hope you figure out the source of your anger and God bless you."

When the woman replied, Fitzgerald was shocked because she had never received a message like this from anyone. Fitzgerald says the woman answered with something to the effect of, "I'm so sorry. You're absolutely right. I am actually going through something, and I should never have been that mean to you. I'm very, very sorry. I'm gonna try to learn from this. Thank you for being discreet and saying this to me. I'm gonna work on it."

Fitzgerald believes that "when people are negative, they're projecting their own issues on other people," and that when there is no foundation for it, emotions like insecurity, jealousy, and fear underlie the hate.

Most psychologists would agree with Fitzgerald's assessment, including Mike Brooks, who, when asked about this type of situation, quotes Gandhi: "The enemy is fear. We think it is hate, but it is really fear." Brooks goes on. "That's what I think happens on social media. When someone blasts another person, they're putting themselves in a position of superior to inferior. . . . But it's also simplifying the universe and that feels good in the moment. But it's contributing, I think, to a lot of ills in society with this kind of mentality of hatred, and anger and vitriol."

In Fitzgerald's case, she acted on the premise that hate was a projection stemming from other toxic emotions. Instead of responding to the vicious content of the comments, she responded to the underlying thoughts and feelings of the trolling woman. In this situation, it worked. However, some experts would argue that responding to those seeking attention only rewards them for their negative comments, increasing the likelihood that they'll do it again.

In the end, it's a personal decision whether to respond to hate or not. Dana L. Cunningham, licensed clinical psychologist and cofounder of Black Mental Wellness, says, "What's healthy for one person may not be healthy for another." For a person prone to getting into arguments, it's probably not a great idea. But for someone else, she says it could be helpful to respond in order to give clarity, provide information and resources, or maybe close out that conversation, so to speak. However, Cunningham emphasizes an important question to ask is, "How much energy do I have to really invest in this right now?"

Colin Wayne Leach believes other important questions to ask include: What is the antagonist's purpose, and what is the purpose of the response? For some people, engaging sends the message of not being intimidated, but often they may not be strategic about it, particularly in assessing to whom they respond. Leach highlights the importance of being tactical in terms of online communication, because "some of these antagonists are basically professional or hobbyist provocateurs and they want the reaction. They want people to lose their heads, to lose their cool, to throw fuel on the fire. That's what they're after, actually."

Chloe: *Siesta Key*

In June 2020, Chloe Long decided to take a break from comments and turned them off. That said, comments still found their way to her via her Concepts by Chloe blog. It's been a harrowing experience for Long, and it has definitely affected how much she chooses to post. For some influencers, passing on the comments isn't an option. Mae Karwowski advocates having someone else read them for you. It provides a barrier while still allowing the influencer to gauge their audience and ferret out issues that might legitimately need to be addressed. It can be hard, however, to follow through with it. The need to read pulls at every influencer, sort of like watching a train wreck.

The sadness and anger are palpable as Long opens up about the hate comments. "I feel like I'm taking on the weight of world when I talk about this stuff, because I feel like it's such a fucking problem. . . . It disgusts me. Quite honestly, I think it's why so many kids, teenagers, and young adults struggle with anxiety and depression, because it's so easy to type something nasty to someone."

Long goes on to talk about how it has affected her. "When people tell you to kill yourself, and how fat and ugly you are, and they hope you hang yourself and your mom finds you in the closet—I mean, I've seen it all—it's just horrible. And it definitely can, if you're not careful, knock you down. . . . My mental health has gone to shit before because of this, for sure, and I had to get help. That's why I went back on medicine when we were filming, because I was really depressed. . . . I think it definitely makes you have a lot of self-doubt and self-hate, which is really, really dangerous. To look in the mirror and not love yourself—I think that's a very unsafe mental space to be."

Long says it was the worst at the beginning, after seasons 1A and 1B came out. The cast was unprepared for all of the hate. The slut-shaming of a particular cast member got out of control. Long and the rest of the cast dealt with it by banding together. Amanda Miller, whom she calls one of her best friends, was particularly helpful to her. Long says, "I'm so thankful that I have such amazing friends and family who are cast members. Because at the end of the day, when it comes to the cast, we can all come for each other, but when you're a stranger and you come for one of us, we're all like, fuck you! I've had moments where I've had to screenshot something and send it to Kelsey, Madison, Amanda, and Julia. The second I do that, there's an immediate pouring in of love and confidence. It brings me right back up. So I think it's really important that if you ever do have a platform like this, where people are going to criticize you, make sure you are surrounded by very uplifting people."

It's hard to get experts to unanimously agree on anything, but social support is something they can get behind. According to a paper published in *Psychiatry,* numerous studies show that social support is important for both physical and mental health and helps people become more resilient to stress.[5]

However, even with excellent social support and the other measures she's taking, the haters still bother Long. But she's slowly but surely getting to the point of believing that "no one's opinion matters, but yourself and God." One thing Long wants for the future: "I think the likes need to go." She doesn't understand the purpose of the number of likes a post gets being on public display; she believes it's only for status seekers and people who want to feel like they're better than other people.

But likes are big business. Even if some platforms are taking steps to take away dislikes or to allow users to hide like counts from the public, there will always be some kind of measure of clout, whether it's the number of followers or comments, or the status of the people liking or commenting on an influencer's post.

Ashley I: The Bachelor Franchise

Ashley Iaconetti Haibon, aka Ashley I, uses compartmentalization effectively to cope with the hate. "I have a little bubble," she says. But that doesn't stop her from finding grating comments posted all the time. "I'll read a comment that's annoying. I'll go on the Reddit boards and be really furious for a little bit. I'll vent it out to Jared or my sister, and then I'm done. I don't carry it with me."

There's a cognitive-behavioral therapy technique called "worry time" that's sometimes used to deal with negative emotions. Rather than a person allowing themself to be bombarded by worry throughout the day, they schedule a set amount of time, like fifteen minutes, to let the anxiety flow. But the second that time is up, they pack away those thoughts until the next scheduled worry time. Iaconetti Haibon seems to be informally doing the essence of the worry time technique. She sees the comment, feels the emotion, vents, and moves on. It can be effective, as long as the person is truly able to move on.

Still, there are comments that tempt Iaconetti Haibon to get into the weeds. She acknowledges, "There are times where I want to just get on there, make an account and fight back for myself. But that just causes more drama. So I usually just let it be." She's thoughtful about what makes her step back and stop: "Maybe it's because on *The Bachelor,* while I didn't always have a good edit—that's for sure—and I was very polarizing; people either loved me or they couldn't stand me—it's changed my life for the better as a whole, so I never let little comments here or there, or the haters that are very prevalent, get to me."

HATE TOWARD THE LGBTQIA+ COMMUNITY

The LGBTQIA+ community is on the receiving end of copious amounts of hate. Isabella Avila, who was at the center of her own controversy (see chapter 9), has been on the receiving end of a "ton of homophobic hate." At this point, Avila mostly takes care of the comments by blocking certain words and not reading them.

As much as Avila tries not to let it affect her, there are unavoidable situations. "One time I got into some weird argument with another small TikToker and I woke up the next morning—I'm not even exaggerating—I had 3,000 Instagram DMs calling me a f—t. Those days affect me." She says that one hateful comment, such as, "You should get a boyfriend," doesn't bother her as much, but a mass of hate is hard to process.

How did Avila handle it? She screenshotted a bunch of the comments and made a video dancing on top of them. That video got almost 3 million views. "It made me feel better knowing that not everybody was against me, because I feel like when that stuff happens, it does feel like everybody's against you," she admits.

When asked about Avila's response, David Ewoldsen, professor in the department of media and information at Michigan State University, thought it was spot on. Avila took a horrible thing and showed the ludicrousness of those kinds of comments. Ewoldsen makes another suggestion for someone who finds themselves in Avila's situation and chooses to respond. They could say something to the effect of, sexual orientation has nothing to do with this conversation, I'm sorry you think that's an insult, and you need to look inside yourself as to why you think that's an insult. Ewoldsen emphasizes that it is important to take a step back and be mindful when responding to hate, so that the influencer isn't responding from a place of anger and emotion.

LGBTQIA+ activist Eli Erlick has experienced targeting for being a trans educator and is always looking for ways to "turn the rhetoric of oppression against itself." She did so by creating an art project that was an image of her draped in a garment of 400 hateful online messages she's received as a trans woman, ranging from "Get AIDS and die" to messages that she is less than human and not a woman. In her post, Erlick says, "I want this dress to represent how every time somebody pushes a trans woman down, our community will jump back up stronger than ever."

Fashion, skin care, and fitness influencer Joey Zauzig, who is gay, has learned how to cope with an influx of hate. It doesn't take long scrolling through his comments to find something like, "Turn from your wrong ways and repent." He says that there are different levels of those types of comments. There are completely outlandish comments that don't even make sense, but then there are the ones that really hurt. It's harder for him to cope with the latter, particularly when they hit an insecurity.

But because of the profession they have chosen, influencers find the most hurtful hate hard to escape. Zauzig says, "When I came out, I was like, if people don't accept me, they're not part of my life. And now having a platform, I don't really have a choice." He copes by stepping back, looking in the mirror, and remembering who he is, where he came from, and what he's trying to accomplish on the platform. "These people that are sitting at home behind their screens saying nasty things are the least of our worries," Zauzig says.

Another important coping mechanism for him is redirecting his energy toward something positive. Zauzig volunteers with the Trevor Project, a national organization that provides crisis intervention and suicide prevention services to LGBTQIA+ individuals under age twenty-five. Part of Zauzig's volunteer training includes responding to texts or calls from young people who are in crisis and often feel alone, which are similar to comments and DMs he gets from some followers. "Using those skills on my platform has become an everyday thing. People message me all the time, telling me about their struggles with coming out or if they're confused about who they are. I've used the skills that I learned at the Trevor Project and transferred them to the way that I speak on my DMs with my audience."

Zauzig tries to reach his entire audience by responding to everybody, even if it's a quick reply, acknowledging them for stopping by his page and supporting him. Interacting with his audience is an important part of who he is online. Responding to these types of comments in an altruistic way helps take the focus off negative comments and can lessen the sense of helplessness toward them. It feels good to respond with action. It's just that the action isn't directed at the hate but rather toward sincere, authentic comments.

Hate toward members of the LGBTQIA+ community and other marginalized communities spawns some of the most malignant comments because they cut at a person's fundamental truth. Often individuals in these populations are already vulnerable in that they may have experienced bullying and abuse offline as a result of their sexual orientation or racial/ethnic background. Now it's coming from the digital world as well.

RACIST HATE

Tyler Moss, aka TMossBoss, who makes everything from reaction to gaming videos, loves being an influencer. He loves it despite encountering racist hate on a daily basis. "I feel like the majority of African American YouTubers will receive racist comments. And it's YouTubers like me, having 22,000 subscribers to YouTubers with 22 million subscribers." In other words, it doesn't matter who you are.

Moss has dealt with racism both in real life and on YouTube. He says for him, it's easier to block out the hate online, as opposed to blocking out a person in the real world who is in your face yelling or being rude. Yet the online racist comments he faces are abhorrent, sometimes violent and threatening—and they keep coming, often from people who are empowered by their anonymity. Moss, who has seen almost everything and prides himself on being able to let the hate roll off his back, talks about a comment he recently received: "You deserve the n***e." Many of the influencers interviewed for this book indicate that these types of comments are par for the course online.

Still, Moss manages to keep his future in focus. "I'm not gonna allow this to ruin the bigger picture," he says emphatically. Keeping a goal in mind while moving through a barrage of racism and hate is beyond challenging. It causes many influencers to wonder if it's worth it.

In 2015, Shanicia Boswell started Black Mom's Blog at a time when there wasn't a space for moms of color to find people who looked like them. Boswell says, "You go to white baby blog pages and we're nowhere in sight. You scroll down twenty rows and there's one mixed, ambiguous baby." She wanted to create something that celebrated Black mothers. Yet when she first started, some white people accused Boswell of being racist and posted racist hate comments on her blog every other day. Boswell noticed some of the worst comments when she posted photos of Black fathers and their kids. White men often said things like, "I'm surprised he's not in jail."

That's not the only hate she had to face. Sometimes, when the hate comes from close to home, it can hurt at a different level. Boswell says some of the most damaging comments to her when the blog was new came from women in her community who disparaged her daughter and tore her down. "You create a business and it's your baby. Especially when you're doing it from this heartfelt place and the very people that you're doing it for don't appreciate it—it makes you want to quit and feel discouraged."

But Boswell didn't quit. Today she has built a career that has branched out from Black Mom's Blog. Now the blog doesn't get nearly as much hate as it did in the beginning, because through hard work, she has built a stronger community. As many influencers acknowledge, her community is loyal and protective. When someone does post something racist or rude, Boswell usually doesn't have to deal with it because members of her community speak up.

How did Boswell get through the lowest times? "I'm a huge believer in balance," she says. She was at a real down point with the platform and was trying to figure out if she wanted to continue, so she chose to redirect her energy to other businesses and to herself. She says, "It's something that I always talk to women about—balancing your energy. So if you start a business, make sure you still find time to do other things. It doesn't have to be another business; it could be forms of self-care. It could be taking vacations, it could be reading a book, creating hobbies—things that you truly love to do. For me, whenever I feel like I'm becoming overwhelmed or exhausted, I tap into my self-care."

On a broader level, in terms of combating racist hate, we spoke with Ewoldsen, who emphasizes the idea of the social contract, which he thinks has been lost. Social contract theory is an unspoken agreement among the members of a society to work together and cooperate for social benefits. Ewoldsen believes that as members of the digital community and society at large, people have a responsibility to speak out when they see things like racism, homophobia, ableism, ageism, misogyny, and body shaming. It could take the form of privately contacting a recipient of the hate to offer support or publicly speaking out against the hate.

An example is writer/activist Kim Guerra, who considers herself lucky because most of her followers are loving and empowering. Still, she does get some disparaging comments. "If I feel like it's just hate[ful] people, and it's not going to bring out a pretty side of me or a kind side of me, I try usually to ignore them. But if I feel this is going to be an educational moment, I do respond with some sass. . . . I say, 'I don't tolerate this behavior on this page, so kindly see yourself out.' I do things like that because I also want—especially younger girls that are following me—to see you're always going to encounter that here and there, but you also get to decide and teach people how to treat you and set those boundaries."

INFLUENCERS SPREADING HATE: "I BECAME THIS MONSTER"

When it's influencers who are throwing shade and fomenting hate, it's like a horror flick where the killer is calling from inside the house. The threat is internal to the industry rather than coming from fans or followers. Infamous gossip blogger and author of *TMI: My Life in Scandal* Perez Hilton came to the realization that he needed to clean his own house.

Forthcoming and self-reflective, he discusses the dark spots in his past and the consequences they've had on his present. Hilton started his career in 2004 and says, "I was nasty, awful, vicious, cruel for six years. I've been much more positive for longer than I was negative, but during those six years, I did so much damage that so many people still only see me that way."

Hilton is not shy about expressing his regret for what happened during that six-year time frame, which included outing people, doodling inappropriate things on photos, giving people nasty nicknames, posting paparazzi photos of celebrity children and people in mourning, issuing personal attacks, and engaging in general bullying. He says, "Bethenny Frankel got really upset at me back in the day when I revealed her pregnancy before she was ready to reveal that to the world, and I ended up being a plotline on *The Real Housewives of New York.*" The litany of celebrity grievances against him is long.

What's interesting is that things didn't start out that way. "I don't think at the very beginning, I was quite so mean. But then I saw that my behavior was being rewarded and it became like this drug. I started getting more out of control and became this monster and I really, truly, deeply, sincerely regret that, and I carry so much shame with me. Being young is not an excuse. I did know what I was doing was wrong, but I did it anyways. Same with a drug addict. Drug addicts know, 'I'm shooting up heroin. That's wrong, but I'm still doing it.' Sometimes we know what we're doing isn't good for us or for others, and we do it anyways. And that sucks."

Hilton needed to hit rock bottom in order to force change in a positive direction. His bottom came in 2010, after a horrific rash of LGBTQIA+ teenage suicides. All the teens who took their own lives had been bullied about their sexual orientation. Journalist Dan Savage started the It Gets Better project, creating videos to help gay teens see that life can improve after bullying in their early years. Hilton was the first public figure to make an It Gets Better video.

He says, "I was doing something positive by making that video. And the response that I got to my video shook me to my core. The overwhelming majority of comments said, 'How dare you make an

It Gets Better video! You're a hypocrite, you're a bully, you're a part of the problem.' It made me change everything, because I don't want to be a part of the problem. From then forward, I stopped outing people." In fact, he stopped a whole catalog of problematic behaviors. Now he's about incisive opinion rather than personal attack. There are even things he won't post; instead of outing Covid-19-positive celebrities who wanted that diagnosis to remain private, he posted without revealing names.

But Hilton's past still haunts him. When asked if he could go back and change something, his immediate response is to the toxicity of those six years. He says, "I hurt other people, and if I could go back and change it for that reason, I would. And also, I like to be honest, that's the main reason why I would change things, and then I would change things for selfish reasons—for my kids. I know that in the future, my kids will suffer because of the mistakes that I made in the past. And also from my own personal selfish reasons, I still, to this day, suffer consequences over my previous mistakes. If I didn't do all of that, I would have an easier time now in many ways. . . . There are still brands that don't want to align themselves with me. Even right now, I'm in between agents, and it's not exactly the easiest process. Some agencies don't want to represent me." Hilton also laments the fact that dating is more difficult because of his past. "Being Perez Hilton is what makes it harder, because most gay men don't like me."

The consequences of his actions online have hit Hilton hard, but he's still in the fight to stay relevant, using everything in his arsenal, except hate. "It's good to do the right thing for many reasons," he emphasizes. In terms of the voluminous amount of hate Hilton still receives, he shields himself with his many years' experience. He used to be more sensitive about it, but "now, you could say the most awful things about me, about my children, about my mom. I don't care. They're strangers. I don't know these people. Yeah, who cares? Yeah, I don't care!"

HATE TOWARD ATHLETES

Athletes are a special category because they're not influencers first. In fact, quite a few might be influencers reluctantly. Athletes also have the added element of fans of opposing teams jumping in and sending hate for no real reason other than team loyalty. Sports manager Jeff Chilcoat sees a particular issue with younger athletes because he argues that's when they're most susceptible to negative comments. Everything new comes at them all of a sudden as young athletes, so distractions can be detrimental. Chilcoat says, "As much as you think you're invincible—because that's the mindset you have to have as an athlete—you're not. You're going to tire out, and you're going to get your feelings hurt." He recommends simply staying away from the comments section.

Some are advocating more than that, including taking breaks from social media. During Super Bowl LVI media day on February 7, 2022, Cincinnati Bengals quarterback Joe Burrow told reporters that his advice for young athletes was, "Focus on getting better. Don't have a workout and post it on Instagram the next day and then go sit on your butt the next day and everyone thinks you're working hard but you're not. Work in silence. Don't show anyone what you're doing. Let your performance on Friday nights and Saturday nights and Sunday nights show all the hard work you put in. Don't worry about all that social media stuff."[6]

How much athletes internalize the negativity remains unknown. As is the case with other influencers, it seems that female athletes bear the brunt of a negative focus on how they look. Chilcoat says, "When it comes to appearance, unfortunately, I don't feel like people are judging guys for how they appear in their sport, and I do think we hear fan negativity regarding how a female looks in their sport. It's completely unfair."

Coaches train individuals in their sport to be both physically and mentally tough, but to what extent does this grit and resilience pertain to social media? Agent Alexa Stabler says, "They play a game that has conditioned them to be so strong, in a sense, you can take anything. They get beat up and hit every day, so if somebody makes a snide comment, or a rude comment, or is trolling you on the internet, is that really something they get upset about?"

Looking back at Maslow's need hierarchy puts Stabler's comments into some perspective. Physical safety needs come before love and esteem needs, so focusing on staying in one piece could put off any rumination about negative comments on social media for the time being. Stabler adds, "We're all human. If someone says something mean about you, that's certainly going to affect you. Maybe it doesn't ruin your day like someone else's."

Of course, in football culture, talking about feelings is not exactly the norm. It remains to be seen how much these athletes or their game are affected by hate. What happens when an athlete, phone in hand, is at home at night on the couch, scrolling though derogatory comments and death threats? As a general matter, Stabler says that she encourages the football players she reps to be open and communicate their feelings.

Douglas O'Neal Middleton Jr., NFL veteran safety, has seen his share of online hate. He remarks, "I've had some games before New York where I get on and I typed my name on Twitter and I see some pretty bad things, so it's tough. . . . Words impact people and people feel words even though they can't see the people that are saying those things. . . . You go on and see those things and you go out there the next day—those things impact you. . . . People expect us to be so strong as athletes, like, oh, nothing hurts those guys; they can overcome anything. And that's true. We're very strong people, very resilient people, but we do feel some of the comments and some of the pain, so I mean I wouldn't completely brush it off, but I will say that it's one of the many things that we're forced to overcome as athletes."

Social media is unique in that it follows players from the game into their home life. Coaching trains them to block out the noise, including social media comments, but some players may be more susceptible to distraction than others. Then there are those athletes who choose not to turn it off and instead use the negativity as motivation.

HANDLING THE HATE: NAME IT!

Licensed clinical psychologists and cofounders of Black Mental Wellness Danielle R. Busby and Dana L. Cunningham both think that naming the hate is the first step to learning how to cope with it. Don't ignore or repress the problem. Instead, see it for what it is. Recognize what's happening and when it's happening, as well as the types of thoughts and emotions it brings up.

For people of color and other marginalized community members, Cunningham says it's important to not personalize it: "It's not about you; it's about something larger that's happening out there. . . . It's a reflection of what's happening in our society." Seeing this helps prevent the comments from being internalized and incorporated into the person's sense of self-worth. It's not within an influencer's control.

Brian Carey Sims, African media psychologist and associate professor in the department of psychology at Florida A&M University, notes that an important difference between now and the past is that real-world experiences of hate may be altered by the digital world. What used to be interpersonal scenarios are now becoming globally publicized events within moments. He gives the example of someone on the receiving end of racially charged nastiness at the grocery store or in their car. Before social media, that interaction might be witnessed by a couple of onlookers. Now it's occurring on the scale of publicly viewable theater. The victim and perpetrator are not only interacting in an interpersonal dimension but are also thinking, "This is gonna be livestreamed on Facebook," wondering what it's going to look like to people now and in the future. "So in any given social scenario, when the phones come out, it's not like that interaction is going to go away, that video is literally going to live forever. . . . The social media paradigm adds additional layers to how individuals are acting and reacting in the moment," Sims says.

Busby states that as with all of these experiences, recognizing what is within your control and outside of it is crucial. "There's a box of things that you can control, which is going to be you. And there's the other box of everybody else and other things you can't control." She urges acceptance of that while doing what you can with the contents of your box. In that way, people can create more meaningful and healthy experiences and perhaps have an impact on the bigger picture.

The experts we talked with emphasized that necessity of having a strategy to deal with the hate before it overtakes the influencer. When they're in the thick of the storm without a plan, it gets too dark too quickly, and the intensity of emotion makes it harder to gain control and composure before acting. Busby says, "Think about what strategies help you to check out for a second or help you de-escalate if you're feeling like you're going up and down, up and down. What are your experiences that help you ground yourself? Is it breath work? Is it mindfulness? Is it going outside and taking a walk when you're feeling yourself reacting? And then being intentional about, 'When I see this, I'm going to try to do one of these things,' and plan out what that can look like and what you would need to make it happen."

BIG PICTURE PSYCHOLOGICAL SOLUTIONS

There are many effective smaller-scale approaches to dealing with likes and hate, and it's worth devoting time to them. However, it's also important to step back and take a look at the big picture. Mike Brooks argues that individuals can't solve societal problems by staying at the same level with them. The influencers must put themselves in an observer's role in order to examine the issue from different angles and find a more skillful approach. This way of looking at things is an aspect of mindfulness and Buddhist nonattachment.

When we step back, what do we see? Brooks says, "Instead of seeing our differences, we need to see how we're alike. And also see how we are all part of the problem. . . . If we can't see ourselves in the other, we're in trouble."

We all share some of the same human experiences. We're happy when we find love. We cheer when our team wins. We mourn when loved ones die. We all know pain and suffering. The question is, can we get past our grievances and empathize with the suffering of others?

Not only is it counterproductive to hold on to resentments and respond to hate with hate, it's also toxic for us. Brooks paraphrases a famous quote saying that hatred is the poison we drink while waiting for the other person to die. Being in a constant state of anger, hate, and stress takes its toll mentally as well as physically, with increasing blood pressure and a suppressed immune system. We won't be able to curb hate online until we curb our own hate and any role we have in it.

Last, Brooks says we need to more fully tap into the flexibility and adaptability that helped us evolve as humans. Technology is changing the world at warp speed—so much so that technological evolution zooms past biological evolution. "We need to really up our flexibility game so that we can more skillfully deal with the formidable challenges we face."

HATERS ARE YOUR MOTIVATORS

In the end, influencers need the practical realization that receiving hate is part of the job. That doesn't mean being complacent; we should still try to effect change. Instead, it's having a breadth and depth of understanding about what the job encompasses. Ewoldsen says that part of coping with the hate might be "the realization that

I'm going to always have people who dislike me and that's just part of being an influencer. That means people are paying attention to me and that overwhelmingly people are liking me, not dissing me. People are paying attention to me."

For Ray Ligaya, "Haters are your motivators!" When he gets hate, one of his first thoughts is "Thanks for the comment. Gives me one extra comment. Took my 100 comments to 101 comments. Great for my engagement." He cautions about the difference between constructive feedback and worthless hate. "Influencers should not care about haters, but they should care about audience feedback. . . . If someone says, 'Hey, the content you were posting before was amazing; what happened to you? Why are you posting this type of content?' If you see a bunch of people saying that, then that's when you really need to listen. That's [the] difference between hate comments and fan feedback."

YouTube megastar Lachlan Ross Power has developed a wall when it comes to the hate, but he admits that he is somewhat less impervious to more constructive negative feedback. He says, "I've had the pleasure of doing this for eight years now. I haven't read anything on the internet that's affected me in the last five. You just get such thick skin. I'm numb to it. . . . I think the comments that hurt the most are comments that you know are true. I mean that in the sense, something you did, like tried to cut the corner on maybe a little bit of production here. And it's like, they see that, and they comment. Those ones hurt the most for me, like imperfection of the craft that we've posted—they're the ones that hurt. XYZ calling me names doesn't hurt at all; don't care, doesn't matter."

For those from every vertical, having trolls and getting hate means you're in the game—you're an influencer.

SELF-ESTEEM AND SOCIAL MEDIA

When Influencers Compare and Despair

Because influencing is a unique career, unique mental health issues go along with it. Joey Zauzig says, "Your mental health gets affected because you're staring at pictures all day long of yourself. You're critical of yourself, but you also have to come up with these videos—different concepts every day, different themes. It's stressful."

The effects of social media on mental health, and self-esteem in particular, have been frequently spotlighted in the media. The topic garnered a lot of attention in 2020 when a whistle-blower shared information from an internal study about Instagram's negative effect on teenage girls' mental health and self-esteem. In an open letter to his staff, Mark Zuckerburg, CEO of Meta Platforms, the parent company of Instagram, dismissed the controversy, saying the report was misinterpreted.[1]

A significant body of research over the years has shown the negative repercussions of social media, including an association with anxiety, depression, and low self-esteem. However, the associations are not cut-and-dried; some correlations are weak, and even positive associations have been found, leaving many questions unanswered.

Colin Wayne Leach says the relationship between self-esteem and social media is something that "psychologists have really been trying to figure out for the last fifteen or twenty years, because at first there was this trend, where, especially for younger people, the more time they were online, the lower their self-esteem. It wasn't a very strong finding, but it was pretty consistent. So people have been trying to figure out what's going on."

The problem is that there can be a rush to judgment when trying to figure out what's going on. Erin Vogel, of the University of Southern California Keck School of Medicine, who has done research in this area, urges caution when interpreting studies linking social media use with mental health issues. She says, "It's hard to tell from those studies whether the social media came first or the mental health symptoms came first, because people who are more prone to depression and anxiety or other mental health symptoms also might be more prone to using social media. So it's hard for us to say whether social media caused that or not." Still, Vogel points to studies, including her own, showing short-term effects of social media use, such as negative effects on mood and how we see ourselves.[2]

Given all that, is social media bad for self-esteem and mental health in general? The answer depends on whom you ask. The research community is divided into different camps, with some who believe strongly in the negative effects of social media and others who think it's not a cause for alarm.

Vogel falls somewhere in the middle: "Personally, I think that it is an issue that warrants concern. I also don't think that social media is ruining an entire generation, or that it's terrible at all times. I think there's a lot of nuance there. And we can't say that social media is necessarily good or bad. So the way I personally conceptualize it, in my understanding of the research, is that social media can be both good and bad, depending on how you use it, and depending on the individual and their own vulnerabilities and their own personalities."

In this chapter, we look at the impact influencing has on self-esteem and body image, and we examine ways influencers buffer themselves when their esteem takes negative hits.

A DANGEROUS COMBINATION

More and more researchers are coming to the conclusion that the effects of social media differ from person to person, depending on an individual's characteristics.[3] In terms of self-esteem, people who value outside opinions and frequently look to others for validation and acceptance are more vulnerable to reacting to negativity expressed by others. Leach says, "I can imagine that there are people who are going online and trying to do their thing, and they're exposing themselves to stuff that they didn't expect. And they don't have the psychological tools and resources to discern whose opinions should matter to them. They're also not protecting themselves from those opinions. If you're open to those views and you're less discerning, and you're exposing yourself over and over again to devastating criticism, this can be really harmful."

He emphasizes that it's the combination of psychological makeup and level of exposure to negativity that largely determines the risk factor. For example, having a mood disorder, anxiety disorder, or personality disorder contributes to a person's risk, but the risk then increases further as they are subjected to more and more online content. The rub? The nature of influencing means that individuals will almost certainly be subjected to a large amount of negativity and forced comparisons with others.

Booktuber Cindy Pham is one of the many influencers with a personality type that puts her at risk. She readily admits to internalizing negative feedback from followers. She takes online opinions to heart even though she intellectually knows that the people with loud, toxic voices only see a miniscule percentage of her real self and her real life. She says, "It's something I've talked about with my therapist. I think I seek them out because it's a way of validating my own negative self-talk. I feel a certain way about myself—whether I think I'm a bad person, or I'm annoying or whatever."

Even though disparaging comments might be in the minority, they hold just as much weight for her—possibly more than the positive comments, because that's where her "brain gravitates to naturally." It's the negativity bias played out with additional vulnerabilities. Depression adds another layer to it.

A tough phenomenon that Pham has had to deal with as a book-tuber is Stan Twitter. The term refers to superfans of things like book series, TV series, musicians, and celebrities. These Stans, usually minors or young adults, voice their opinions online in not-so-subtle, sometimes fanatical ways. Pham says, "I don't think that demographic realizes the impact of that kind of behavior against people, because a lot of people don't realize that content creators actually have feelings beyond what they show on camera, or issues or drama that they might not know about. I think there's this degree of separation where people feel like they can just say whatever, and there's no impact. And they might not realize the level of impact because they're young, or they're dealing with their own personal issues. It's a lot easier to project that on to someone on the internet, who you don't know as a person, so you don't think it's as damaging."

Despite Stan Twitter and other types of negative feedback, Pham doesn't overlook the power of the positive comments. She gets joy and fulfillment from posting her videos and having high engagement. At times it bolsters her self-esteem. She says, "I deal with depression a lot. I think my issue specifically is that I have a very negative outlook on myself, where I view everything negatively, but I also view myself very negatively. I have a tendency to dismiss myself a lot and not acknowledge any of my positive attributes, or even be aware of my positive attributes. And as I'm doing my channel, every now and then I get a lot of comments that are super kind, like not just saying that my videos are funny or entertaining, but also really long comments that talk about how they appreciate me. And they just say really nice things about me, like I am smart or pretty or funny or whatever. And it's things that I wouldn't associate with myself. But to have a volume of people who say those things kind of makes me realize the discrepancy between the way I negatively view myself and the way that others actually perceive me." This type of feedback actually serves as a reality check for her, reminding her of the positive qualities that get swamped by her attention to the negative.

Pham found a way to use the positive comments as a tool for psychological growth: she collects them in a folder so she can refer to them whenever she feels down. It's a way for her to challenge the instinctual negative self-talk and to allow herself to reevaluate her identity. It's not easy to make it stick, but having the comments in a folder is a concrete way she can look back on them and force herself to remember the good stuff.

Pham is clear about the pitfalls of relying too heavily on the opinions of others—positive or negative—but is working on a healthy balance. Part of Pham's balance includes engaging in offline hobbies and keeping in touch with friends from college because they give her some distance from influencing. Being outside is also a healing experience, and a reminder that there's a "whole other world out there."

Pham is realistic and reflective about the downfalls of influencing in combination with her underlying mental health issues. "I have to accept that as a condition that comes with being a person on the internet. It's a matter of me trying to keep perspective so that it doesn't swallow me whole and that I lose sight of the bigger picture, which is that there's way more beyond the internet. I think that's why I don't want to be a full-time content creator—because I hesitate to devote my entire income on other people liking me or not."

A familiar story is one in which at-risk younger people use social media as a lifeline. The short-term effects can be positive, but in the long term, without help, the vulnerabilities are still there, and the very aspects of social media that were formerly helpful can turn harmful.

Kyle Hernandez is an influencer who credits social media for bringing him out of the depths of depression. Born in Louisiana, he moved to a small town in Colorado after high school because he was unsatisfied with his life. "I didn't know where I was going with it, per se, and so I decided that the best situation for me is to move and get out," he says. After his best friend moved away, Hernandez found himself alone in Colorado. Secluded and smoking weed every day, he descended into a dark place. "I just started getting down on myself," Hernandez says.

His self-esteem plummeted and the depression built. He recalls, "I just started noticing that every day, I'll start to get a little bit more sad, more sad, more sad. It was a Friday in November; I decided that I was going to go commit suicide in the middle of the forest. But that day, that exact day, I was on Facebook scrolling or whatever—and TikTok was only out for about three months at this point, two months, I think—and I'm scrolling, and I see this ad for TikTok."

He had heard about the short music clips on TikTok, but the advertisement was geared toward comedy clips, which is something he had done on his YouTube channel in the past and liked. "I decided, you know what, screw it. I'm just gonna do it. And I downloaded TikTok. . . . So the first video that I made got like sixty-something views and I'm like, no way! Who are these sixty-something people? . . . I had no clue if I was gonna get any views, and I didn't care if I was gonna get any views or anything. I really just wanted to make myself laugh at the moment. . . . And then I'll post the second video. And the second video gets like 1,400 views and I'm like, this is insane!"

His mood changed and he continued posting. "I'm freaking out—let me just do the same exact thing tomorrow. So the gun that I bought, I literally put by my bedside table. And I literally just left it there. . . . I ended up getting on this path of every single day: I'm just gonna post three to five videos every single day, and I didn't skip a beat for six months, and that gun stayed exactly where it was. So I'm not saying that I fully would have committed—I probably would have gotten scared right at the end and not done it. But at the end of the day, something told me to go download TikTok. For some reason it started doing well." As of 2022, @kyleblockbuster had 1.7 million followers on TikTok.

In this situation, social media obviously turned out to be a posi-tive force. The danger is that Hernandez's mental health issues were helped by a surge in followers, which is a surface solution, whereas a more in-depth one is needed. Hernandez did find purpose and self-worth in that moment and beyond, but what happens when that purpose and self-esteem are threatened by something like a drop in followers? Tools and techniques are needed to help Hernandez and people in this vulnerable position with the inevitable ups and downs of influencing.

COMPARE, BUT DON'T DESPAIR

In 1954, psychologist Leon Festinger proposed the social comparison theory, which centers around the idea that people have an innate drive to evaluate their opinions and abilities in relation to others. By drawing comparisons to the those around them, people form judgments about themselves and define who they are. When people want to feel better about themselves, they tend to seek downward comparisons with individuals who are worse off, but when they need motivation or inspiration, they tend to look for upward comparisons with individuals who are better off. The tricky part is that upward comparisons, especially when there are a lot of them, can damage self-esteem, causing feelings of inadequacy and self-doubt.

Before digital spaces, people mainly compared themselves to those around them at school, at their jobs, at social organizations, and in places of worship. Movies, TV shows, and magazines drove home a glitzy, seemingly unattainable celebrity culture. Even so, it didn't seem as ubiquitous and invasive as social media.

The question then becomes, how does social comparison differ online versus in the real world, perhaps in a common scenario like walking into a party, sizing everyone up, and immediately comparing yourself to the other guests? First of all is sheer number. At a party, only a finite number of people are there, available for comparison. Online, that number is infinite. Online, there are also a massive number of richer, prettier, smarter, and more talented people. In a global online community, there aren't many spots open to be the best. In contrast, in someone's town or neighborhood, statistically, it's not as hard to be number one. In their own area, people are more likely to come across others who are relatively equal regarding social status, economic status, and education level. It's the difference between being a big fish in a small pond, and a big fish in a vast ocean of fish, sharks, and whales.

Second is the amount of time spent online. Years ago, even if employees of a large company spent time and energy comparing themselves to their fellow workers, home could still be their refuge. Now, influencers live in a world where their career and home lives are enmeshed, with few boundaries between work time and downtime. With the constant barrage of images, videos, and text that they must attend to, influencers are less able to get away from the inevitable comparisons. Leach notes that people are tying their self-esteem and self-worth to "day-by-day, hour-by-hour, minute-by-minute feedback, and attention from other people, and when they're not getting it, feeling really bad."

Third, the comparisons aren't apples to apples. Years ago, a party-goer wasn't likely to know details about every single guest in attendance. Online, there's an abundance of information about people's lives that, for some, borders on TMI. Erin Vogel says, "On social media, we have so much information about people that we barely know. We're not just seeing how somebody is presenting themselves at a party; we're seeing everything that they're sharing about their life on social media, which can be a lot. And when we see all that information, it's easy to forget that they're not sharing absolutely everything. It's still kind of a highlight reel. So those comparisons are still there, but we're really getting a lot of rich information about people that we barely know, or people that we've never met in real life."

Instead of comparing real life to real life, we're comparing real life to highlight reel. However, because we may not fully recognize that it's just a highlight reel, it's playing a cognitive trick on us, making us think that we know more than we actually do. The highlight reel isn't necessarily fake, but many people do tend to post the positive, celebratory moments in their lives, marking holidays, anniversaries, weddings, birthdays, and parties.

Fashion influencer and curve model Kristina Zias says, "There's a comparison game that I struggled with in the beginning. Oh, for sure! When I was trying to build this, I definitely struggled with my self-esteem because I felt like I couldn't compete with people who looked a certain way, or who had more money, and were wearing the designer bags, getting invited to these cool events, and going to fashion week in Paris. That definitely takes a hit to your self-esteem because not only are you not making money, but you just can't compete. But I think when I stopped trying to be someone else, when I started owning who I was and carving out my own path and realizing that I didn't have to [fit] the mold of that person—I'm not that person; I don't want to be that person—that's when I really started to grow. And that's when my self-esteem and my business and everything grew as well."

Again, personality type plays a role. People use comparisons as part of their self-definition to varying degrees. Some people are more externally focused, and some are more internally focused. The key seems to be striking the right balance.

Celeste Viciere, aka Celeste the Therapist, a mental health advocate and podcast host, stresses the importance of "creating affirmations for yourself and reminding yourself that the goal is to be better than who you were yesterday, not better than your neighbor or anyone else." However, this can be easier said than done. She adds, "Kids are literally looking at people their same age group on Instagram or Facebook and starting to say, 'Why not me?' . . . I think that logic kicks out and the emotion comes in. And all of a sudden, they feel insecure because they're seeing something that they want and that they don't have. They really have to work on reminding themselves that if they don't wake up and be intentional about programming their mind, then they're choosing for society to program their mind."

Each influencer has a unique way to deal with the despair. Laura Vogel had a client who deleted Instagram from her phone because of the negative psychological hit she took from the comparison game. Vogel says, "For some people, even if you have more than 5 million followers, you don't have 10 million, you don't have 20 million. It's very easy to compare and despair." This particular person decided to let the team handle her social media, but that's not an option for most influencers.

To get himself out of the downward spiral, fashion and lifestyle influencer Ooreofe Oluwadara challenges some widely held assumptions, focuses on the motivational aspects of comparisons, and tries to live in gratitude. He says, "If you're not strong-willed, it's easy to get swept into a cycle of insecurity and wanting to be somebody else, or wanting to have something somebody else has, or feeling like you're not enough, which I sometimes find myself falling into. But then I'll snap out of it because I live in a decent apartment in New York, and I'm doing better than a lot of people are doing. . . . It's really OK to be average. You don't need to have Jeff Bezos's money. There are plenty of people who make $200,000, $400,000, a million dollars a year, that nobody talks about that do perfectly fine and live perfectly well. I think everybody wants to be all the way at the top, but you don't really need to be at the top."

Oluwadara uses his training as a track athlete in college to lift himself up when self-doubt creeps into his psyche by using competition as a source of motivation. He mentions another influencer who had 10K followers and posted a picture of a $5,000 check he got for a single post. "I'm like, OK, if he can do that, I can do that too. A couple days after, I started listing brands that I want to work with and what I need to do to get there. So that motivates me even more," he insists.

Dana L. Cunningham believes that some influencers can use the comparison with peers who are more or less equal to generate motivation because at times the internet can be a relatable space. "So you can say, oh, look at this person who's very similar. I can relate to them. I kind of vibe with certain things that they post. They're doing it!"

Aditi Oberoi Malhotra thinks that social media has been positive for her in this way. She says, "It has affected me by helping me to see how you can make your dreams come true. There are so many success stories out there, whether or not people are ready to accept it. There are many influencers who have literally turned their thing into successful businesses. You see many influencers being picked up by big stores like Sephora and Nordstrom." Rather than comparing and despairing, she uses others' platforms as a blueprint for success.

The paradoxical mix of influencers' self-esteem dropping on the one hand but elevating on the other was a consistent theme with the influencers we interviewed. For example, disability lifestyle influencer and actor Lauren "Lolo" Spencer, says, "For me, it actually helped my self-esteem, because the more vulnerable I become in my content, the more I share things that are not that social media standard. . . . It's a tool for me to say, I've already shared this, so you can't weaponize that against me, because I've already owned this part of who I am or this experience."

However, careerwise, Spencer sometimes finds herself caught up in the comparison game. She will ask herself, "Am I doing enough? Am I posting enough content? Is the content still helping people? I'm seeing some other influencers who are also disabled have certain levels of successes that I'm wondering, what are they doing that I'm not? . . . Are they more ambitious than me?"

When these questions begin to chip away at her self-esteem, Spencer has a toolbox that she reaches into to deal with it. "If it's something really concerning for me, I'll talk with my team, or I have a lot of different mental health and spiritual practices that I tap into. I have built up my awareness of when I'm getting a little off track, like, OK, I'm thinking about this too much—let me put this down and go watch TV for a second, or I need to journal now, or I'll book an appointment with my therapist. Therapy has helped me tenfold. Or I'll meditate, or those kinds of things. So I just have my different rituals and practices to get me back on track and feeling better," she says.

FILTERED BEAUTY, BODY IMAGE, AND STEPPING INTO POWER

Of all the comparison games, ones revolving around body image are among the most common. Influencers' disordered body images, fueled by social media–driven comparisons, may lead to eating disorders or body dysmorphic disorder, an obsession with perceived flaws in physical appearance. Individuals with preexisting body concept issues are particularly susceptible to the house odds in this game, but everyone is vulnerable to it.

Ashley Iaconetti Haibon describes herself as a shy student. She was someone who hesitated to raise her hand in class, although she got more comfortable in grad school. Once she became part of the Bachelor franchise, however, everything changed. Nerves went by the wayside. Now, doing live TV doesn't even cause a butterfly in her stomach. In terms of looks, she deals with insecurities common to most people, but she has a "pretty healthy body image and self-esteem." Still, it doesn't make her impervious to the pressure of perfection that exists online.

She says, "My concept of beauty has definitely been affected by social media. I mean, the filters! I follow this one account; it's called Goddess Women [goddess.women on Instagram], and it's the most beautiful celebrities that there are. They take them and they Photoshop them to look even prettier. And I'm like, how do I achieve this? And I'm like, reality check—they didn't even achieve it! So I will say that social media—just seeing all the pretty people in this world that exist—for some reason, it's different than magazines used to be, because magazines used to tell you this is all manipulated, and these are models. But now with Instagram, sometimes you don't know if it's manipulated, but [also] . . . these are regular girls, apparently not the elite. So are regular girls supposed to look like that?" (Point well taken, but it's more waxing nostalgic than factual that magazines were that transparent about photo manipulation back in the day.)

How much does the need to keep up with the fabulously unflawed affect Iaconetti Haibon in her everyday life? She indicates that it's a constant drip, drip, drip, but nothing devastating. "I'm not carrying it around with me, but I'm probably more critical of myself in the mirror just because I see this perfect imagery every day, not just when I pick up a magazine, not just with models, but with girls who apparently are living their everyday life looking that good all the time," she says sarcastically.

As the years go on, these feelings of insecurity get worse for Iaconetti Haibon. The filters people use to enhance their looks really get on her nerves, to the extent that she's making a conscious choice to limit their use. She says, "It's insane. I try not to use filters on myself as much because I think I'm putting a bad message out there. I'll use one little filter that just blurs your skin a little bit extra. But these ones that totally distort your face, like make your cheekbones so high, and your eyes so wide, and your lips really full—I try not to do that because I know that I'm being a bad demonstration for the girls who follow me." Sometimes she'll show filtered and unfiltered photos side by side, "just to keep it real."

Lately, the trend has been to call out influencers who are overfiltered. For example, the Kardashians have been in the media quite a bit for fake-ish photos with headlines that read, "Kim Kardashian Accused of Photoshopping Now-Deleted Instagram Photo"; "Kourtney Kardashian Deletes Photo of Her Backside after Getting Called Out for 'Bad' Photoshop"; "Khloé Kardashian Fans Are Claiming They've

Spotted a Hilarious Photoshop Fail in Her Latest Instagram Post after She Was Left 'Embarrassed' When an Unedited Bikini Picture Went Viral."[4] It remains to be seen whether this type of backlash will lead to any kind of significant change, or whether it amounts to nothing more than pointing out a Photoshopped needle in a stack of filtered hay.

Mary Fitzgerald of *Selling Sunset,* who projects confidence in herself, also isn't in love with filters. She says, "I don't do Photoshop or anything like that. If I haven't done my makeup or something, I'll use a filter to try to make myself look a little bit better. I try not to fall into that. I see even good friends that have to approve every photo to make sure they look the best and then they take in their waist, they accentuate their lips and stuff. . . . I've just never been that person. I think people follow me and they like me because I think I'm more grounded and down to earth. If I ever do fall into that mindset, I hope someone gets me out of it because it's really not healthy. I see these young girls and even friends where I'm like, why are you doing that? That's not you. Some of the photos don't even look like them when they post them."

She stresses that the photo may be beautiful, but it's not the real person. On occasion, she'll say something to a friend, but they often ignore her advice to "just post you." Fitzgerald isn't new to this mindset because it's prevalent in LA. "It's all about looks and everyone's trying to be more beautiful and outdo someone else, like get all the plastic surgery and stuff to fix it. I don't have anything against plastic surgery or fillers and Botox, but I think if you do it, it should be to accentuate yourself, not to change yourself," she says. Even though the youth/beauty ethos is endemic in LA, Fitzgerald believes that "social media has definitely made it worse."

Beauty filters, which are the photo-editing tools used to adjust and enhance photos and selfies (for example, the FaceTune app), along with real-life editing and enhancement through fillers and plastic surgery, are contributing to what is known as the Instagram Face: the uniform look that boasts full, high cheekbones; large, blank eyes weighed down by lengthy lashes; a small nose; smooth, plump lips; and plasticky, poreless skin. In an article about the Instagram Face, Jia Tolentino addresses the racial aspects of Instagram face, noting, "It was as if the algorithmic tendency to flatten everything into a composite of greatest hits had resulted in a beauty ideal that favored white women capable of manufacturing a look of rootless exoticism."[5]

Along with Instagram Face, Instagram Body is also taking hold. In teen boys and young men, a phenom colloquially known as bigorexia has fueled an obsession with bulking up and building muscle, thereby creating a particular type of body that can now be seen across social media.[6] The point of all the workouts and protein shakes is not to compete in a sport; it's to compete on TikTok and other platforms. Research shows that an unhealthy fixation on this six-pack-based social media standard may increase the risk of muscularity-related eating disorders.[7]

But Instagram Face and Instagram Body are business. That business, along with the desire to have the power and status that go hand in hand with youth and beauty, propels even younger people toward more radical fixes. Even millennials and Gen Zers are racing to plastic surgeons, images of their favorite influencers in hand, showing them how they want to look, so that they too can measure up to a sculpted standard, rendering them image ready.

For influencers with a history of eating disorders like anorexia, bulimia, or binge eating, viewing an endless feed of perfect images can heighten the problem. Many find successful, creative ways to cope. Kim Guerra is a queer woman of color who holds a license in marriage and family therapy. As someone with personal experience dealing with an eating disorder, Guerra has a conscious way of engaging in social media. She says, "I think when you're on social media, it's very easy to disconnect from them being a person. You see their picture; it's very curated. And not only do you see that, you see other people's reaction and response to it. You see the likes. You see the comments. You see sometimes paid sponsorships, and my goodness, they're getting paid this amount of money to wear this little bathing suit and look like this! . . . I cannot let myself compare because that's going to be detrimental to me. Growing up, I overcame disordered eating and issues with loving my body and being comfortable with myself, so I have to be extra careful. And then I also have to be mindful with the stuff I post. If I post myself in a bathing suit, I want to make sure that at times, I show some of my rolls and some of my hairiness or imperfection so that I don't make other people feel that way. I want them to see a woman that's loving herself fully without having to alter her image. And that's also been a journey, because it requires you to be vulnerable with yourself and with the people in your circles—in your network."

The beginning of Guerra's journey as an influencer wasn't an easy one. The negativity sometimes bled into her offline life with other influencers. "It was, how many followers do you have? And what do you look like? . . . People wouldn't hang out with you if you didn't have a certain amount of followers." It was all new to her at the time.

When she started to share her work, Guerra had to remind herself that "social media can have power over you, or you can step in with your own power. . . . At least my little corner of social media is going to be a source of empowerment, and a source of joy and goodness. It's going to be a source of love. And that's what it's become for me. And a lot of times I have to filter who I follow and how they're impacting how I feel, or how I see myself, or the world around me, and I want to make sure that when people come to my page or when they encounter my work on the social media world that they feel joy, that they feel love, that they feel empowered."

Spanish American blogger, mental health advocate, and eating disorder survivor Lorraine Ladish has both ageism and body negativity to deal with online. Ladish, who is in her late fifties, notes that the kind of criticism influencers get when they're older is somewhat different. "It's interesting because when you're young, maybe the discussion is something about weight or having stretch marks or whatever. When you're older, sometimes the criticism is, 'You look horrible and old and full of wrinkles,' or 'You look too young for your age; you had work done. Why did you do that?' There's no winning," she laments.

A growing number of celebrities with big online presences are pushing back against ageism. For instance, former supermodel Paulina Porizkova, born in 1965, has been a leader in antiageism; she dares to post untouched photos, speaks out against the cult of youth obsession, and shows that people over fifty don't need to walk in the shadows.

Thanks to her strong sense of self, Ladish has no intention of stepping foot in the shadows. She is OK with being online now, but she believes that years ago, when her eating disorder was more virulent, it would have been too much to handle. Today, she speaks out about normalizing aging bodies. Next to a post of herself confidently posing in a bikini, she writes, "When I first saw my aging and sagging skin in pictures I was horrified. Eventually, I accepted it and am working on not being upset by the physical marks of aging. I've said it before and will say it again. I did not waste time and energy in my youth in the grips of an eating disorder and crippled by depression only to do it again, this time over the passage of time. No thank you!" She encourages followers to look at current close-ups juxtaposed with photos of herself at twenty-one, when she was in the throes of bulimia.

For Chloe Long, being able to relate to followers who struggle with their weight gives her solace, although she also has had to deal with frequent "nasty" comments during times when she weighed more. In order to maintain her mental health, she tries to focus on the positive side. "I know it definitely has helped because the amount of people that message me and DM me who are not the typical size double zero. . . . You don't have to be a supermodel stick-thin person to be on a show or become whatever. I'm still human, so of course I have insecurities, but I really am a very confident person, whether I was fifty pounds heavier, whether I weighed this way, or whether I'm 125 pounds—

I know that there's no reason to beat yourself up. . . . So I think being that I've been heavier and being confident has helped so many people. Hearing from them literally makes my world go round."

It's comforting for Long when she gets messages from people saying things like, "Seeing you and watching your posts makes me feel so much better. I struggle with anxiety and depression in my way, and you give me motivation."

SAVE YOURSELF: DIVERSIFY AND DISTANCE

Wanting social approval and having it affect self-esteem in both positive and negative ways are part of being human. Defining ourselves by those around us existed long before social media and influencers, but because influencers depend on likes and comments for their livelihood, it adds an extra element of risk to the psyche. Erin Vogel believes that it doesn't necessarily give influencers a false sense of self, but self-esteem is much more fragile if they're frequently relying on others for their esteem needs.

This is why diversification and a little distance are so important. Vogel says, "If people can diversify where they're getting their money from, as well as where they're getting their self-esteem from, that can help. So not putting all your eggs in one basket, and not relying on all those social media likes might take some of that pressure off, at least in terms of making money, but also in terms of how you view yourself and your self-esteem."

For some influencers, the idea of diversifying income is jarring and unpalatable. Going from full time to part time may seem more like giving up than diversifying. Viciere says, "Unfortunately, sometimes people may look at it as a failure, if they have to get a part-time job, if they already went full force into the social media influencer role. But at the end of the day, your mind is fragile; you only have one. . . . A lot of times, people tend to get to their breaking point and won't all the time come back from it. So I think if we can really think about what we're doing to our mind, when the hate and the things that are being said are harming us, we would take better care of ourselves."

Balancing money and mental health is not an easy process. Whether influencers are part time or full time, it's important to be mindful about where self-esteem boosts are coming from. Is a large percentage coming from online sources? For a better balance, influencers need to look to offline friends and family for approval. They also should move toward different sources of esteem, like taking up a hobby or simply engaging in activities that they're good at.

However, even after taking measures to diversify, whether it be income or validation, influencing and social media can still change how people view themselves, which fortunately, according to Erin Vogel, isn't necessarily a bad thing, depending on the way an influencer approaches social media. She says, "It's important to remember that their followers don't know them in real life and don't know everything about them. And that their entire self-esteem shouldn't necessarily be dependent on their followers' opinions of them." This is where the need for space comes in. Vogel continues, "For influencers, it can be important to have some separation between their work life and their personal life. So even if they are really trying to be authentic on social media, it's still OK to have aspects of their life that they're not comfortable sharing. It's still OK to have some things that you're private about. And I think that creating a little bit of distance from your following of people that you don't know and your actual self and your relationships in real life can be really healthy."

A major theme that runs through all the techniques used to combat social media's effect on self-esteem and mental health in general is awareness of the problem and influencers' awareness of their own vulnerabilities. It's unhealthy to go into this career path unaware of the social and psychological mechanisms at work. Mindfulness, education, and counseling are major steps in this direction.

CANCEL THIS!

Influencers React to Cancel Culture and Deplatforming

Cancel culture is on the mind of many interviewed for this book. Some are worried it could happen to them. Some have had it happen to them. Mississippi native and TikToker Logan Isbell, who is in his early twenties, says, "Influencers have to make sure if they post something that it's not coming off offensive to the person they are sharing it to. It's a lot of pressure because cancel culture will come for you, and they can end everything you worked for."

Cancel culture is a modern form of exile, but instead of sending Napoleon to Elba Island, society kicks individuals out of cultural relevance and deplatforms them. The canceled may lose their careers and their public voice. For some, the purpose of cancel culture is to call out unjust, unethical, or immoral behavior. They think it's a way to speak truth to power and hold people accountable, but many think it has gone too far. Barack Obama said this of cancel culture: "That's not activism. That's not bringing about change. If all you're doing is casting stones, you're probably not going to get that far. That's easy to do."[1]

This chapter examines cancel culture's effect on influencers, how influencers avoid being canceled, and steps influencers can take toward making a comeback.

IS CANCEL CULTURE A NEW THING?

Cancel culture is not something that was invented with the internet. Colin Wayne Leach says, "For the whole time that humans have organized themselves into communities, we have paid attention to people's ethical behavior—unfair behavior. And the greatest punishment we have is social punishment, is ostracism, is criticism, is damaging someone's reputation, talking about their reputation. Gossip plays this role." It's a way of socially regulating behavior, which is not new to Twitter or Facebook.

What's new is the context in which it's happening. Leach says, "We have villages within villages, so there is so much polarization in our society, and in many societies, that we have competing community standards now of what's right and what's acceptable." Because divergent virtual communities are competing to set the standards of moral and ethical behavior, there is less agreement about right and wrong than in the past. Leach argues that this is what cancel culture is really about: disagreement over standards.

Isn't today's way of doling out punishment more immediate? Not according to Leach, who poses the question, "Is it any more immediate than living in a village and being caught stealing, and the whole village pours out and bashes you?"

Because today the punishment is often coming from the outside, instead of within a small village, offending influencers may be less amenable to accepting their punishment; they may not want to have another group's values imposed on them. More voices can lead to more ambiguity and more conflict. After all, who gets to decide what constitutes a crime and what constitutes the punishment? Further, how can the canceled become the uncanceled? The virtual world is new enough that these issues are still being worked out online, in real time, with no certainty on the horizon anytime soon.

CANCELPROOF

Are there some people with immunity to cancellation? Perez Hilton is first in line to declare his invulnerability, and he has a good case to back it up. He argues, "I'm cancelproof because for the entirety of my career, I have been disliked more than I have been liked. I don't trade in my popularity. My popularity is not what determines my success. My giving people what they want and need and providing that service for them—that distraction, that entertainment—is what determines my success. . . . If I was somebody like Reese Witherspoon, whose image is so important, cancel culture really matters, but I'm not."

He also believes that there is more bark than bite in all the calling out. "Cancel culture, for the most part, doesn't do much. You're canceled for the week and then there's a new person that's canceled. . . . Nobody's ever permanently canceled anymore. You look at frickin' Mel Gibson—if Mel Gibson can still work, then anybody can have a comeback!"

Comedian, writer, and producer Judy Gold's answer to that? "Mel Gibson is a privileged white male. So how many women have had their careers shut down or people of color?" Some influencers believe that cancel culture hits harder at microinfluencers and those who are marginalized. Eli Erlick says, "I have seen many trans women who have small to medium platforms that will never come back. I have known people who have killed themselves because of online harassment due to saying something problematic at some point. . . . The fact is that the only people who really get canceled are the ones who don't have much to start out with in the first place."

Erin Vogel warns us of the potential psychological effects of cancel culture, particularly on younger people, who are sensitive to social rejection. She says, "Getting canceled can feel like the end of the world and like they don't know who they are anymore."

A STORY OF CANCELING AND A
COMEBACK: ISABELLA AVILA

In our first interview with her, it was easy to tell that twenty-something Isabella Avila (who uses the pronouns she/they/he), a TikTok star, was on a fast track to success. She goes by OnlyJayus online, which is derived from an Indonesian word that means someone who tells a joke so unfunny, it's laughable.

Seemingly mature for her age, she talks about her modest roots and the perks and pitfalls of newfound fame. At the time, she had about 9 million followers on TikTok alone, not including other platforms; a Netflix podcast, *Know It All;* and was considered an up-and-coming star by management at Viral Nation.

Born in Las Vegas, she lived for stints in New Jersey. In middle school, she moved to the Central Valley of California, which she describes as the "Bible Belt of California." In this conservative area, it wasn't unusual for kids to get dropped off at school from trucks with a Confederate flag on the back. It also wasn't unusual to use racial and sexual slurs in everyday conversation, according to Avila.

In high school, Avila learned her way around YouTube, posting live stories. It didn't go far, just a couple thousand followers, but she taught herself how to edit and how to gauge what the audience wanted. "I would post a video, and I could see that it didn't do well so I tried something else. And then look at a video that would do really well, and I would go through the comments and see what people liked about the video. I'm trying to replicate it so if they like the way the story was told, I would try to copy how I wrote it, or if they liked the editing behind it, I would try to improve upon that editing. . . . I was just building off of what feedback I was getting from people."

Then, in college, she got in a competition with her little sister, who had about 10K followers on TikTok. Avila had a gut instinct that she could beat that. It turned out she was right; it was an epic win. She began producing unique content that included fun facts provided with charismatic delivery, and engagement soared. "Quality content" is her mantra.

The lifestyle that came with the followers is a big deal because, as Avila puts it, she comes from a "background of absolutely nothing." One out of eleven siblings, Avila says, "My dad was able to feed all of us. We had a roof over my head all the time, but we never had little luxuries, like we didn't go out to eat, or we didn't go see movies. We didn't do extra stuff. And then when I was sixteen, I got put into foster care, so then I turned from kind of nothing to like, I literally had nothing. And then I aged out of the program at eighteen. I got a job, had to pay for community college myself, and all that stuff."

Fast-forward to fashion week in Milan. Dolce & Gabbana paid for Avila and a friend to watch the fashion show. Her requirement for the trip was creating three videos, one for each day, along with posting on Instagram. In addition to this sponsorship coup, she started to be recognized as a celebrity. People came up to Avila on the street at home in California, although fans weren't standing outside her house—yet. It was an exciting time, but it was also a time filled with the online hate that inevitably comes along with the accolades.

Everything turned sour when some of Avila's text messages that included sexual and racial epithets resurfaced, written when she was fifteen or sixteen years old. In a second interview with us, conducted over a year later, Avila acknowledges, "Realizing that that was even part of my vocabulary was obviously hurtful to a large majority of my fan base." The consequences cascaded. She lost her podcast, and her talent agency dropped her. Avila says her management got tired of her haters going after brands that had worked with her. But the repercussions weren't just professional; they were personal. Her relationship with her longtime girlfriend ended about a month later.

It took an enormous emotional toll. She says, "The entire internet turned on me. I was awake for five days when I posted my apology." She's struggled with depression her whole life, and although she doesn't think the depression worsened because of this, she believes it hurt her in other ways. "I think the anxiety got worse, though, because I still would get recognized out in public—would turn into negative interactions. And my phone number got leaked and my address got leaked and people were coming to my house, and I had to move, so there's still some lingering anxiety." Avila got doxed, which means that users published private or identifying information about her online. Doxing has become an ugly and dangerous part of cancel culture.

Taking steps to rebuild her support proved daunting because her attempts yielded acceptance from some and disdain from others. Avila describes the apology video: "There's no excuse for it. I'm sorry. I feel gross for this. I feel disgusting. There's nothing really I'll say except I'm sorry, and that I'm going to try and do better. And part of that was saying that I'm going to try and uplift Black voices because I have this huge platform. And I feel like it'd be the right thing to do just to give these smaller POC [people of color] creators a place to say what they want. And so for a few months, I tried doing that—reached out to a bunch of different creators. Creators reached out to me. We did podcasts. We did some interviews. We did livestreams. I let some people post on my page."

The apology video itself got backlash, with some people commenting that Avila faked looking awful. Avila maintains she appeared awful because of her insomnia. She's concerned about being viewed as "performative" and wants to strike the right balance between addressing the controversy and posting normal content.

Criticism about not doing enough collabs with Black creators has also followed Avila. "I got a lot of people wanting to collaborate with me after I announced that, and I was responding to a lot of people, but then at the same time, I had to move because I got doxed and there was a lot of different stuff. I ended up changing medication for my sleep and my ADHD. And I didn't get back to a couple people. And a couple of those people went very viral for saying that I ghosted them, when in reality, I just didn't check my email. So I got canceled for not checking my email at one point, and that wasn't something I expected. But it's now something I have to be more aware of. I have somebody that checks my email now for me, so this doesn't happen again."

Not only has Avila shored up professional issues to bounce back, but she's also attended to personal psychological issues. Avila admits, "I also said a lot of homophobic things, which was surprising to some people because I'm gay. And then looking back on that, it was like, I did have a lot of internalized homophobia from how I was raised. Years of therapy kind of unworked that, so I was trying to be a better ally to POC, to people in my own LGBT community and just trying to do better, but controversies just seem to follow sometimes."

Raised as a conservative Catholic, the message Avila got from the church and her parents was that she was wrong, and throughout certain points in their life, she has taken it out on others. Avila reveals, "Growing up and being told by the church that this is a sin, this is an abomination, you cannot do this, and then growing up with those feelings that like, I knew I liked girls—it was really hard. And I repressed it for years. I would bully people at school in elementary school who I thought was gay . . . but I knew I was gay and that I just had a crush on these girls, looking back on it. It was a lot of unlearning different things. I'm still in therapy, trying to figure it out and grow as a person, but I've gotten a lot more comfortable in my sexuality since I came out as gay when I was fifteen, sixteen—so, around the same time that I was saying this like awful shit. But when I came out, my parents disowned me. I got put in foster care because I was gay. And so there was a lot of mixed internal fighting going on with that too."

Because of the personal work Avila has done, which includes broadening her experiences, she feels like she's different now in her early twenties than when she was a younger teen in terms of both LGBTQIA+ and racial issues. She says of her teens, "Looking back at how I felt and those times, I never would have considered myself a racist, but I definitely wasn't a fucking ally. I wasn't a good person. But I think once I got to college and started meeting Black people on my basketball team and just like hanging out with them on weekends and understanding, oh, this is what they go through; this kind of language that I've been using and was taught—it was normalized—isn't OK at all."

The key question for Avila's career is, are fans and followers accepting what Avila views as change and growth, or is the audience just done? It seems now that many are willing to forgive her past. Interestingly, Avila noticed that some of the reaction was platform dependent. On TikTok, the younger audience has the attitude that they understand this kind of speech is wrong at their age, so Avila should have too. On YouTube, where the audience is older, Avila got more understanding, as her audience there emphasized that it happened a while ago.

For the most part, Avila believes that she has bounced back pretty well. She says, "I had like 10 million, and then I lost about a million followers from all the controversies, and then today, I'm almost at 17 [million on TikTok], so it's great. . . . I've just been trying to stick to my content and really figure out what my values are and what I want to do with my platform."

When asked if she thought she would have been in a better position had it not been for the canceling, Avila's response is, "I definitely feel like if I was a less controversial and problematic person, I would have more followers and have more of a reach. But again, it's kind of just a consequence of learning and growing—learning how to be a social media person, I guess."

Avila believes acts that are completely illegal or completely immoral are impossible to come back from, but "the fact that I had said it so long ago when I was a teenager, I think a lot of people understood that everybody makes mistakes, and everybody has stuff that they're ashamed of."

CRISIS MANAGEMENT

It's not just influencers who have to be vigilant about cancel culture; so do their managers and agents. Because influencers put out content hour after hour, day after day, the risk of putting out the wrong content is high. Nechelle Vanias says, "It's hard not to make a wrong turn; there's so many. . . . It's stressful for them and it's stressful for us."

In some cases, Vanias says she and the influencer may not be aware that what they are doing is offensive to some groups, such as cultural appropriation, until it's too late. "Girls were wearing bandanas as a top, but apparently [this is] highly inappropriate, because you're appropriating Mexicana culture. I didn't know it. . . . Not all of them are avoidable, because some of them, we don't even know. It's hard to catch every last one. Yes, it's impossible!"

Like many in the industry, Vanias stresses intent. Does the influencer mean harm? Does the influencer learn from mistakes? Vanias says, "It's a challenge for me. As an individual, as an agency, we believe in the right of redemption. At some point in time, it's got to be there; especially if you want it for yourself, you've got to be extending it to others. And when you're thirteen and fifteen and eighteen—that's the big question. When are you old enough to know better?"

WALKING THE TIGHTROPE

Ashley Iaconetti Haibon and her husband, Jared Haibon, are very much in the public eye, and accordingly, they take cancel culture seriously. Both are from the Bachelor reality series and both host podcasts: iHeart's *The Ben and Ashley I Almost Famous Podcast* and *Help! I Suck at Dating with Dean, Jared &* . . . on Apple podcasts. In our discussion, which took place before former *Bachelor* host Chris Harrison's cancel culture controversy that led to his removal from the show in 2021, it seems like balance is one of the most important things to them.

Jared Haibon says, "I think there's certain elements that are good, like we don't want to offend anybody. We don't want to make anybody feel sad or use a term that was socially acceptable to use just a couple years ago, but now would not be." However, on the flip side of it, he doesn't like the rush to judgment. "I see a lot of people in the public eye who make mistakes and people immediately want them to be deplatformed." Both would like the temperature to come down, with people stepping back and looking at the intention behind a comment or action.

Iaconetti Haibon describes an incident that happened on her podcast with fellow Bachelor alum Ben Higgins. The discussion was about former Bachelor Colton Underwood's ex-girlfriend's taking out a restraining order on him. "Ben said casually, but with no intent to excuse his behavior, 'Love makes you do crazy things.' And just saying that sentence made our audience flip out, thinking that he was trying to excuse his [Colton's] behavior as an act of love. It was not what he was trying to do. And me knowing Ben—I thought the audience knew Ben enough to not flip out at that. But we had to do an entire apology episode, where we did learn a lot. It was worthwhile, and I'm glad we did the episode, but it was amazing how sensitive the audience can be these days."

Iaconetti Haibon, who is a naturally vulnerable and authentic person, thinks that sometimes cancel culture makes her fearful about that authenticity. She says every so often, complaints arise from the audience, such as, "They never say how they're feeling anymore." It's because not only she, but numerous other influencers, think they can't.

In terms of the podcast, she says, "I'm so much more filtered," and later adds, "You want real and raw, but then you freak out every time we accidentally use a word not in the right place. . . . If we accidentally say something that you guys are going to interpret wrong, then we have to deal with this, and it's just not worth it for us."

Jared Haibon calls for "just a little bit more understanding" and being "willing to have conversations," while Iaconetti Haibon interrupts and asks for a little bit of "grace."

IT'S NOT FUNNY!

Cancel culture has hit comedians hard online and off, since freedom of speech is at the core of their craft. Judy Gold, author of *Yes, I Can Say That: When They Come for the Comedians, We Are All in Trouble*, is passionate about the topic. "When you think about Lenny Bruce, Richard Pryor, George Carlin, and Joan Rivers and the shit they went through so they could say whatever they wanted to—what they did for us so that we could get on stage and say what we want—that we can tweet what we are thinking. And they were jailed. Lenny Bruce went to jail. And so did George Carlin. . . . I believe when there's no discourse, which is what we're ending with all this kind of stuff, then there's no evolution. We don't evolve, and we're just going to repeat the same mistakes."

For Gold, however, intent is all important. She doesn't believe comedians need to apologize for a joke when their intent was to make people laugh, but she draws the line at so-called jokes that mask real racism, sexism, and homophobia.

A challenge with posting jokes and skits online is that intent gets blurred because the nuance of a live performance is lost. Gold says, "First of all, you're working with a finite amount of characters. And you have to compensate for the fact that you can't whisper or yell in a tweet. I mean, you could do all caps, but that lack of nuance and looking at it and seeing a hundred ways someone could take it the wrong way, and then saying, all right, I'm gonna do it anyway. You're opening yourself—it's a Pandora's box sometimes. . . . I have definitely checked with my publicist and comic friends before I've tweeted certain things."

The room for misinterpretation plagues comedians and can be particularly hard for those influencers and content creators who don't test their material in front of live audiences first. Many comedians consider the comedy club their home, a place where they can experiment with their most controversial jokes. Actress and comedian Mary Lynn Rajskub likes to run through new material during late-night sets, where the comedians before and after her are beyond "nasty." She says, "You want to still have that face—where I'm in a room with people, and it's not going to be blasted on social media. And then you try to hit that line and not cross it and be sure that's your point of view."

For her part, Rajskub says, "There are really good things about cancel culture that are necessary and then there are really horrible parts of it." But does it cause her anxiety? Only a little. A part of her finds it kind of thrilling. She references a controversial joke that she posted online. "It's kind of more exciting especially when you've been doing it as long as I have, and you're honing in on your voice and the things that excite you. You kind of just have to go for it. Before that God joke, pushing the button, I was like, OK, this is so edgy. But then once it was up there, it felt really good." Also, after logging so many hours onstage, and with the benefit of hanging around other comics, Rajskub is relatively confident that she's not going to post anything too crazy.

REDEMPTION, OR THE MOON COLONY

After an influencer is canceled, if and how they find their way back onto their platform is at the crux of the issue. Most see former film producer and convicted sex offender Harvey Weinstein as the prototype for someone who should be canceled, and stay canceled. He's a horrific 10 on a scale of 1 to 10, but it's the 4s through 7s that cause the most uncertainty and conflict. What about the influencers in between? Some prefer the term "consequence culture" because it eschews the permanent connotation of being canceled. It's the prospect of being lost forever in the abyss that influencers fear most.

Laura Vogel is a proponent of rehabilitation for offenders. She says, "Unless we're going to create a moon colony for everybody that ever fucked up, we're going to have to reckon with it at some point. The people that are most called out for screwing up are the people in our society who have made the biggest impact thus far. They're only in a position to fuck up because they're talented. So we hold the people that have had success to a higher standard, or to the same standard but in a more public way, which I think that we should. We also need to have a means for them to be rehabilitated."

Increasingly, finding redemption takes more than a rote apology; it requires authenticity and action, but depending on the offense and the personality of the offender, there is no guarantee of a way back. PR powerhouse Liza Anderson says, "Humility, an apology, and sincerity goes a long way. . . . You also have to see, are they really sorry? Did they regret what they did? Is there a learning moment there? A lot of times there isn't, and a lot of times you can't help somebody like that." She mentions a case of an actor who was on hiatus from a show when a damning video leaked. The individual said some "terrible" things in that video. "I don't know how you come back from that," she says.

For egregious offenses, it's a hard road to redemption. Even the most skilled PR professionals can't necessarily help. After a certain line is crossed, Anderson says, "I don't care how much money you have and who you're gonna hire." She tries to avoid these situations by taking on authentic clients and not working with people who want to "manipulate the system."

For lesser offenses, the path has more structure. Anderson likes to ask, "Where did it go wrong, and how do you not make the same mistake again? I always think smart people make mistakes, and stupid people make the same mistake twice." She stresses explaining to fans and followers what happened, and she urges clients to do their due diligence. She thinks if a person apologizes with heart that comes through, it leads to a path forward.

MAKING A COMEBACK AND REPLATFORMING

Even though industry insider Laura Vogel believes in second chances, she doesn't think they should come easy. The following are actions she says influencers can take to rehab and replatform.

Be Vulnerable

It all starts with an audience telling influencers they screwed up. Influencers likely feel under attack and scared. If they have a conscience, they're upset they hurt people. Anger also plays a big part thanks to the barrage of negative comments, which often include violent threats and directives to go kill themselves.

This mix of emotions can easily lead to defensiveness, with influencers walling themselves off rather than being vulnerable. But vulnerability on the influencers' part gives both sides a chance to heal in a real way. Opening up rather than closing off allows influencers to listen to other perspectives and put themselves in someone else's shoes. It's necessary to let in constructive comments and feedback without harsh judgment of the audience or themselves.

Get Educated

Some influencers may not understand why their content is perceived as offensive. They need to find out. It's the influencers' responsibility to dig deep and educate themselves. They need to talk with experts and do research on the subject to develop a true understanding of the dynamics at play.

Apologize for Real

Crafting half-hearted nonapology apologies is one way some influencers deal with the issue. However, audiences are growing weary of shady "I'm sorrys." It's not meaningful to say, "I'm sorry *if* people were offended." People *were* offended. Also, only focusing on what other people are feeling, rather than on the offending action, is a way of obfuscating and shifting the focus. A real apology should include these elements: "This is what I did. This is why it was wrong. I am apologizing to those who were hurt."

Stop Doing It

Influencers should use the things they've learned to stop it, move on, and produce a different kind of content.

Don't Expect Forgiveness Immediately

It's OK for influencers to ask for forgiveness; they shouldn't demand it. The audience might not be in a place of forgiveness. If not, influencers may find a new audience who respects them for how they handled the situation.

Create Content that Does Something Positive

A great way to move on without demanding forgiveness is to create positive content. It should go something like this: "I made a mistake. This is where I was coming from. I was wrong. This is how I'm going to do better. I don't expect you to stick around. But if you do, you will see me doing better. And if I screw up again, let me know."

Vogel told a story of informally advising a gamer called out for being sexist. He ended up posting content about his history of childhood abuse, which was productive, interesting, and helpful to many. He also gave a sizable donation to a transgender woman to open a gaming store, essentially putting money behind an individual from the group that had been harmed or could have been harmed by his actions.

These steps that Vogel outlines aren't necessarily a blueprint. Vogel stresses that they need to come from a place of honesty and authenticity. She gives fallen YouTube star Jenna Marbles as an example of this process done right, and wishes she would resurface. Vogel says, "What she did was she shut the fuck up! For a minute, she stopped talking and listened to the people with a large voice and to all of the comments of people with a small voice. . . . And then read about it and learned about the history of blackface, learned about sex positivity, learned about all the different things that she was called out for. She put herself in their position. And she educated herself as to what she was doing that caused the reaction, whether it was right or wrong. And then she decided that they were right, and that she did not know then what she knew now."

Vogel likes the way Marbles looked back at her past actions and took full responsibility by acknowledging that even though she wasn't intentionally coming from a place of racism or sexism or slut-shaming, it was that, it was wrong, and she regrets it.

HOW NOT TO GET CANCELED

One of the best ways for influencers not to get canceled is to educate themselves. They need to be aware of not just their community but other communities. They must ask questions, do research, and have empathy. Gen Z thought leader Gigi Robinson states that doing due diligence to ensure that offensive content isn't created is of the utmost importance. "I'm the kind of person that frequently is doing that work and learning about marginalized communities. I'm learning about different things that I can do to be an ally and different ways that I can talk about chronic illness or body image in a way that is not triggering. . . . I think just being conscious and doing things with intention is so important, and nowadays I feel so many people are creating content without any sense of intention. They're just doing it because they want to be TikTok famous." For Robinson, it's about understanding how to honor different people's space online.

However, the reality is, no matter the due diligence, mistakes, both intentional and unintentional, will be made. Mae Karwowski tries to buffer her clients against being deplatformed; diversification is key. Karwowski wants "to really be sure of other ways that you're building a career, making money off this, so you're not living and dying by a negative message here or there. It becomes important, especially now when there can be a huge, swift movement to cancel someone. Then you can handle it."

FREEDOM OF SPEECH AND POLITICS ON SOCIAL MEDIA

Many people look at the issues of being deplatformed, having their posts deleted by social media companies, or even having their accounts blocked as a freedom-of-speech issue. This has been a particular issue for debate when it happens to politicians—and even regular people who are voicing political views that may be considered unpopular by many on social media. The courts in the United States have regularly upheld that comments and posts on social media sites are not subject to the protection of the First Amendment of the US Constitution, which protects freedom of speech, particularly as it relates to religious speech or political speech, as well as the freedom of the press and the right to peaceably assemble.[2] That is because the Constitution protects freedom of speech from being impeded by the government, not private corporations. Social media sites are run by private companies, and therefore, they can set their own use standards and codes of conduct. If these are violated, they can take action against that person or the posts. However, in recent years, banning some politicians from social media platforms, either temporarily or permanently, has sparked a renewed push for changes to the laws—changes that some say could open the doors to blocking legitimate views or public debate. Many legal scholars have also weighed in, with research analyzing how freedom of speech is addressed in regard to social media sites regulating content posted by their users.

"Striking a balance between undeterred free speech and censorship to protect values considered worthy of protection is indeed a difficult exercise. Censorship of social media speech may not outweigh the benefit of forbidding a particular speech but allowing complete free speech on social media may also have negative impacts, such as fostering cyber bullying or hate speech," according to attorney Marie-Andrée Weiss.[3]

Protecting religious speech and political speech is at the center of a larger current debate; there is a growing movement seeking to expand the protections of the First Amendment to private companies, such as social media platforms. David L. Hudson Jr., a law professor and First Amendment Fellow for the Freedom Forum Institute, notes in an article, "Certain powerful private entities—particularly social networking sites such as Facebook, Twitter, and others—can limit, control, and censor speech as much or more than governmental entities. A society that cares for the protection of free expression needs to recognize that the time has come to extend the reach of the First Amendment to cover these powerful, private entities that have ushered in a revolution in terms of communication capabilities."[4] The debate likely will continue; it is difficult to get people to agree on a best path forward, and in addition, the laws on the books find it hard to keep up with changes in technology.

Evelyn Douek, an associate research scholar at the Knight First Amendment Institute at Columbia University and a doctoral student and lecturer on law at Harvard Law School who has written about the issue of freedom of speech on social media, notes, "Online speech governance is a wicked problem with unenviable and perhaps impossible trade-offs. There is no end-state of content moderation with stable rules or regulatory forms; it will always be a matter of contestation, iteration, and technological evolution."[5]

CHASING THE NEXT POST, CONTENT BLOCK, AND THE ANXIETY OF ALGORITHMS

The scale of the original content that influencers produce is huge compared to that seen during the history of arts and entertainment. Putting out a book or a film every year versus posting around the clock yields different psychological consequences. Most traditional writers experience pressure to be continuously creative, but they're not going public with it several times a day. One of the closest analogies to influencing is producing a daily TV show, but even that has its differences, like living according to a set schedule and always working with a team. Output that's released to the public may still be created every day, but not around the clock.

Influencers are constantly chasing the next post, all day, every day, and it's not without a price. Sarah Penna says influencers "burn out, and it's really grueling. It's so hard to try to build an audience. And then when you're at the top, it's hard to maintain that audience. All the pressure is on you. Typically you don't have a staff. You don't have cofounders. They're not companies. They're just young people putting themselves out there, and you get the hate comments and everything. It just wears on you."

In this chapter, we look at the psychological consequences and remedies for chasing the next post. We'll also look at the ways in which algorithms drive influencers to post, as well as influencers overcoming the new form of writer's block: content block.

HOW MUCH DO INFLUENCERS POST?

It depends on whom you ask, but there is a general range that industry professionals often advise when considering how often to post content. Ray Ligaya says, "YouTube is longer form. It takes a lot more time to edit the video, so it's healthy to post one to two YouTube videos a week. Instagram—it's good to post every day, but at least three times a week. Instagram Stories has to be every day." Then add on livestreams, blogs, and other platforms like TikTok, Twitch, Twitter, LinkedIn, Pinterest, and Snapchat. Ligaya acknowledges that "it takes a certain mental toll because you have to keep putting smiles on people's faces, and you tend to forget about the side of things where you've got to take care of yourself first."

The process of posting comes more naturally to some people than others, and therefore can be more or less stress provoking. For instance, Kristina Zias, a self-described "sharer," loves the process of documenting her life and engaging with people, to the point that she would choose to do it even if she wasn't an influencer. Her posting schedule depends on her day-to-day activities, but sometimes she puts as many as ten to twenty-five posts a day on Instagram Stories, with the purpose of taking her audience along for the ride.

For Aditi Oberoi Malhotra, writing comes naturally and she loves it, so in terms of her blog, she's been writing articles every day. In terms of Instagram, she felt the pressure of posting around three times a day when she first started. However, she says, "Very early on, I realized that I have to find balance because I'm also a mom. . . . So when I used to feel that I don't think today I can post a quality image, then I used to just skip it. I used to skip a day. . . . Why should I feel pressured? I'm not working for someone else. I'm not working in a company where I need to. It's my business. I can take a day off if I want to, and think about content that can add value."

In terms of number of posts and when to post, for most influencers, it seems to be a mix of art, science, gut instinct, and magic. Influencers have their own unique takes on posting. For Ashley Iaconetti Haibon, it's putting quality over quantity and following a plan that works for her. She says, "I have a very weird strategy. I like to post stories two to three times a week, and I do it all at the same time—all at 6 PM Pacific time. And I'll upload, like, twelve stories at once. So I collect throughout the week because I find that has a way better engagement rate. You want to show advertisers that you get a lot of views. So I'll do stories two or three times a week if I can get by with that. And then I think, two to three Instagram posts are ideal because you lose followers every time you post. So you want to have really high engagement on those pictures. They have to be really good."

Iaconetti Haibon says posting can be a series of three steps forward, one step back: "It doesn't matter how loyal the base; you pretty much always lose followers every time you post. I think people will just think, 'Oh, this popped up in my feed. I don't care about her anymore.' If you're not posting, then they don't even know that they're following you."

For Instagram alone, Iaconetti Haibon spends about three hours a day recording content, editing it, and posting it. There are always details to consider, like the overlays, creating account links, coming up with captions, and sending the post back and forth to get approved. She does recognize the importance of lessening the load every now and then. "There's totally times where I think it's smart to take a break. There are little things you can do to help. Even the other day, I was like, I don't feel like having social right now. So I moved my Twitter and Instagram app over to not the main page. So whenever I opened my phone, it wasn't there sitting in front of my face, but I'd have to scroll over and have to cognitively be like, 'I'm going to go to Instagram and Twitter,' without it being an impulse decision." She has friends who will actually delete the app (not the account) off their phones for a weekend, just so they can't access it for a couple of days.

From her point of view, on Instagram, Iaconetti Haibon believes it's OK to take a short social media break and then come back because you get more features—not a fact, just an educated guess. However, many influencers believe that not posting for a while on a variety of apps hurts them. Why? Because of algorithms.

ALGORITHMS: THE HOLY GRAIL

Influencers live and die by the algorithm—a word that a few years ago most laypeople probably wouldn't have known much about. Now in social media circles and beyond, it's a mainstay in the lexicon. But what is an algorithm exactly?

Social media algorithms are a way of mathematically sorting content, so users see posts that are deemed relevant to them and their interests, as opposed to random posts. Platforms use algorithms to keep their audience's attention, thus keeping them on the site—the longer the better.

Different sites use different algorithms, and they are constantly in flux, which lends to the air of mystery that surrounds them. Influencers like Iaconetti Haibon and marketing agencies make it their business to try and crack the code. They try to figure out the algorithm that particular platforms are using in order to optimize the ranking of their posts and reach as many people as possible. Table 4 lists a few factors that can affect the ranking of posts.

Sometimes apps let influencers in on the algorithms, but often they don't. More than a few aspiring influencers have no idea what needs to be done in order to increase their rank on a platform or come up in a search. Rey Rahimi says, "It's definitely a trial-and-error

Factor	Algorithm
Timeliness	New content gets priority over less recent content.
Interest	A user or content someone engaged with in the past through likes, shares, comments, or views takes priority.
Watch time	Videos that are viewed longer take priority.
Number of followers	The more people you follow, the less you'll see posts from the same people.

Table 4. Factors that can affect the ranking of a post

thing. Something that you gain over time with experience on the platform. You see what works, see what doesn't. . . . And it's nothing that anyone ever knows. It's nothing that they will tell you, like, hey, if you post during this time, if you post consistently, we're gonna help you out." She adds that people who are creating quality content but who fail to focus on search engine optimization and aren't aware of the algorithm get discouraged and quit even though they have the talent to make it big.

Not only do algorithms affect individual influencers, but they can also affect online culture, including content and platform trends. Penna details a major shift caused by YouTube's change to favor watch time in 2012: "If somebody watched the majority of your video and that led them to watch another video, your video would get pushed higher in the algorithm, so what that did was favor much longer videos. This is why everybody in the top now is video game playthroughs, because they're very long and people watch the whole thing. So a lot of YouTube talent got very disheartened. . . . There was a lot of disillusionment that happened at that time. And I think Vine came in at a pivotal moment. People like DeStorm were very frustrated with that change in the algorithm. And they were able to quickly rebuild an audience over there, monetize it, and engage with it. And while it was still a lot of work for a video, it was a lot easier than beating your head against a wall and trying to play that YouTube algorithm game."

The bottom line is that algorithms affect careers. One of the biggest financial hits influencers take is if they don't post consistently. Digital media producer Laura Vogel says, "If you don't post regularly, you will see a financial impact on your ability to monetize—on your ability to have ads." This doesn't bode well for taking time off as a cure for influencer burnout. Many of the influencers we interviewed felt anxious after taking even a couple of days off because they thought that the algorithm wasn't favoring their videos after their return. Several YouTubers we interviewed said that they were discouraged from taking time off because they believed their videos didn't appear to be recommended as much after a few days of not posting.

MANAGEMENT HEADING OFF BURNOUT

Managers of influencers always encourage consistent posting, but the good ones also try to help their clients fend off burnout by encouraging necessary time off and advising them to have a life outside of influencing. Raina Penchansky says, "We're very sensitive to making sure that there's never any sort of pressure to produce content or to work with brands or to do anything if you're dealing with something. . . . Let's pause brand deals for a month if you're having a baby, you're moving, something just happened to your family."

Platform diversification is also a must with managers; however, again, the good ones have their clients pace it—it's a marathon, not a sprint. Penna's attitude is, if you're going to add more work, try to balance it out in other ways. During her Big Frame days, she always said, "If you want to do Vine, or you want to try something new, that's great. Let's also try to take something off your plate, like if you're not really getting a lot of views and engagement on Facebook, can we chill on that, and then you can put more of it into Vine." Piling on is neither a good quick fix nor an optimal long-term strategy.

Gaming influencer Lachlan Power would like to see things trend toward a more balanced lifestyle in the gaming space, including those who aren't signed to an organization. He says, "One of the harsh realities of esports is the amount of time required to be good at these games, such as *Fortnite,* and that does create a little bit of an unhealthy lifestyle. We are trying to make moves in providing a healthier lifestyle for our players, trying to show them the right ways of structure and balance, because a lot of the times these players will [be gaming] fourteen hours a day, and the only thing that matters is the most amount of hours on the PC instead of breaking it up into getting a workout in there, getting some good food in there, getting some good sleep in there—trying to preach those practices."

Mae Karwowski acknowledges the challenge of constantly chasing the next post and the danger of having it overtake an influencer's life. She says, "It's hard to document something rather than experience it. So you need to make sure you're not documenting every single thing. That's a big thing for me. I'm like, here's your schedule; stick to it. Make sure you're enjoying your life outside of it too."

In terms of the rigor of collab houses, she cautions, "Filming twenty-four hours a day and editing—that works in terms of growing your audience. You're gonna become famous. It also takes a huge toll. And with TikTok, the volumes are so much higher, and video is hard to create, so it can be really hard. . . . They need even more resources because more people are influencers."

Because the industry is so new, and because influencing isn't yet taken as seriously as it should be, given the number of influencers, the research and resources don't yet match the need.

INFLUENCER OVERFLOW INTO REAL LIFE

Influencing overflows into real life all the time; that lack of separation is a source of stress and anxiety. The ironic part is that it often floods into the most significant life events. Ashley Iaconetti Haibon talks openly and honestly of the business pros and personal cons: "Having to constantly be filming is annoying. . . . We can't just go to Thanksgiving without having our phones out. We have to document the food and the family activities and stuff like that. And you're just kind of like, I wish that I could not have to have every part of my life be documented. But you always know that days like that is when you're going to get high engagement. So you can't waste days like that. . . . For our anniversary, I knew it was going to get a lot of likes. So I felt like I was on my phone most of our anniversary. And it did. We had a huge engagement day. I was getting, like, 300,000 views on my story. I don't think I had that since our wedding day. So it just kind of sucks that the important days that you wish you could just spend in real life, that you've kind of had to document it all."

It's so all-encompassing that it takes away some of her enjoyment of the events. She says, "Being on your phone sucks. And then you always have to excuse it with your friends, like, I'm so sorry, I'm so sorry. . . . On the East Coast, 9 PM is my posting time, and it also happens to be a popular time to be hanging out, having dinner and drinks with friends. . . . We don't want our friends to feel like we're not present in the moment if we have to document things or be on our phone at a certain time."

The connection influencers have to content and posting can lead to disconnection from other important people and events in their lives. Celeste Viciere says, "A lot of people are trying to stay on top, so everything around them is about content—about what's next. Their brain never settles. If there's a flower that's coming out of the ground, they're not able to see the beauty and life because they're so focused on creating the perfect thing for their viewers."

Some might argue that the act of influencing becomes their new here and now, but that's a question for philosophers. According to most psychologists, the idea of not being fully present in the moment has implications. The distance created by being on the phone all the time and viewing everything as content creates a barrier between the influencer and their own psychological state, as well as the influencer and their relationships with other individuals, nature, and the spiritual realm. Once the space between gets big enough, it becomes harder to get back; it gets harder to connect with others and develop a healthy, deep sense of self.

When we lose the ability to be fully present in the moment, we lose the ability to achieve what psychologist Abraham Maslow calls "peak experiences," which is a state of intense joy and wonder, often accompanied by a feeling of oneness with all that is. During peak experiences, individuals are often in a state of flow, or immersion in an activity to such an extent that all distractions seem to fade away. In some cases, influencers might achieve a state of flow during the content creation process, but all too often, chasing the next post can get in the way of peak experiences and flow.

How do influencers prevent disconnecting from themselves and the world? Viciere says they need to learn how to stay grounded in the moment, and to do that, they need to make time for it. She says, "We'll make a calendar for content and X, Y, and Z, but nowhere in our calendar is time for us. It's not like you gotta stop everything to smell the roses. But you gotta be intentional creating time. You can't tell me you can't create time for yourself. You choose not to create time. Where are we rushing off to? Where are we going? . . . When you think about it, anxiety loves to either dwell on the past or worry about the future. So if people aren't in the moment, they're struggling with a lot of anxiety."

There are those for whom the present moment is a struggle. People who are unhappy in the moment may use influencing as an escape. To this, Viciere says, "It's so important to make sure we're leaning into our suffering. Our mind wants us to run away from our suffering and seek pleasure, but then we just keep suffering. And so if we actually just pause and pay attention to what's happening, we'll actually begin to have more control. It won't feel like things are just happening to us."

INTENTIONALITY, THE WEAPON AGAINST PERFORMANCE MOODINESS

Not only do influencers stress about their next post, but they also stress about it doing well; it affects their happiness level. Rey Rahimi says, "I know a lot of other content creators say this: your mood really depends on how your content online is performing. So if I post a video now, and it doesn't do well, I am down for the rest of the day. The rest of the week, honestly, until I post my next video and it does better." When asked what she does to combat this, she says, "It's very, very close to impossible, because it's not like you can ignore the numbers, because you have to look at the numbers to see what you need to do better and see what's performing well, so you can repeat that. But yeah, I try not to look at it too frequently and too fast. What I used to do is, I would just sit on it, refresh it, read the comments, reply to comments. And YouTube, on the home page, it tells you how your video is performing compared to your last ten videos. . . . So I try, again, not to check that too frequently, because a big portion of trying to prevent that downturn in your mood is to not refresh it too much—not try to think about it too much and just start thinking about the next one." Yet thinking about the next one is a Catch-22 because even though it's important to move on, it's the very thing that leads to the chase.

In order to combat one's mood being dependent on social stats, Danielle R. Busby and Dana L. Cunningham say it's necessary to be intentional. What does being intentional mean? It's about approaching life and livelihood strategically instead of willy-nilly. Being intentional about mood management means recognizing that outside forces are controlling your emotions, identifying the triggers, and developing a plan for when it happens. If you don't develop a plan before being knee-deep in tumultuous emotion, then it will spiral even more out of control. Catching the mood descent early is critical, like medicating a migraine at its first sign.

In terms of developing a strategy around self-care, Cunningham suggests casting a wide net. "There's a lot of different components when we think about that—mental, physical, spiritual, workplace self-care, emotional self-care. When we think about all these components, are we filling all of those buckets with different things? So social media and my work as an influencer shouldn't be in all of those different circles. Where else can I plug in?"

CONTENT BLOCK

Writer's block is the insidious plague that all writers dread; it squelches creativity, leaving blank pages in its wake. Today, influencers struggle similarly. They stare at their phones, needing to post, but there may be no ideas in sight. How do influencers come up with ideas consistently, even when they are uninspired? The following are ways influencers overcome content block.

Be Real   One way to get around content block is to authentically be the content. Kristina Zias acknowledges, "There's definitely writer's block and creator's block. But I do think that the more I've allowed myself to be who I am and show up authentically, that doesn't happen as much, because I don't feel this pressure to write some really deep, inspirational, motivational caption every single day or share very editorial photos, because sometimes, honestly, if I just take a photo on my balcony in my sweats, that's more relatable and that's more real life, and I don't necessarily feel like I have to keep up with this perfect feed that everyone tries to do. The more I let go of that, the less I struggle creatively."

Chloe Long also keeps it real to avoid content block; she advised her friend and costar on MTV's *Siesta Key,* Amanda Marie Miller, to do the same. Long shares, "She was telling me about how she feels like she needs to be more consistent on Instagram. And I actually said to her that although it's very important to engage with your followers, I think it's also very important to protect yourself and your mental health, first and foremost. And so my advice to her was, why don't you jump on Instagram Live, or post the video of you telling your fans that this is how you're feeling. That you wish you could post every day and you want to engage with them, but you have so much going on in your personal life and with school and filming, and all of this stuff, that sometimes it's just not on the front line of what's the most important for you. But that doesn't mean that you don't think about them, and you love them."

Long still realizes the importance of posting consistently, but she advises that influencers learn to put their phones away so they can laugh and have fun without the pressure.

Find What's Trending   It's common for influencers to scour what's trending when trying to come up with new content. For instance, Zias looks at Pinterest for creative inspiration. When Logan Isbell runs out of ideas, he searches what's trending, or he'll look at Instagram's Explore page for photo ideas. It's a natural part of the process, but it's still a slippery slope. The trick is to be trendy, but still unique and yourself.

For Rey Rahimi, the hardest part about doing YouTube videos is the idea creation process. But once she comes up with the idea, she gets a boost and a sense of excitement. She says, "Everything after the actual creation process is so much easier for me. I enjoy filming, I enjoy editing, I enjoy everything, except for sitting down and trying to come up with a video." The key for her is originality, but sometimes she'll go for what's on the popular page and make videos about what's trending: "It boosts your channel, and you can show it to a newer audience that way. So every now and then it's nice to follow a trend, as well as adding your own unique twist to it. If you make a really good one that's unique to you, and you don't just do it because everyone else is doing it, or you put actual effort into it, that's a way to garner a whole new audience." However, she notes the importance of balance and cautions: "If you do that too much, you kind of blend into everyone else who's doing the exact same thing, and there's nothing making you stand out."

There's also a different culture on different platforms. For example, on TikTok, copying a trend, like a dance, and then posting it is what you're supposed to do. This is not the case on YouTube. Closely copying what another influencer is doing can be looked down on as uninspired, unoriginal, or just plain annoying.

Relax, Don't Do It Joey Zauzig describes himself as a "fast-paced, impatient human," but he says he has to tamp that down a bit when creating content so it doesn't work against him. He says, "When you start spiraling in your head, you're not actually coming up with anything good. My best ideas come to me before I go to sleep, so I have trouble sleeping, because I'm thinking about, oh, I can do this TikTok video tomorrow and then I can make it into a Reels video, and then I can do a static post to coincide with both of them. My mind is spinning. So sometimes just to clear your mind up, meditate, listen to a guided meditation—I live for those. And just take a step back from your work for a second. Everyone needs to do that."

Long walks also help Zauzig step outside the content creation process. Still, he's trying to figure out which works better for him when facing content block: taking the time to relax and get away from it, or scrolling though apps like TikTok to spark new ideas. Perhaps it's a balance of both.

Look to the Audience Successful influencers have an open, flowing dialogue with their audience and can call on this relationship when they feel stuck or need inspiration. Part of overcoming content block for beauty, lifestyle, and fashion influencer Aysha Harun is listening to her community and bouncing ideas off them. She says, "I really like to go back through my content and see what's been doing well, what hasn't, and just make more of that. So if I notice people are really enjoying home content, I figure out a way to incorporate more home content within my channels and Instagram and all of that kind of stuff. So it's really just knowing your audience and studying your audience, but at the same time focusing on what's trending at the moment."

Find Inspiration in Others   Simply being around other people in the industry can spur creativity. Getting out, talking with other influencers, sharing insights, and, at times, collaborating can be great ways to ward off content block. In this scenario, content or collab houses can be an advantage. Rave Vanias, part of the Vault collab house, says, "I definitely think, as a house, it benefits us a lot because we have somebody to always talk to or someone to always get with that feels the same way we do because they do the same thing that we do."

Lean into It   A big part of working though content block is the realization that it's part of the process. Leaning into it rather than fighting it can go a long way toward reducing the block time and increasing the productive time. Tim Montgomery, best known for his comedic TikTok videos, has gotten to a point where he recognizes the ups and downs of creating fresh content. He says, "I myself get into polarizing states of creative booms and extreme lulls." What helps him move through it in a natural way is not falling into the trap of caring about what other people think of his content and rather making the content he enjoys.

Create a Backlog   Recognizing that there are going to be creative booms and lulls means preparing for them. Mary Fitzgerald has days when she is in a time crunch while working and doesn't want to post selfies of herself sitting at her desk. She says, "I had a photographer do some extra photos because I don't look great every day. Also, I try to mix it up. But I try to get some stocks, where I have a backlog of photos and things to post in between, where I can post every day—that's what you're told you're supposed to do. So I try to have some good photos that people will like and want to see, like kind of a backlog, because there are some days, where from the second I wake up, it's until midnight when I finally stop working."

Catch the Lifestyle When It Creeps Up   The freedom of an influencer's lifestyle can be intoxicating. It may lead to late nights, late starts to the day, and copious amounts of partying. It can also lead to just being lazy—and, for some, entitled. Ray Ligaya cautions influencers against getting too comfortable living that influencer life, which can lead to content block. He says there is a creative price to pay for influencers who passively watch brand deals coming in and "not doing anything all day, drinking, smoking marijuana, but not really thinking about the monetization side of things." He urges influencers to keep their head on straight and be proactive.

Developing Structure and Meaningful Purpose   Busby and Cunningham are mental health professionals and also content creators for their website, Black Mental Wellness. Both have experienced content block. Busby finds it helpful to create structure by going back to the mission statement. She says, "What is your purpose? Why are you doing this? Let that be a part of your drive of the content you create so that it can feel authentic, but then also, it can feel meaningful, which can help. And it's yours, right? You don't have to go out and find it or figure it out. It can still be hard, but I think it creates some structure for you. What is the mission here? How is this feeding the mission? And if it is, how do I want to execute that? But maybe I'm trying too hard on something that's not in alignment with the overall vision and goal?"

Cunningham deals with content block in a similar way. She adds to Busby's strategy the question, "What are you passionate about?," then using that to drive the content. She also likes to go back to what previously resonated with the community for ideas. She says, "If there was a conversation or some topic that folks seem to be really engaged around, there's no rule that says you can't go back and revisit that again, or bring up an issue. Also, I think considering current events—what's happening right now in real time. . . . So sometimes just thinking about and reflecting on what's happening in our community or in society as what to post about or what to do next can be helpful."

FROM DISCRIMINATION TO THE EMPOWERMENT PARADOX

Experiences of Influencers from Marginalized Communities

The issues that marginalized populations face in the real world are harshly reflected online. Racism, sex-based discrimination, ageism, disability discrimination, religious prejudice, and body shaming are a dark side of the culture—and a dark side of the influencing profession. Outcry from social media users and influencers is shining a light on the subject. For instance, in a June 15, 2020, post, Instagram CEO Adam Mosseri addressed the issue: "The irony that we're a platform that stands for elevating Black voices, but at the same time Black people are often harassed, afraid of being 'shadowbanned,' and disagree with many content takedowns, is not lost on me."[1]

Shadowbanning refers to social media apps' blocking or restricting a user's content without informing the user. The content is usually deemed inappropriate and a violation of guidelines; however, there have been complaints from marginalized groups and individuals who think that shadowbanning is unfairly used against them for putting out content that shows their experience and viewpoint.

Yet even with an undercurrent of bias, prejudice, and discrimination, there are waves of positive forces within the influencing industry for those whose voices have traditionally not been at the forefront. It's the empowerment paradox. People who have been disenfranchised, marginalized, ignored, and in general pushed to society's sidelines are carving out a space for themselves in an effort to be heard.

In June 2020, YouTube CEO Susan Wojcicki posted a blog story supporting the Black community and announcing some new initiatives to amplify Black voices and protect people on the platform from hate and harassment: "Our platform has been a place where people come together since YouTube first launched 15 years ago. And in the midst of uncertainty, creators continue to share stories that might not otherwise be heard while also building online communities. We have always been proud that we are a platform that celebrates a broad and diverse set of voices. And we have implemented many policies and product features to protect our communities. But we recognize we need to do more, in particular with the Black community. . . . We're committed to doing better as a platform to center and amplify Black voices and perspectives."[2]

In this chapter, we'll look at issues around bias and discrimination in the influencing industry, including pay inequities, the psychological effects of discrimination on influencers, and the steps being taken to combat these issues, together with instances of online empowerment.

ALGORITHMIC BIAS

Algorithms are an automated decision-making process that used to be thought of as neutral. Not anymore. Algorithms, and their impact on what voices are heard, or not heard, on social media, have been written about in media outlets such as *Forbes, Wired, Washington Post,* and *Harvard Business Review.* Critics have said that recurring, systematic errors in algorithms can create situations that favor some groups at the expense of others, perpetuate social biases, and in general set up an environment ripe for discrimination, even if unintentional. For example, algorithms tend to recommend videos similar to those that viewers have previously watched. Therefore, if people choose videos that lack diversity, this choice is going to be reinforced and amplified.

In *Algorithms of Oppression,* Safiya Umoja Noble argues that digital decisions "reinforce oppressive social relationships and enact new modes of racial profiling." She calls it "technological redlining."[3]

It's hard to find an influencer from a marginalized community who isn't talking about algorithmic bias. In some cases, it leads to a sense of helplessness and hopelessness among influencers because it seems like an amorphous entity that's impossible to get a handle on. Rave Vanias, a Black influencer, states, "We do have to work ten times harder . . . because we aren't represented enough, and also we literally have algorithms against us."

Kevin Kreider is angry about this technological bias, calling algorithms "racist." He says, "I get this message a lot from people, women especially, like, where have you been? And I said, buried underneath algorithms, because algorithms do not favor Asian men and Black women and people of color."

His general sense is that the algorithmic bias tends to mirror bias in the culture because, he says, "white men have so many more followers, engagement, brand deals than I could ever imagine. And technically—and this is not to be vain—I am now a celebrity, and I still don't have those privileges as a white guy who has nothing. And so that's what's really discouraging even today. . . . You know, 'I don't want to follow an Asian man, I follow a white guy.' And even though this Asian guy is super attractive, and he's got a very successful show, I find that there's still a bias—an unconscious bias."

Kreider echoes the sentiment expressed by many in marginalized communities: he has to work harder while maneuvering around the way things are. He's had acting and literary agents reach out to him, but he thinks that as an influencer, the brands just aren't there for him. Kreider says, "I mean, there's no deals coming my way. I still continue today having to carve my own path and go for what I want."

As the topic of algorithmic bias is coming to the forefront of the mainstream conversation, researchers, academics, and professionals are stepping up in an attempt to find solutions. For example, the Brookings Institution issued a report on "Algorithmic Bias Detection and Mitigation: Best Practices and Policies to Reduce Consumer Harms."[4] Organizations that develop guidelines for ethical algorithms are also surfacing, like the Algorithmic Justice League, whose mission is "to raise public awareness about the impacts of AI, equip advocates with empirical research to bolster campaigns, build the voice and choice of most impacted communities, and galvanize researchers, policymakers, and industry practitioners to mitigate AI bias and harms."[5]

PAY INEQUITIES

Unfair and unethical disparities in pay are another thing many influencers from marginalized communities talk about. People in every marginalized community say they bear the brunt of it. Anecdotal evidence of pay inequity is widely reported, and more research is being done that backs up what influencers already know. For example, Bloomberg's *Businessweek* found that Black influencers are paid less than white influencers and more often get paid in product rather than money.[6] They also found that Black influencers sometimes get less money than white creators who mimic their content.

At the end of 2021, a research study came out revealing that white influencers earn more on average, with a pay gap between white and BIPOC (Black, Indigenous, and people of color) influencers of 29 percent.[7] The gap between white and Black influencers is even larger, at 35 percent. The study reports that influencers with more than 50K followers and earning $100,000 on average are nearly twice as likely to be white, and that 77 percent of Black influencers have fewer than 50K followers and average around $27,000 annually.

Women also experience pay inequities. In a Klear survey, it was found that even though women make up 77 percent of influencers, men are paid more, with women charging an average of $351, while men charge $459.[8] These disparities were highest on YouTube.

In the trans community, Eli Erlick argues that there is a lot of exploitation and many incidences of influencers being underpaid. She says, "I've been very fortunate. I am a white, cis-passing trans woman, and so I think I do get paid more, or I should say I know I get paid more than many Black trans people with comparable followings."

The male/female pay gap extends to the world of sports influencers as well. University of Oregon's T. Bettina Cornwell says, "If you look at the top fifty influencers in sport, it's predominantly male. There's a good smattering of females, but if you look at what they earn for their relationships, it's really night and day. There's the rare top of the heap in everything, but for the most part, women don't earn as much—end of story." Some of the disparity has to do with the amount of exposure a sport or athlete gets. The more exposure, the more popular the athlete. The more popular the athlete, the more followers and brand deals. Daniel Rascher says things are changing, and more female athletes are able to grow their brands today; however, still, not many professional women's sports get the kind of exposure men's sports get. He points to professional women's soccer as a sport that's doing well, but there's still no female equivalent to men's football and baseball today.

In terms of esports, women are underrepresented. Lachlan Power says that the content side of gaming is "evolving" and that the industry is making "great strides in the content creation fields of females and gaming, and we're trying to support that as best we can." In 2021, Team PWR signed Kathleen Belsten, aka Loserfruit, whom Power has collaborated with over the years. Belsten is a popular gamer and is passionate about inclusivity and positivity. Among female gamers, she has the second most followed channel on Twitch, and she was the second gamer to get her own *Fortnite* skin/outfit as part of the Fortnite Icon series.

As far as the competitive side of things, Power says they don't see much female representation in competitive gaming, although "it's definitely getting better." He cites *Fortnite*'s all-women tournament and other such events and initiatives.

It's important to keep in mind that pay inequity comparisons aren't always apples to apples. It's not simply a white person getting $1 per impression and a marginalized community member getting 50 cents per impression. Laura Vogel, who was formerly an employment discrimination lawyer, says that when looking at pay inequities, the bigger picture also needs to be addressed, including access to things like managers, agents, and representatives who can be advocates, as well as the degree to which marginalized community members are positioned to advocate for themselves. Thus, she emphasizes addressing "the culture and the industry that has created the circumstance in which a pay disparity is a reasonable result."

The pay and treatment differential is something that has stood out to Black Muslim influencer Aysha Harun, particularly earlier in her career, but she believes the Black Lives Matter movement has improved the situation somewhat. Harun also credits the change in her status with having a good manager, who ensures that Black creators get the same pay as their non-Black counterparts. She says, "I definitely noticed it early on, especially before I had a manager and before I scaled out my business a little bit more. I'm originally from Toronto. I currently live in Los Angeles. But just based off of the creators in the Toronto space and the budgets that they were getting and how much more work there was for them as opposed to myself, I definitely noticed a huge difference."

Viva Fifty's Lorraine Ladish has also noticed that mainstream budgets ("mainstream" meaning here that they're not catering to one community) have more dollars for Latinx influencers now, although it's still an uphill battle. Ladish gives an example of a brand that paid her a third less for doing Spanish-language versions of English videos in a series. She went against her agent's recommendation to not do the Spanish version. She says, "I decided to do them because I felt bad for whoever didn't speak English, and I wanted to make that information available to them. . . . Sometimes you have to make this call, where you really want to do something that's beneficial for your people. But there's never an explanation, which I find not OK, [for] why there's less money for Black creators or for Latino creators."

Ladish believes that one of the ways to combat pay inequity is for influencers to be more transparent with each other. She says, "I'm an open book because I feel the more information we all share, the better it is for all of us." Ladish has had experiences where brands have made her an offer but demanded an immediate answer. She believes it's because they didn't want to give her time to research or ask peers what the pay should be for that type of project.

To encourage more transparency and accountability, and to further expose the disparities that exist between Black and non-Black influencers, Adesuwa Ajayi founded the Instagram page @influencerpaygap, where influencers can anonymously post the pay and treatment they receive from the industry. It's an informal way for influencers to gauge how their peers are doing in comparison. What they're finding is that there are deep-seated inequities in pay and treatment.

The million-dollar question for most influencers is, how tough should you be in negotiating pay? When do you ask for more? When do you take what you can get? What's the number where I outprice myself? Ladish considers herself a tough negotiator, but she understands the reasons why influencers, especially those from marginalized communities, often take what's offered to them, no questions asked. Ladish says, "I have friends who are making $300 per blog post, and they've been doing this for ten years, but they don't dare ask for more money, or they need those $300 so they'd just rather have that than nothing. I had stopped doing the $300 thing years ago. For example, for me right now, one blog post with social media shares is $3,000."

It's a challenge. The more influencers fail to negotiate, instead accepting whatever is offered, the more the average fee for everyone goes down. People want to get paid what they're worth, but they also may be driven by fear, afraid that if they push back too aggressively, brands will go away. This is not an unfounded fear. Kim Guerra says, "I've negotiated some, and some responded well, but then others just stop talking to me after I asked for higher pay. . . . A lot of times, what the culture has been like—it's either you risk asking for what you know you deserve and what other people are getting, or you risk not getting anything. . . . Especially with immigrants, you're just told, oh, you should be grateful we're even asking you. You should be grateful we're even thinking about you." Guerra would like to see more intentionality when it comes to amplifying Black and Brown voices, and not just when it's trendy, in order to make it a safer space for everybody.

Jessy Grossman sees getting paid equally, getting paid fairly, and getting paid on time as big issues in the industry. She would like to see diversity in influencing be addressed from both the top down and the bottom up. In terms of leadership, Grossman wants more women to continue to have a seat at the table, but with a focus on women of color, because "as much as this is a pretty female-dominated industry, it is a lot of white women who have leadership roles." Conversely, Grossman believes that changes at the top are also influenced by changes at the bottom. She says, "The more that we have women of color influencers in programs and things like that, it's actually also influencing who's running those programs to understand where those women are coming from and how to best navigate those programs."

For actual change to happen, advocates say the people representing influencers need to step up and make sure their clients are getting equal pay. Lisa Filipelli says, "We literally had to talk about this the other day—about how do we explain to brands that we will not be underselling our diverse clients? Sorry, it's not going to happen. If you're offering a white woman more than a Black woman, we're totally going to tell you about that. . . . We came up with language internally that we'll use in emails that just says, 'You've paid X client this, you're offering X client this; this is no longer fair.' We came up with some verbiage all together as a team so we could make sure that we had a response that was both professional but direct. . . . It's something that we discussed as a team. Our roster is diverse, and that's how we want it to be. And our team is diverse, so that's been important to us. And I think it's important for a brand to know if we think that they're taking advantage of somebody."

LaToya Shambo, of Black Girl Digital, says, "Brands don't value Black content the way that they value white content." The way she likes to position her influencers to combat this is less about their following and more about the production. She says, "If the industry would shift their mindset for a second on what they value, then there'd be less inequities. It's like you pay for a commercial—you're paying megadollars to that production company. . . . I tell the influencers they should also position themselves as a production company be-cause you are actually producing content. You have to maybe hire a photographer, maybe hire a videographer, maybe hire an editor. You have to spend time editing. . . . So for you, [the] brand, not to value the production that goes into making this content—that's rude!" With this shift in viewpoint, inequities are buried because race, ethnicity, gender, sexuality, age, and physical ability—all these are taken off the table, because, she says, "all that matters is if the production of the content is quality. If they approached it from that perspective, then if you have $10,000 for an influencer, then you've got $10,000 for all influencers."

Shambo would also like to see the wild west environment curbed by some sort of standardization in terms of pay scale. She gives an example of the measurement ad agencies work from, CPM, which refers to cost per mille, or thousand, meaning that it is the cost advertisers pay for 1,000 views or impressions of an ad. Critics of standardization or regulation say that such a strategy doesn't encourage innovation and can put people who don't deserve it higher on the pay scale while also lowering the rates for those who do.

Some professionals in the influencer industry say unionization is a way to achieve equity, and an important step for marginalized members of the influencer community in particular, who may benefit from being under the umbrella of a union. As the number of influencers grows, the work is increasingly becoming recognized as a profession, including by the Screen Actors Guild–American Federation of Television and Radio Artists (SAG-AFTRA), a union that traditionally represents actors. In 2021, SAG-AFTRA approved an "Influencer Agreement" stating that anyone who makes money as an influencer selling products on platforms like TikTok and Instagram may join the union and qualify for benefits, including the right to earn union income, as well as health and pension benefits.[9] However, some influencers like Eli Erlick complain that the fees are "absurd," which is prohibitive for many.

COMBATING THE PSYCHOLOGICAL EFFECT OF DISCRIMINATION ON INFLUENCERS

Discrimination of all kinds, be it ableism or sex-based, age-based, body-based, or race-based discrimination, doesn't happen in a vacuum. Consequences reverberate through the individual, within families, and across society. Research has shown that discrimination can have deleterious effects on both mind and body. Danielle R. Busby points out that the negative impact hits people from all sides and can range from mental health outcomes like anxiety, depression, and low self-esteem to physical outcomes like hypertension, which is connected to stress. With regard to influencers, Busby says, "Having an unfair experience based solely on your race or ethnic background—it's taxing, and it requires you to use a different amount of energy to do your already probably taxing job. And you're expected to still do it just as well as anyone else without that tax." All of this leads to compounding stress.

Dana L. Cunningham also brings up the fact that there can be racial trauma, which leads to internalized oppression. The result is a host of disruptive, negative thoughts. She says, "People may start to think and question, 'Well, what's wrong with me? Why am I not good enough? What concerns are with my product? What do I need to change about myself to do something different?'—which is not obviously helpful either, but it's oftentimes a reflection of our system."

Internalizing racism rather than looking outward can also lead to imposter syndrome. Mental health advocate and influencer Celeste Viciere, says, "A lot of times, especially people of color, and I speak for myself personally—I think that imposter syndrome can kick in when you've never been in a certain arena or been in this kind of influencer world before. . . . It was hard. I have to really remind myself this is what I deserve."

In the article "Discrimination Can Be Harmful to Your Mental Health," UCLA experts view the correlation between discrimination and an increased risk of mental health disorders as a threat to the individual—but they also raise it to the status of a public health concern, stating that there is a domino effect with things like depression, anxiety, low self-esteem, and substance abuse.[10] A person who abuses alcohol will have trouble forming healthy relationships with their children. A person who is depressed and lacks confidence won't perform to their full capacity on the job. This is why the experts say discrimination affects others beyond the subject of the discrimination.

What is the healthiest way for marginalized influencers to cope with the discrimination they face? One thing experts say needs to happen is opening up about the reality of the situation and shining a light on it. During our discussion, Busby comments, "We need to name it, like how we're having a conversation about it. We're talking about it. We're giving voice to it because this is a lot of people's experience, and a lot of times when we don't name it, when we don't talk about it, it creates this space of 'I'm alone,' or 'I have hopelessness,' 'There's no way to get out of it.' And until we start talking about it, we can't really do much about the realities of it. We need to bring awareness to it."

A big part of awareness is not just the external factors at play but also the internal reaction within the individual. This is where mindfulness comes in; it helps create a full, healthy picture. This well-researched technique is about learning to be in the here and now, without distractions but with acceptance of your present state. Viciere says, "If I'm mindful and know who I am—know all the work that I've put in, I can actually challenge the system and say, 'It's the system. It's not me!' But a lot of people don't do that because they're not mindful of what's happening in real time. They hear it, they're affected; before you know it their esteem is low." She recommends paying attention to states of being, like mood changes when influencers encounter discrimination, so that they can become aware of how they are affected emotionally, physically, and spiritually. This will help prevent internalizing the hate and injustice while also providing a springboard for coping.

Experts agree that coping strategies are not one size fits all. It's something that's highly personal and depends on individual preferences. Busby says, "I think it is very person specific. Are you someone that needs to be doing work related to a cause you're really passionate about? . . . I think people should take the time to be intentional and say, 'what's going to be my outlet?'"

The outlet might not always be community action based or related to advocacy. Often it will be internal—meditation or other therapeutic coping strategies. If the influencer does choose the community action–based route, a key is that it fosters a sense of hope even though the reality is that change is slow.

GETTING TO GREAT ADVOCACY

Influencer advocacy runs along a spectrum, with some staying away from it completely. Reasons for that include wanting to keep things light, worrying that brand deals will be affected, or simply preferring to stay out of that lane. Those who choose to advocate often cite a sense of responsibility to use their influence toward a common good; without it, influencing seems empty to them. Quite a few influencers and influencing professionals we interviewed believe that advocacy should go hand-in-hand with being an influencer.

Travel influencer Johnny Jet says, "I got political a couple times. . . . I was like, I'm not staying silent. And I've definitely lost followers. . . . I don't care; I'm going to use the little influence that I have." It isn't always easy to take a stand, and sometimes it comes at a cost.

Many influencers grow into an advocacy role once they get to know themselves better, get to know their audience, learn from audience comments, and develop an understanding of what matters to their followers. Others have a sense of what they want to advocate for when they start out; they become, first and foremost, advocacy influencers.

Venezuelan-born disability activist/influencer Paula Carozzo has a PR background and lives in Miami. She developed cerebral palsy as a child after a tonsillectomy gone wrong led to inflammation of the brain, permanently affecting her balance and mobility. For a portion of her life, she used a wheelchair, but she now walks with a cane.

Carozzo says, "Growing up with a disability, things are pretty much done for you. If you have difficulties getting dressed, your parents will come in and help you get dressed. If you have difficulties opening the door, they will come in and help you. So I would say my life was pretty inclusive and pretty accessible, until I became an adult with a disability. And these are things that many people don't talk about. That's when I was like, OK, maybe this is something I need to speak about. . . . We start having less support from our parents and our peers, not because they don't want to give us support but because we also want to be independent. We also want to have access to the things that everybody has access to—some of the same opportunities. . . . I thought to myself it would be nice to represent my community just by being who I am—this very fashionable girl, that kind of always has an issue getting dressed, because the clothing I want to wear isn't always adaptive. By adaptive, I mean, clothing that is made for people with disabilities, with limb differences. . . . So there was that conversation I wanted to have in the fashion industry. And then there was, of course, the conversation of how infrastructure is built without thinking about people with disabilities."

At first, when Carozzo started posting with her cane, followers thought it was a prop and were perplexed by the way she walked. Carozzo took these opportunities to steer the conversation in a way that redefines disability as a condition that is a lifestyle, not a life sentence. She has since built a community of other advocates, disabled celebrities, moms of kids with disabilities, and people without disabilities who want to be part of the conversation and effect change. "They have realized that we have been put away for too long, and this was like a rebirth," she says.

For Gigi Robinson, body image, chronic illness, and mental health influencer, outside circumstances helped shape her role as an advocate on social media. She says, "The pandemic happened, and I couldn't just post about my daily outfits in quarantine that were so normal at the time. . . . So I said, OK, I'm going to do something more. Then obviously the resurfacing of the Black Lives Matter movement emerged, and I did a deeper look into, not only the brands that I worked with, but also the people I followed and the way that they were showing up on social media. So I said, you know what? Social media is not just about posting your fucking outfits. Social media is about making a difference and being an influence over other people." Going forward, Robinson has made the decision to create more consciously and take targeted stances.

What are the most effective ways to take those stances? Individual influencers find different approaches that work for their audiences, but in general, the theme of being "relatable" pops up when talking about successful advocacy.

Eli Erlick finds relatable posts, which evoke emotions such as inspiration or anger, draw attention, as well as posts that are entertaining. A little humor and sarcasm go a long way. She also says, "Usually, as far as algorithms go, you do need to include photos of faces, and I found that to be very interesting because we're actually not controlling our own modes of advocacy as much as algorithms."

Relatability is important as well to Lolo Spencer; she also finds that blowing people's minds by giving them something they don't expect is a great way to advocate and elicit a response from the audience. She says, "High-fashion photography is incredibly effective and engaging because people don't expect people with disabilities to look fashionable—to dress fashionable and be glamorized. So when those examples are shown through my photos, people—they go fucking crazy. They go wild. They love it! So there's that piece of it that makes it effective and engaging."

Looking for topics hidden below the surface but that need to come out is a version of mining for gold. When it strikes, it produces a wealth of engagement. Aysha Harun experimented with posting about mental health issues, which gained traction with her audience because it's something this community didn't really talk about. She says, "I think mental health had such a huge taboo in the past, especially with the Black community, and more so the Muslim community. I think that a large Muslim creator sharing their struggles of mental health and just advice on that is really important, and I'm glad that I can be part of that movement. And I definitely think it's gonna be more focused on in the future, as well, especially with this Gen Z generation. I think it's so beautiful how vulnerable and open they are about mental health, and it just makes me excited for the future."

With more and more influencers advocating for their causes, there is the danger of cause fatigue. Does too much advocacy blur the voices so that no one is heard clearly?

Liza Anderson says it's an age-old question that started with actors and other artists. If you show up to hear your favorite band in concert, do you want them to start talking to you about politics? When you turn on an awards show, are you interested in hearing the actor's worldview during the acceptance speech? People have different preferences. Anderson thinks it's a deeply personal decision for each influencer. She says, "If that's a platform you feel like you want to use and you feel like you have a social responsibility because you have an audience, then please, by all means, but does one necessarily necessitate the other? I mean, not everybody needs to change the world. Some people can just, you know, work out, or sing, or cook, without feeling obligated that they have to change the world."

A SPACE AND A PLACE

Some people think social media and influencer platforms are evil, plain and simple. Others believe that the inherent bad outweighs any potential good that might come from this medium, causing them to dismiss certain phenomena without taking a closer look. The groups with these points of view, however, may be missing significant cultural changes that have arisen as a result of online interactions.

Rather than seeing social media and the internet as inherently good or bad, Erin Vogel views it as a "tool that we can use in ways that either benefit us or harm us or both." The question then becomes whether that tool is used responsibly or irresponsibly. Too often it's the latter, unleashing a violent spread of hate and misinformation.

The internet isn't the first arm of the media to be used in nefarious ways. All forms of media have had their moments of shame in history. For instance, yellow journalism in the 1890s emphasized sensationalism over fact to sell papers, and it's well known that during World War II, the Nazis were adept at using the latest marketing techniques of the time to spread their propaganda through the arts (like theater, film, and music), radio, and printed material. In the 1990s, extremists used radio as a tool to broadcast hate speech. The spread of hate rhetoric and misinformation through media isn't something that's new. What is new is its speed and reach.

Laura Vogel believes that social media is democratizing and useful. She says, "If you have something valuable to say, anybody can say it. And if people listen to you, you have power. . . . Now, somebody might be more likely to listen to someone that is beautiful or white and attractive in the traditional standards of beauty, but if we're going to change this society, giving power to people that otherwise are locked out is exceptionally important. One of the ways that we can create change is by giving people a voice. Well, social media does that. It allows people to take their own voice and to use it however they want, and so I find it very equalizing."

One of the best examples of this type of equalizing is Black Twitter, which is an informal digital community on Twitter that started around 2009, bringing Black people together virtually to discuss topics of interest to their community—and often effecting change. Brian Carey Sims's understanding of Black Twitter is that it is the "space on Twitter, where Black folks feel free to be the way that Black folks are outside of the white mainstream gaze. Because most of American society, since its inception, has not been designed by or with Black cultural elements or aspects in mind. Most of the time, Black folks feel the need to sort of assimilate and accommodate and adjust who they are." Before social media, there were Black actors portraying characters on screen and other forms of scripted content, but these types of raw, authentic exchanges, seen in real time on social media within the Black community, were revolutionary.

In a *PR Week* opinion article, "Why Black Twitter Matters for Brands," Esther Akinola says, "Without too much effort from brands themselves, Black people drive campaigns through their engagement as long as the content sits within a topic and/or tone that resonates with them."[11] If brands don't factor Black Twitter into the equation, then they're missing out on authentic engagement, some of the latest trends, and a wider audience.

Of course, it's not only Black people who have found a place on social media. Sims says, "If you've got a marginalized or oppressed group, there's a space for you on Twitter that allows you to be, quote–unquote, 'yourself' and engage with other members of that community in an authentic way. And I think that's a general sort of positive in a world where connection is at a premium."

MORAL, ETHICAL, AND GOOD FOR BUSINESS

More people in the industry are approaching diversity as not only a moral imperative but also as just plain good for business. For example, FabFitFun has partnered with influencers from every community, including people who have intellectual and physical disabilities. Jolie Jankowitz believes that commitment to inclusivity goes beyond the influencer program and has to be a commitment for the marketing strategy as a whole. FabFitFun has an ethical strategy, but it's also great for business because they're about customizable subscription boxes. Recruiting influencers from a variety of different backgrounds shows a variety of different ways that consumers can customize their boxes. Presenting more options and reaching more communities can lead to more sales.

Jacques Bastien argues that diversity in influencer marketing simply makes great business sense because in every ethnic group and subculture, people have money and are willing to spend it. Most of the brands that work with their agency recognize this. They come to them for the right reasons and have the right budget. However, there are instances where it's clear that brand reps are reaching out not because they have the intention of hiring, but because they have to check off a box indicating that they had reached out to a Black and Brown agency.

Bastien says the issue is that a lot of companies are not "intentional about focusing on that subgroup and creating something for them, or even if it's not just for them, just include them in the process—be very direct about the fact that when we created this thing, we thought of you."

Bastien experiences situations where brands want to work with his influencer talent, but then in the process of researching the companies, he finds that their websites lack images of a Brown or Black person, or that the wording is geared to a single narrow audience. These are signs that show inclusivity to be an addendum. For Bastien, that kind of outreach has come too late. He states, "We've said no to many opportunities because we know our creators are not going to want to work for that project. . . . I want to make sure that you also thought of me when you were creating this thing. But it seems more like an afterthought. You built this thing, you built this business; then you say, let's try to get this to some Black people. Let's try to get some Brown people to see this."

He gives Fenty as an example of a brand that got it right, both in terms of inclusion and in terms of influencer marketing. Megaartist and megainfluencer Rihanna is the founder. Launched in 2017, Fenty Beauty is a cosmetics brand that took off as a result of its inclusivity regarding gender and skin tones.

Bastien says that when you're talking about diversity in influencer marketing, it means not only hiring diverse creators but also having a diverse staff with different backgrounds and experiences, which they can pour into a campaign to make it successful. Coming from one myopic perspective can lead to other issues as well, including people getting canceled because there's no one there to catch insensitive, unethical, or inappropriate comments.

Bastien views his agency as a first line of defense; they make sure many things never reach the influencers. After several years in the business, he's picked up a pattern of "keywords" that tip him off to discriminatory practices. He recalls one situation with a makeup line that was looking for natural Black influencers, but he believed the brand turned an influencer down on the basis of her skin tone.

At every level of the influencing industry, there are still those that hold on to a narrow approach from the past. A high-level executive we spoke to told us, "It's difficult to force diversity onto the influencer business. . . . You can't force diversity on a brand if the product is not a product that that category would use." A newer approach that seems to be taking hold is that diversity is just good for business; it's not something that needs to be forced.

When asked if diversity can be "forced" on influencer marketing, Bastien's reply is that it "should be diverse naturally." He describes diversity as a "bunch of different things coming together to create something beautiful. So if you look at it as music, a drum works phenomenally by itself. A guitar works great by itself. And those things are celebrated and appreciated for what they are individually. And then when they come together . . . we just hear amazing, beautiful music. . . . So the thing that music itself figured out is that we're better that we're different, because imagine a song where . . . all of that was being played by the drum." He goes on to say that in influencer marketing, the differences should be used in that sense, as well as celebrated intrinsically.

THE LIFESTYLE AND LA

Influencing isn't just a job; it's a lifestyle. Manager Naomi Lennon describes it as a tight community with a singular focus. "We love to talk about content all day and social media. What I love is that I can go to dinner with all of them, and we're all on our phones, and no one complains! . . . It's very engrossing—so all-encompassing. I noticed that it's hard for them to have any other hobbies." Influencing is imposing a new autonomous structure on work life—arguably one that is blurring the lines between career, home, and play more than other industries.

Even though influencers can be found everywhere around the globe, the epicenter of influencing is Los Angeles, California. Many of the influencers we interviewed were either thinking about moving to LA, in the process of moving to LA, or already lived in LA. This chapter focuses on the culture of influencing in LA and beyond, including glam events, personal relationships, and influencing's collision with the acting community. We also look at the dangers and lifestyle issues that influencers face.

THE INFLUENCER INVASION AND BLURRED LINES

The culture of Hollywood is changing at warp speed, and it's because of influencers. Traditional entertainment and entertainers are crashing into an exploding industry. As the dust settles, lines between old and new are blurring.

Many of Hollywood's veteran actors are left soured by the change. Former *Friends* costar and popular actor Jennifer Aniston told *Hollywood Reporter* in 2021, "It's not the same industry that it used to be. It's not that glamorous anymore. It's slowly becoming about TikTok and Instagram followers. It's like, we're hiring now based on followers, not talent?"[1] On October 5, 2019, Aniston joined Instagram and set a Guinness world record for hitting 1 million followers in five hours and sixteen minutes.

Max Levine talks about the movement toward digital content and the people who are behind it: "The studio or network model, it's obviously shifting. . . . Legacy companies historically just move at a much slower rate than newer types of companies. And I honestly don't think it was even until Covid hit that a lot of these talent agencies really started putting more and more resources into it, because productions were shut down. But digital content—people can really create from anywhere. . . . Society, it has shifted, in terms of how people approach content creators."

Influencer Eli Erlick has lived in both LA and New York and has watched the evolution in influencing: "I think it's changed a lot over the past few years. It used to be a lot more combative, where influencers weren't seen as legitimate, but now actors realize that part of their self-promotion is also online. So hanging out with influencers is much more welcome. On the other hand, in New York, there's a bit more snobbery still, just as there is against TV or film actors versus theater actors."

Stephanie McNeal, who describes herself as obsessed with internet culture, has a similar take. She says, "It's probably considered a little bit more prestigious than it used to be, or a more valid career choice. . . . But I think just from talking to influencers that I know, they still struggle with a stigma of it being a frivolous and stupid career." When asked if there was a difference in how people view influencers in LA, she said any contrasts could be broken down into general New York versus LA differences, which she has experienced by living in both cities. McNeal says, "New York tends to be a lot more serious, a little more judgmental, a little more buttoned up. . . . I think the same person moves to New York or LA. But I think people in New York move there for success. A lot of people move to LA for not fame, per se, but for a more exciting lifestyle, but it's the same. They're both driven by the same underlying goals. And so I think maybe in LA, it [influencing] would be a tad more accepted."

Kevin Kreider sees a change happening, but he is frustrated by a hierarchical system that he thinks puts actors on top, reality TV stars in the middle, and influencers at the bottom. He says, "TV is changing, people are crossing over, people are becoming brand influencers. And I think actors—and coming from the experience of being that arrogant actor—you really got to get over yourself! They gotta stop being so arrogant about it. It's art, whether they realize it or not. It is an art form. It is entertainment, just like what they're doing. . . . I think what ends up happening is people are rewarded who are the risk takers."

He believes the success of reality TV and influencing is leading to "jealousy" and "insecurities" among traditional actors. In the end, Kreider plans to maintain his future-forward approach despite the outside noise. "There are some reality people who are doing everything. I hope to be that reality guy who turns into everything: actor, writer, influencer."

The fact is, the definition of who is and who isn't an influencer is up for grabs at this point. For Aditi Oberoi Malhotra, anyone who is a celebrity, writer, content creator—really, anyone who has an Instagram or other social media channel where they are posting content to influence other people—is an influencer, whether they accept it or not. Of course, today there is more acceptance.

Malhotra says, "Initially, the first couple years when I started—wow, there was a lot of negativity! Everybody was writing off influencers, but the weird part is, even magazine writers have become influencers. Literally, I tell you editors are posting their outfit of the day, every day. The lines have blurred."

Levine sees the blurred lines as well. Even though influencers tend to hang out with each other, he notices that they're also involved with people from acting and music. "They're all starting to intertwine a little bit more, because it's kind of all homogenizing," he says.

The rungs of the hierarchy's ladder are also shifting. Malhotra says, "If you click with an actor, for example, if there is an actor who's commenting on my post and I take the time and effort—if I like that person's content and I reply back to them or comment on their picture, then you can cultivate a relationship. There are still people who are very snooty, I'm sure, but that is also true in the case of influencers. If some influencer is really big and kind of high-headed [sic], they will not talk to actors who are just starting off." No matter what rung on the ladder a person occupies, Malhotra believes the key is humility.

For some, the cultural analogy is less like a ladder and more like high school. That's the way it is for Rave Vanias, an influencer who is moving toward the actor space. She explains, "You have your cliques. Here's your popular people. Here's your jocks. Here's your nerdy dude. It's the same space in the influencer crew. You have your Instagrammers. You have your TikTokers. You have your YouTubers. You have your actors that post on social media. You have your singers that post on social media. . . . Some people will interchange. Someone like me will have influencer base friends, but then I'm acting, so I have to go hang out with the acting people too."

Vanias also puts her finger on the trend of actors getting cozier with influencers because of their followers, musing about the actors' attitudes: "I couldn't tell you they're sitting there like, 'I got to go hang out with little kids that are just dancing on screen and doing nothing,' or if they're sitting here like, 'Wow! This is cool that I have this opportunity.'"

For most, the relationships are mutually beneficial. Of course, some pairings are more cringy, seemingly manufactured attention grabs than others; consider reality star Kourtney Kardashian's much-photographed friendship with TikTok megainfluencer Addison Rae. Actors/comedians are also getting into the mix; take YouTube star David Dobrik, who posted a video of himself chilling with Chris Rock as they watched *Madagascar* together.

Some collaborations seem less forced and more like the natural progression of the entertainment industry. For instance, on her podcast, *Good for You,* Whitney Cummings has more than the regular roster of interviewees—rosters that usually include actors, musicians, and comedians. Cummings's guests also include popular influencers, like Hannah Stocking, Liza Koshy, and Amanda Cerny.

The influencing community and the acting community are increasingly mixing at events. As with any industry, networking professionals want to put their best foot forward. Eli Erlick says that in LA, that means "you need to constantly have a smile on your face, enjoy everything, and promote that you're happy so you get hired again."

Kim Guerra says that when she goes to an event, it's easy to spot other influencers because they are "a lot more extra." She recalls a premiere that included actors and influencers: "You could tell the difference in that space because I actually was hanging out with an actor and a music producer and they're more chill, and then you have the influencers taking videos and everything. . . . That's why they invited me—to take videos. And I took a picture of the snack bar. I felt like I was a bad influencer." The actor Guerra was with wondered, "Oh, my goodness. Am I supposed to be doing that too?"

LA-based influencer Aysha Harun describes the unique thrill of encountering famous people. "Just going to an event and seeing a celebrity that I've maybe watched their movie or their show—it is a little weird and strange. It's just a very full-circle moment. I went to an event summer before last, and I was in a room with Mandy Moore and Sophia Bush, and I'm like, damn! I've watched these two women since I was a child, and it's crazy to be in the same room as them."

As the tables turn, influencers are the celebrities that get recognized. For several influencers we interviewed, their new celebrity status takes some getting used to, especially for their significant others, who are often pushed to the side and ignored when fans approach. It causes strains in relationships as well as breakups.

TikToker Kyle Hernandez dated his girlfriend for two and a half years before they decided to be just friends because of his influencer career choice. He says, "I wanted to do something bigger with my life, and I told her that I wanted to be an actor, I wanted to be an entertainer—I wanted to be something really, really big. And so, for her, she always wanted to be rich—everybody wants to be rich— but she just never wanted to have the issue of walking outside and somebody's running up to me and wanting to take a picture. She didn't want that lifestyle. I told her I totally understand. And for four months, I straight up told her I could figure out a way to fix that." But unfortunately he couldn't find a way around the fan element of influencing—the same scenario as any traditional celebrity.

BRAND EVENTS: SEEING AND BEING SEEN

Brand events can be the crown jewels of the profession for influencers, or they can become a chore. The events themselves, over time, may seem simultaneously glamorous and mundane. But no matter; they're an integral part of the profession. It's all about seeing and being seen in person, with the added extra layer of ensuring that the whole spectacle and/or product is seen by followers online.

For Ashley Iaconetti Haibon and her husband, Jared Haibon, events are a great way to keep their names out there and stay relevant. They have a "say yes" attitude toward invites: "There's so many events that are just geared toward influencers these days."

The Haibons get invitations all the time asking them to show up for things like gifting suites, cocktails, and private screenings. She says, "Hollywood uses influencers as advertisement, and not all of it is going to be paid. . . . If we get invited to a premiere, even if we don't care about the movie and we kind of want to stay home that night, we're still going to go because the pictures of the red carpet— the connections and the mingling that we're going to have there—is worth it just to keep relevant. . . . I will say you run into a lot of the same people at those places. And they are places that actors and musicians aren't going to show up to. It's people who are just trying to stay where they're at."

Kristina Zias often goes to product launches for beauty and fashion influencers, like a Cover Girl event introducing a new foundation. She says you'll end up meeting someone you know, or someone will know someone, and things take off from there.

Seasonal events are an important part of her yearly rotation. The time at the end of November and the beginning of December is especially busy as brands and PR push holiday content. There is also a glut of events around once-a-year festivities like Coachella Valley Music and Arts Festival, where brands try to showcase concert fashion.

How many of these events influencers attend depends on what stage of life they're in and what they are trying to accomplish. Are you married with kids? Are you single? Are you wanting to party? Make friends? Make business connections?

Zias estimates she goes to about five events a month. She prefers intimate dinners, which permit real face time with people, to huge parties, where it's unlikely she will get to know anyone from the brand. She says, "I started becoming more selective because I realized how valuable my time was. And if you're out going to events all the time, then you're not creating content. That's time you're taking away from building your business. . . . I still think events are extremely valuable, but I think it just depends on the type of event, and the type of relationship that you have with a brand or PR agency. . . . I don't care about free drinks."

Malhotra has a similar take as Zias on events. She prefers to go to events that propel her career or help her grow in some way; she's not in it for the "free goodies."

IMMERSION EVENTS: SOAKING UP THE EXPERIENCE

The idea behind immersion events is that if you up the engagement of influencers, you up the engagement of their audience. Immersion events allow influencers to take a deep dive into the brand experience, either by trips that are essentially glitzy company conferences or unique events and experiences that fit the brand, like fashion shows, concerts, and red-carpet events. It's a way for influencers to develop a more authentic connection with the brand and keep a savvy audience from getting bored with the ordinary way products are usually rolled out.

For the launch of a new lipstick, luxury brand Givenchy flew about sixty influencers from all over the world to Paris, then put them on a private jet to London for an immersion experience. Malhotra felt privileged to be one of two influencers from the United States to be chosen for the special excursion. Givenchy had different events planned for them each day, including a presentation about the product and a treasure hunt that had them flitting to different locations as they tried to solve the puzzle. The trip culminated in a full-on luxe launch soiree.

Malhotra says, "They just didn't want us to be paid and create an Instagram post sitting at home. They wanted us to be more interactive." Thanks to the time spent together doing different activities, Malhotra bonded with other influencers and made friends on that trip. She emphasizes, "It was a lot of fun, and at the same time, it was a work trip."

Joey Zauzig also points to immersion events' aspect of work melding with fun. When Dell introduced a new laptop, the company wanted influencers to get to know the new computer at more than a surface level. Zauzig describes that trip: "We land, we go to a hotel room, we get a lot of times to shoot content, we have a time to learn about the new product, and then [we] post about the product—just to provide an experience."

He says that some of his noninfluencer friends don't get the point of the trips. Why do brands need to pay for getaways? Zauzig argues that it's about "keeping people's attention going and making it a longer story," rather than just introducing a product and moving on with your day.

During these brand-saturated experiences, there's always a precarious balance between having fun and working. Zauzig details the breathless pace of a "crazy" influencer trip to Brazil:

> You get ten outfits to shoot in twelve days. You wake up, you have breakfast, there's free time for an hour to shoot photos. . . . You get on a bus and go to lunch somewhere cool. You take more photos, you go back, you upload your photos, you submit them for approval, you post your photo, you tag them, you do your swipe ups, you do a little checklist on your phone—make sure you get everything that you need to do for that day done. And then you have dinner that night, hopefully have a few cocktails, and do the same thing the next day in a different location.

Zauzig makes it clear that this is not a vacation. It's exhilarating, but it's a lot of work. To his followers, the trip simply looks like a compilation of stunning beaches and beautiful clothes; they don't see the hours he spent in his hotel room, editing and selecting photos. To counter this, Zauzig shares posts of himself doing the actual work to give his audience a more accurate depiction of his experience.

The wow factor of these trips for the influencer depends on their stage of life, how long they've been doing it, and their life experience. Influencers we interviewed from modest or low-income backgrounds were more awed by the events than influencers who weren't new to luxury or who had been doing the job for a while.

SEXUAL MISCONDUCT: IS THIS WHAT PEOPLE IN POWER ARE LIKE?

Because of the nature of the influencing industry, there's a lot of partying and a lot of power differentials. Newbies are working alongside people who have already made it or are in a position to open doors for them. It's a situation ripe for sexual harassment and sexual assault.

Reporter Stephanie McNeal says, "I think it's about the same as any other industry where people are given a glut of money and power—like it's Hollywood, the music industry, politics. It's not something that I think is unique to the influencer industry."

Kyle Hernandez has experienced the abuse of power firsthand. Growing up in Louisiana, he says that he was taught to respect others, so he was surprised to find he was getting disrespected by some in the industry. When we asked him what he meant by "disrespect," he opens up about experiencing two incidences of sexual misconduct at out-of-state events, one he describes as being perpetuated by a fifty- to sixty-year-old man running the event. He says, "We were all above twenty-one and we were in the casino. We were just having a conversation and he wanted to go drinking. I just finished flying and I was super tired, and I was like, 'Hey, well, I just want to go home.' And he's like, 'Oh, no, just stay out. Just stay out.'" That's when the "CEO of the entire event" started drinking more and flirting with him. Hernandez says. "Then he touched my private parts."

The man apologized the next day, but for Hernandez, it wasn't over. The incident, which he equated to a "no-respect boundary type of thing," put him in a doubtful frame of mind and made him wonder, "Is this what a lot of people that are in power are like?" He reports that he told some of his social media friends about the incident, and a couple of them who were from LA said, "That's pretty common in the entertainment industry, like people just touchin' on you." They went on to say that it was less common in the influencing industry. Of course, this is anecdotal, and this may or may not be the case.

There have been some high-profile influencers who have found themselves at the center of sexual misconduct allegations. Some of them are influencers using their fame and status to allegedly create a situation where they are able to take advantage of fans; others are famous influencers who have been accused of enabling a culture of misconduct.

One of the highest-profile people caught up in a controversial situation is David Dobrik, a YouTube and TikTok star with more than 50 million total followers, known for a particular brand of prank-humor video. He lost some of his sponsors and posted several videos online apologizing in 2021 after a young woman claimed she was raped by one of his collaborators while filming a video in 2018. YouTube then temporarily suspended the ability of Dobrik and his cohort to monetize their channels, noting, "We have strict policies that prohibit sexual harassment on YouTube and take allegations of sexual assault very seriously. We have temporarily suspended monetization on David Dobrik and Durte Dom channels for violating our Creator Responsibility policy."[2] Dobrik also faced allegations of sexual misconduct from a member of his Vlog Squad, Seth Francois, who in February 2021 alleged that he was tricked into kissing another member of the squad in a video. Francois, who goes by Seth online, also alleged he faced racial abuse from people online and said there was a fear that if he spoke out, he would be cut from the squad. Dobrik later apologized to Seth, saying consent has always been important to him and he "missed the mark" with that video.[3]

Just a few months after he was suspended from making money on his channel by YouTube, however, Dobrik was back on that platform, making videos that were regularly getting more than 5 million views. He even signed a deal with Discovery for a new series on its streaming service.

Influencer and makeup artist James Charles has roughly 47 million combined followers on his YouTube and Instagram channels. He has twice been canceled (temporarily) for allegations of misconduct. The first was in 2019. Then in 2021, he faced allegations that he used his fame to attempt to "groom" underage boys. He posted a video, apologizing for what he called flirting and for not understanding how his celebrity influenced his fans to potentially do or say something they wouldn't do normally. He apologized to the victims and pledged that something like this wouldn't happen again.[4]

These are just two examples that made headlines, but they provide insight into the dangers that exist in the industry. In some cases, the platforms take action, as they did against Dobrik, but influencers are often left to handle issues as they arise on their own.

STALKING: A DARK SIDE OF INFLUENCING

Most of the time, cyberbullying stays cyber. It lives online on an influencer's post. However, in some chilling cases, it comes to life in the form of real-world stalking. A variety of mental illnesses can be the driving force for this type of behavior on the part of fans, including the delusional disorder called erotomania. People with this disorder have the unwavering, false belief that they are loved and adored by someone—usually someone of higher status, like a celebrity. They may even believe that they are in a relationship with the object of their delusion, even if they don't know them. This leads to attempts to make contact, which leads to stalking. When people with erotomania are thwarted, they get angry.

Because of influencers' visibility and frequent interaction with the public, they are at high risk for being stalked. Andreea Bolbea, aka Andreea Cristina, a popular lifestyle and beauty blogger (SimplyAndreea.com) is, sadly, a typical example. Her stalker began by sending deranged emails, the contents of which got darker and darker. She disregarded them, but he let her know that he would not be ignored, threatening to come find her. He did. She writes that he flew to where she lived and spent a month leaving packages and letters at her home.[5] She got a restraining order, but the authorities couldn't find him to serve him.

The details that influencers post about their lives can leave them vulnerable to stalkers. In an eerie Tokyo case, a fan analyzed images that a pop star posted online to identify her whereabouts. Through a reflection in her eyes on a selfie, he noticed a train station sign, zoomed in, and used Google Street View to locate the station from which she commuted. According to news reports, he waited for her at the station, followed her home, and assaulted her.[6]

With every post influencers make, there is a chance that they are providing clues that permit insight into their habits, hangouts, and everyday patterns. Influencers post so much personal information that it's sometimes hard for them to draw the line. One of the most famous cases was a harrowing incident in 2016, where Kim Kardashian was robbed at gunpoint in her Paris hotel room. News reports of the time indicate that she believed the thieves stalked her before the robbery to gain critical intel for their plot; she seemingly regretted announcing on Snapchat that she was home alone and set to leave Paris the next day, which provided them with a tiny window of opportunity for the robbery.[7] After the trauma, Kardashian changed her online habits to avoid oversharing; she believes she can still be authentic while protecting her and her family's privacy.

Some influencers experience a twinge of guilt at not leaving it all out there because they desperately want to form a close connection with their audience. Kristina Zias says, "There are a lot of people who feel like the influencers they follow are their real-life friends and real-life family." Kristina has genuine affection for her community of followers, but she knows it can only go so far. When she was pregnant, she had some followers asking her for her address so they could make her something or send something for the baby. She says, "I don't know what to do in those situations because it's so thoughtful and so sweet, but I'm like, OK, this is dangerous. I can't give out my address to people."

The issue of superfans showing up at their home uninvited has become a nuisance for influencers. Usually the goal is simply to get a selfie with a favorite influencer, but how are influencers supposed to judge who is dangerous and who is not? Besides, it's a gross violation of privacy and just plain annoying.

During the pandemic, overzealous fans showing up posed a different kind of threat. Beauty influencer Bretman Rock posted a series of videos begging fans to stop coming to his house asking for photos, especially with the threat of Covid looming.[8] He said he's willing to talk to people and have his picture taken in public places, but he draws the line at fans showing up at his house uninvited.

Another phenom that rode the social media wave is doxing. Originally, in the 1990s, hackers "dropped docs" on each other as a revenge tactic to expose their rivals. Now, doxing refers more generally to publishing private or identifying information about someone (often celebrities and influencers) online. Doxing can be as elementary as a vengeful person finding out the address of someone famous and posting it publicly, or it can be elaborate. In one notable case, hackers obtained emails and phone numbers of some Instagram users, including well-known celebs, and set up a website revealing the personal information. Doxing often leads to influencers' having to change their phone numbers and email addresses; in the worst-case scenario, they have to move.

Influencers who have an infrastructure of agents, managers, attorneys, and security behind them are far better equipped to deal with stalking than an influencer working alone. Manager Jeff Chilcoat has a protocol in place to help determine an athlete's risk from a stalker. He says, "From a social media standpoint, we've picked up on people that we think are stalkers or maybe even dangerous. . . . We really want—if we can—we want to shield the athlete from that. . . . We've had a couple of instances where we've had to have some sort of security check into someone to make sure that the athlete was safe, and we didn't have anything to worry about."

For influencers without that kind of backing, learning to set boundaries becomes even more important to ensuring their personal safety. Too often, though, influencers, especially younger ones, equate oversharing with authenticity. It becomes a race to overshare, with danger instead of a win at the finish line.

Influencers barraged with hate on a daily basis may try to ignore all the threats that come their way. Somehow, they need to strike the fine balance between not focusing on the hate but staying vigilant regarding individuals who pose a real risk to their health and safety.

BEATING BACK THE ISOLATION

When people think of influencers, they're more likely to associate them with excitement and glitz than isolation—but isolation is a big issue, particularly if their sole occupation is influencer and they're not living in a city like LA or New York. In big cities, you can choose to go to an event every night. And if you're living in a collab house, there are people all over the place, all the time. However, that's not the reality for many influencers. In between events, there's a lot of solitary work to be done.

Rey Rahimi, a graduate of the University of Toronto in Canada, keenly understands the introverted aspect of being an influencer because her friends have more traditional lifestyles and structured schedules: "If I choose to stick to solely creating content on YouTube,

I would definitely like to move somewhere where I'm surrounded with people who are doing the same thing. Because right now, all my friends—everyone around me—they have their school, they have their full-time jobs. And it can certainly be very isolating to just stay at home all day, edit videos, create videos, film yourself. I would love to move somewhere with people who have the same energy around me of creating content because it can definitely be very isolating."

It's not only location that creates the loneliness. Kristina Zias, a married mom, is in a different stage of life than Rahimi and lives in LA. She contends with isolation too: "It can be a very lonely career because you're sitting behind your computer and you're taking photos. Honestly, sometimes I miss working at Nordstrom because I was around people every single day—talking to other people. It can be a little isolating, so I think trying to build a real network for yourself is very important."

Of course, now that the pandemic has altered the traditional work environment, resulting in fewer people likely to be anchored to an office desk, influencers won't seem so out of the norm. Still, that doesn't change the need for contact with people on a regular basis and the importance of forming relationships with peers. That's why influencers all around the world are finding each other and making connections.

PEN PALS FOR THE MILLENNIUM

For many, like booktuber Cindy Pham, influencing breaks down traditional geographic obstacles—sort of like a 2000s version of pen pals. Pham is part-time influencer, full-time art director at Twitter. She started posting videos casually a few years ago, which gained traction. At about 10,000 to 20,000 subscribers on YouTube, brands like Book of the Month, Squarespace, and Native started reaching out to her.

Along with the expanded reach came an expanded social circle, online and off. Pham says, "Now, because I have a bigger audience, I know if I visit a new city or new country, if I wanted to, I could just reach out and hang out with someone who either makes videos or knows about my channel." She says the book community is a pretty small group.

Pham has extended her influencing to travel and now aspires to the life of a digital nomad: "I would move to a new city or new country every few months and work from wherever I am living. . . . I can do that as a remote worker for my full-time job at Twitter, but also have that freedom to do so as a YouTuber. I know that I can actually make content from my travels and be able to support my travels through that."

There's something special about sharing common goals with people and finding connections across the globe. TikToker Logan Isbell is clear about what these relationships mean to him. He says, "Over half of my friends are social media influencers. I've never had a big friend group, so having all these people from around the world doing what I do and having the same connection/humor as me makes me very happy."

NETWORKING EVENTS

More formal opportunities to gather are also popping up. For instance, on college campuses, social media clubs are becoming an option. At the University of Southern California, Reach is an organization that aims to create a community for influencers, digital marketers, and anyone interested in social media. They offer guest lectures and workshops on building a following and creating viral content; they arrange social outings to get adventurous Instagram shots; and they develop video projects.

Gigi Robinson, a USC alum, was a member of the Reach community during college. In high school, Robinson mainly used social media as a digital scrapbook, but she took note when she came across Reach at USC's Involvement Fair. For her, it was about using social media to leverage her photography so that she could work with brands and, she hoped, eventually shoot commercials. The club played an important role in helping her shape her personal brand, which centers around chronic illness, body image, and mental health.

Reach was also vital to Robinson in terms of fostering a sense of community among digital influencers and creators. She states, "It's kind of a brutal industry. It's very cutthroat. Nobody wants to share their secrets." But having a formal organization helps break down walls by creating a sense of shared experience. In the end, it's influencers who can best relate to the experiences of other influencers.

Robinson sensed a vague sense of resentment coming from a few of her noninfluencer friends in college. "I had trouble with some friends really understanding how I manage social media and how I manage my life," she laments. One friend confronted her by saying, "You're so self-centered; you're always on social media!"

The need for community also extends to other professionals in the influencer marketing industry. That's why Jessy Grossman started WIIM, Women in Influencer Marketing, a networking group comprising professionals from ad agencies, public relations firms, media companies, influencer networks, talent agencies, and brands—basically anyone who touches the influencer space but isn't an influencer themselves. Their goal is to create a supportive community for leaders in the industry to share information and network with like-minded women. Grossman was always passionate about women in business supporting each other, but she is also interested in demystifying an industry that's so often dubbed the wild west. "We have to figure out how to make it not that anymore," she says.

What are some themes that come through in both virtual and in-person events? Many relate to demographics. The influencer industry is not only female dominated but also fairly young. The age of people in the influencer space makes it the perfect incubator for imposter syndrome, which refers to feeling like a fraud in one's position, resulting in an inability to accept success. Grossman says she often hears things like, "I feel confident in what I know, but I have this really high-up position at this company. Am I the right person for this job?"

Grossman also hears concerns from young women who are enjoying the intense focus on their career, but who then wonder when starting a family might fit in, and if it does, how they'll manage it in a 24–7 industry.

Burnout is a major issue in general and in the management space specifically. Grossman says, "It's an industry of today for tomorrow, and everything's last minute. It's draining on people. Usually clients are all over the world. . . . What is Monday-to-Friday anymore? Everybody is always on, and it's really easy to burn out. . . . As women, we're very much inclined to get the job done and to prove ourselves, and our wellness is last on the list. I see everything from physical stuff to mental stuff where people are just really struggling to keep up."

Unfortunately, Grossman sees a lot of talk around prioritizing wellness but not as much implementation. Wellness events tend to be their least attended.

AN LA STORY

What's it like when someone decides to become an influencer, picks up his life, and moves to LA? That's twentysomething TikTok star Joshua Suarez's LA story. Suarez started out as an influencer by happenstance. An injury in college rendered his original career choice impossible. Wondering what he would do next, he came upon a YouTube video and decided to try making comedy videos himself. It wasn't easy sticking to it at first because of the hate he received from the people in his own neighborhood in Ohio. But getting results changed his mind. "I was like, wow, I'm just gonna keep doing this because I see hate, but I'm also seeing followers. I'm seeing income, finally! You know what, it's kind of worth it," he thought to himself.

As a result of his desire to expand his audience further, coupled with the in-person and online bullying he was getting in Ohio, Suarez made a spur-of-the-moment decision: he told his supportive mom that he was moving to California in two days.

Things didn't go smoothly at first. He says, "I was staying at this place with a couple other influencers, who were just starting off. . . . So we tried it out for a month, but the house didn't work because people weren't really focused. They weren't determined to work. And I told everybody the only reason I'm out here in Cali is to work. I'm not here to play games. I'm not here to just have fun. . . . I want to work, and I want it to then pay off."

After scraping up the money, Suarez moved to his own place in Koreatown, an LA neighborhood. He recalls, "I had no real friends out here. I didn't know anybody. So I ended up just doing TikToks by myself. I was doing everything by myself, and somehow, I don't even know how it happened, but I started making friends. And as soon as I started making friends, I started getting more connections to people who are in the same mindset and also driven. And from that point, that's when I strictly focused on TikTok, 24–7. I started posting five to ten videos a day."

When he hit around 7 million followers on TikTok, he started doing collabs with his girlfriend (@queenstaralien) and another couple, and signed with influencer marketing, media, and talent management agency Six Degrees of Influence. After about a year and a half, Suarez had over 11 million followers on TikTok. The four of them then moved to a temporary house in North Hollywood in an attempt to recruit couples to create a couple's content house.

Suarez met his girlfriend after she popped up on his Instagram search, and he swiped up on her story about getting a lip injection. He says, "We planned out a date to do a little collab day because we were both at the time, literally, influencers." As they got to know each other, their friendship turned into a romance, and their intermittent collaborations turned full time. He says, "We both were doing TikTok in the beginning occasionally, and then we both saw that there can be a career in this. So we both started hitting the videos hard and working hard to make it."

Being in a relationship and working together has its advantages and disadvantages. Suarez says they end up fighting over a lot of petty work things, like who gets to film first. They also have different attitudes when it comes to the type of content they post. Suarez's boundaries about what you need to do to get followers is different than his girlfriend's, which causes problems. He also likes to be safer about the content they post, so there's no chance it will get taken down by the platform, whereas she takes more risks. Finding a resolution isn't always easy, but they try to compromise. Suarez acknowledges influencing is a lifestyle for him, an all-day, every day thing, and it might be difficult to have someone in his life who isn't from that world.

Overall, Suarez is clearly pleased with the direction his influencing has taken him: "I'm very happy. I don't have to really worry about money at all for a very long time. TikTok—I always say this—but it literally changed my life."

A DAY IN THE LIFE OF AN INFLUENCER

When we asked influencers and industry insiders what the biggest misconception is about influencing, the majority said, "That it's easy." Asking serious influencers what a typical day is like for them usually busts that myth.

We asked YouTube megastar Lachlan Power what a typical day is like for him. He makes the important distinction between being a content creator and, then, as the business grows, being a content creator plus running an organization. Power says, "I think the hardest days were back in the early days of my career, like those days where you really had to try and prove—especially when this wasn't a career at all and was still in the very early days of gaming on YouTube. Those days were very, very hard. We're talking gaming twelve hours a day. We're talking sleep schedule nonexistent. It's all over the shelf."

These days allow him more structure, although because he has to work with US time zones, he's up until around 2 or 3 AM most days. Power runs down what a typical day is like for him now:

> It's pretty stock standard. I'm up at 10 AM. Today, on this lovely interview at 11. Probably going to go play some *Fortnite* for a couple hours—used to play a lot more *Fortnite* during the start of the *Fortnite* era of my career. But now, these days with PWR, there's a lot more other things to focus on, such as concepting content for the group, our competitive endeavors, and everything we're doing in creative, such as the Coca-Cola collaboration.
>
> So yeah, it's kind of just like, wake up, interview, talk with staff on my Discord. Probably a couple hours of *Fortnite,* try to film a video if I can, and then sync up with the team in the afternoon for what's on today. There's always something on today. And that's normally just like, you have a competitive event.
>
> Tonight, we're doing a filming session. Tonight, we are concepting a map release. There's a lot of things going on in the organization. And that's including our apparel as well. So it's always something to jump on and get ready and help push along with the team, and then try to just fit in filming content—my own channel—around that schedule.

Because Power started his career out of a passion for creating content, the managerial role is new and has taken some getting used to. He says about running the organization,

It's a different game—different game completely. The manager's role sometimes is a little frustrating, you know—kind of getting behind, and especially with my own YouTube presence of my own YouTube channel, that sometimes since the inception of PWR has taken a backseat. And that's a bit hard at times because I used to have this philosophy of posting every day. And with everything going on, it's just not possible anymore. So I've had to swallow that pill in a way of just like accepting that I can't post every day and just try to get a better-quality video out every two days, every three days, maybe get these dailies here and there. . . . I've been learning a lot about how to manage people in an organization over the years. Because realistically, I got into this game, just playing video games, and it's a completely different experience having a team, having an organization and work with everybody; but it's fun.

While Power has about thirty people in his organization, Kristina Zias's life probably resembles that of more influencers out there who don't have as large a team. The following is a description of a typical day in Zias's life. It definitely puts the misconceptions to rest.

Typically, I wake up; I have my coffee; I'll answer some quick emails. My management team is based in New York, which I love because I like to wake up early and get work done right away. So I love that emails come in at 7 AM on my time. And I try to do that as much as possible. I'll take my dog for a walk and then honestly, just sit at my kitchen table and create content, whether it's going through creative briefs and trying to figure out what I have to shoot for the week or drafting Instagram posts and Instagram captions.

Normally, I like to shoot in the evening because there's better light, so if I have a shoot prepared with my photographer, I'll be prepping for that for a few hours. That'll be getting looks together, looking at creative concepts, finding photo inspiration, location scouting, styling the look, and then heading over to the shoot. And so, you've noticed I've been by myself all day with my dog. And then I'll meet up with my photographer. We'll shoot the content. After that, come home. You have to break everything down, put it all away. And then I'll have to go through photos and selects.

And it's that process over and over again. . . . It really doesn't stop.

As her remarks show, the bulk of Zias's day is computer work, with a lot of prepping for photo shoots and styling. She works from the time she gets up until she goes to sleep, which is around 11:30 PM. On a typical day, she might be sending in video concepts and photos for approval right before bed. However, she points out that she has flexibility in her schedule. She can take off in the middle of the day if she wants, or she can be as regimented as she chooses. For Zias, it's all about trying to find balance among all the moving pieces of her life.

"EVERYTHING IS CONTENT"

As the realities about the lifestyle emerge, it's clear why connections with other influencers become so important. In the early days of YouTube, Sarah Penna managed Joe Penna, then her boyfriend and now her husband. Despite the possible pitfalls, Penna found it a fun experience. She enjoyed going to work every day with him and talking about his deals over dinner. She says, "It's a weird career to have. And we certainly saw a lot of relationships where someone was in the YouTube world, and someone wasn't. That's challenging. There's this perception that, oh, it's so flexible, which it is, but it's also always on, especially if you're a blogger or someone who's sharing your life with your audience. Everything is work. Everything is content. And again, it can be really exhausting. So you have to have people in your life understand that it's not just a fun little hobby that you can put down any time."

COLLABS AND CONTENT HOUSES

Avoiding a S**t Show

There's something seductive about collaborations among creatives. Individuals filled with passion about what they do combining their energy and playing off of one another can lead to an eruption of ideas. Throughout history, artists and entertainers from every genre have often separated themselves from the rest of society and occupied the same space to get energy and inspiration from one another, as well as extrinsic things like social capital, status, and a wider audience. Take SoHo in the 1970s, defined by artists like Andy Warhol, or Paris in the 1920s, known as Années Folles, or the "crazy years," a term used to describe the wealth of artistic collaborations at that time, led by the likes of Gertrude Stein, Ernest Hemingway, and Picasso. However, along with the artistic spoils that go with the closeness, there can be dark repercussions of a collective lifestyle, including destructive partying, alcohol and drug addiction, the spread of disease, mental and physical abuse, and the proliferation of mental health conditions.

Still, the need to be in the same space with other like-minded creatives pulls at many in the arts and entertainment community. It's part of the artistic journey, and it's no different for influencers. By choosing the right collab partners and engaging in some smart cross-promotion, influencers can mutually benefit by broadening their audience. Ray Ligaya says influencers use collabs "to get an edge, to get more followers and get . . . clout." Sometimes, if influencers perceive that the person approaching them only wants the collab to gain status or clout, it can be seen as a negative.

1, 2, 3—COLLAB!

There are different kinds of collabs in an influencer's world, and according to Nechelle Vanias, "it doesn't matter whether you're in the house, not in the house—just doing content with other creators will grow numbers. The fan base loves that. And you're mixing different fan groups, no matter if you're big or small."

Individual collabs happen when a couple of influencers partner for a project. For example, the wildly popular comic artist/YouTuber Zachary Hsieh, aka ZHC, is known for gifting customized items to megainfluencers. He gave YouTube star MrBeast a customized Tesla, and he customized the FaZe House, the esports collective, in twenty-four hours. On occasion, one-on-one collabs can be significant enough to alter a person's online life. OG YouTube star Brittani Louise Taylor credits her connection to YouTube celebrity Shane Dawson with her career's taking off. "I met my friend Shane Dawson and then the videos we did together blew up, so it was really because of him that I even have a following."

Then there are the collab houses with different content focuses, including gaming. In 2022, Lachlan Power started PWR House in Sydney, Australia, temporarily, for the Fortnite Champion Series finals in Oceania, as a way for them to have all of their *Fortnite* players live, train, and compete together. It served as a test for their organization. He says, "It was really awesome. Having everybody under one roof—definitely going to do it again. . . . That was the first time a lot of players had met each other, met me, met the staff."

Power is interested in branching out from models of other gaming houses he's seen in the past. "I've had the experience of visiting a lot of gaming content houses, like, say the Sidemen, Click, back in the day, like all these other famous gaming content groups, and it's definitely a lot different. We had the strategy of, let our players focus on winning, and focus on practicing, because that's the purpose of it. And then we flew our content team out for a week-long filming session. And you know, a lot of the professional players got involved there as well. But we were able to split it up in a way so that the players can focus on what matters most to them, which is their competitive endeavors, and then get our content team in to help get some content going."

When influencers don't want to be together full time, they may choose to go the content studio route, which allows partnerships and brand promotion without having to live in the same space. Amp Studios, cofounded by Max Levine and YouTube megastar Brent Rivera, is an example. The company develops creators, produces content, and amplifies that content to millions. At this point, they're generating over 1 billion views per month and have worked with brands including Chipotle, Coca-Cola, and Disney. Their target audience is the Disney-meets-MTV crowd.

Levine says, "We were one of the first content creator collectives out there. . . . We actually launched our own studio space. It's secondly a house, but no one lives there. I view it as a studio space. I think it's a great place for us to create content and give everyone the resources that they need to create what they want/need to create. . . . We have a YouTube room, we have a room for a character we're gonna create, and we have a room for podcasting. They have an outdoor area that we do a lot of TikToks at. So we kind of view it as different sets." Influencer/creators at Amp include Ben Azelart, Lexi Rivera, and the twins Alan and Alex Stokes. The key differentiator between Amp's type of studio space and other content houses is that they don't live there together. When home is with other influencers, whether it be a content house, influencer house, or collab house, things can get really . . . challenging.

Levine has a well-thought-out take on this type of collab: "We were talking about a house for a while, but we didn't end up doing it. I think if we were to do it, it'd be more of a studio space versus a house. When you have all these people living together, it's kind of a shit show . . . because it's just a lack of infrastructure and you're throwing people together, and there's drama. And people running those companies aren't necessarily legitimate a lot of the time. It's a very slippery slope. A lot of them have gotten into trouble with their landlords, or the cities that they live in, or the people who run the company, or the people who are living in there."

Still, Levine credits the houses with making influencers more visible in the entertainment industry. "It definitely added a spark to TikTok as a platform. When you bring powerful people together, you're bringing more eyeballs on something, and it makes it more electric. So I think it brought the creator culture and ecosystem more to the forefront and even TikTok as a platform. . . . You just have to be careful about doing it," he warns.

Even an out-of-town excursion with a bunch of young influencers can be eventful. "We went on this trip to Las Vegas a few weeks ago, and I was the chaperone. And you know, it's very interesting, I'll say that," Levine laughs. He goes on to say, "Their job is to create content and to entertain, and they're trying to do that. And with that comes a lot of thorns, because sometimes they do things that young people might do, but it's in the spotlight."

As the influencing industry expands, the coverage of it is getting more fervent. Levine notices more journalists popping up around the space in the last few years. Stephanie McNeal is one of them. She writes about internet culture and influencers now, but she started out as a breaking-news reporter. Over time, she realized that she enjoyed writing trending news and viral stories because of the "quick hit of dopamine" you get for having a lot of page views and the validation you get by finding a topic that's interesting to a lot of people, then writing about it. From a personal standpoint, McNeal had always been into influencers; she enjoyed reading blogs, and she followed different people and talked about them with her friends. Around 2015 or 2016, she and her trending news team did a couple of big stories on YouTubers that did really well, causing her to wonder if people would be interested in influencer scandals. They were. "We started to report on that, and it just did really, really well," she says.

Are influencers hesitant to talk to the media? McNeal thinks compared to other types of celebrities, they're about the same. She says that with other celebrities, "once you establish your reputation in the industry, you can pretty much get who you want. And that's what I found with influencers as well. Once I had a body of work, people were more willing to talk to me."

HISTORY OF SCANDAL

The Hype House launched in 2019 and was one of the first collab houses to make a splash as the group of teen TikTokers, including Chase Hudson, Charlie D'Amelio, Dixie D'Amelio, and Addison Rae, found their way to the top of pop culture. An LA Spanish-style mansion built on a foundation of drama, the Hype House has had numerous scandals, one of which was its feuding cofounders. Daisy Keech filed a federal lawsuit against Thomas Petrou and Chase Hudson, alleging they tried to cut her out of deals. One day she showed up at the mansion to collect her belongings, flanked by an armed guard.[1]

The Hype House, however, wasn't the first house. Many consider the O2L mansion, created in 2014 by YouTubers known as Our2ndLife, to be the first. A short time later, the biggest stars on Vine moved into an apartment complex and lived collectively on 1600 Vine Street. Other infamous early houses include the Clout House, part of the esports unit FaZe Clan; the Vlog Squad, founded by David Dobrik; and Jake Paul's Team 10 mansion.

While the houses generate content, they also generate controversy. For instance, in 2020, the Team 10 house was raided by the FBI as part of a federal investigation, which was widely reported as being connected to an incident in Arizona where Jake Paul was charged with a misdemeanor related to a looting incident. The Team 10 house has also been involved in a number of public feuds with other houses, including FaZe Clan's Clout House.

A major issue with Team 10 and other houses are the wild parties that annoy both their neighbors and city officials. A number of Tik-Tok party houses created controversy in 2020 during the height of the Covid-19 pandemic, when some houses had large parties with no social distancing or mask wearing. Two popular members of TikTok's Sway House in LA were arrested in connection to several parties, with Blake Gray and Bryce Hall charged with misdemeanor crimes related to pandemic violations and facing fines up to $2,000 and potentially one year in jail. The house in the Hollywood Hills where the two hosted parties had its power shut off by the city of LA after the mayor authorized utilities to be cut to houses violating the pandemic regulations.

The so-called party houses in the Hollywood Hills had other controversies as well, with many neighbors living near some of the houses complaining of raucous behavior. One neighbor told the *LA Times* about "drag racing at all hours and used condoms everywhere," as well as girls changing clothes in the streets and lots of noise issues.[2]

Bryce Hall found himself on the wrong side of the law again in 2020, when he and fellow Sway House member and TikToker Jaden Hossler were arrested in Texas. The two were charged with drug possession after allegedly being found with marijuana.[3] The Sway House ended up being disbanded in early 2021, lasting just over a year after its founding. During its short life, the house saw infighting among members and public controversies around arrests, although in an interview with *People* magazine, TalentX and Sway House co-founder Michael Gruen said the house was disbanding because the members had grown and were moving on.[4]

ANATOMY OF A CONTENT HOUSE

In the beginning of 2020, Six Degrees of Influence (SDI), an influencer marketing, media, and talent management agency, started their first content house. The Vault (@thevaultla on TikTok), a TikTok facing collective, brought together thirteen young influencers ranging in age from fifteen to twenty-one, although in its second season, they upped the minimum age to eighteen.

Nechelle Vanias, SDI chief solutions officer/cofounder, says that while the influencers on their roster are primarily Gen Z on TikTok, their goal is "always to move them over to Instagram and YouTube because while TikTok is the most popular platform, the majority of influencer marketing dollars are still being spent on Instagram and YouTube. So from a longevity perspective, or careerwise, we want them across all three platforms."

The content house turned out to be a win for SDI. It was everything they thought it would be, including a talent incubator. It put them on the map in terms of their visibility within the influencer community. They grew their roster from about ten or fifteen influencers to managing over fifty in 2021, although not all the talent in the content houses will be signed with their agency.

Their strategy is to have multiple houses across different topics. The Vault is unique in that they offer a variety of content, which differs from the original dance-oriented TikTok houses. Vanias says there is always a long line of influencers waiting to get into the Vault. Next, SDI plans on Twin Flames, a house with four or five couples. As part of the content, they like to add in a romantic couple or two later on; it adds drama and increases audience engagement. Vanias likes the "couples" vertical because it's growing on TikTok; it has proven to be successful on long-form video as well.

Other houses in the works include the House of Allure, which is a Playboy mansion for a new generation; a gaming house, which is a great vertical with a dedicated fan base; a beauty house along the lines of the paused Rihanna Fenty TikTok house; and a fantasy house. SDI's plan is to max out at six houses in the United States, then go abroad.

Building Up a Concept, Not an Individual

An important premise for SDI is that they don't generally build content houses around particular talent because influencers have the potential to be canceled, and they often do things they're not supposed to do. As an agency, SDI wants to develop the content house as a brand with different seasons—something akin to the TV series *Love Island, Survivor,* or *Big Brother,* where the audience might have a favorite contestant, but they keep watching the next season because they are following the concept, not a single individual.

This lesson is learned, in part, by paying attention to the comments left for the members of the Hype House. Vanias says, "They have a big challenge, which is having a relevant brand when it was so closely tied with former members the D'Amelios and Addison Rae. . . . The comments say a lot, just to cue you in on a secret. The comments on any page—the Vault pages—say a lot about what's going on. If you go on the Hype House's TikTok, you'll see comments like, 'We want the old people back,' 'We don't like these people'—those sorts of things. They're struggling to maintain a brand, when it was so closely tied to influencers. We saw that right away, which is why we made sure that we were establishing a brand versus building it around any specific talent, because inevitably that talent is going to move, grow up."

Location, Location, Location

Real estate is a key factor in the success of content houses. In terms of picking a location, Vanias wanted to find a place for season 1 of the Vault that had a great backdrop to showcase products—a place brands could get excited about. For the audience, the space needs to be aspirational, with decor that inspires people. At the time of this interview, LED lights and cute pillows are the thing.

For season 1, they chose a modern 5,200-square-foot house with five bedrooms, one block from Melrose in West Hollywood. At that time, none of the influencers had a car, so they were able to peruse the famous entertainment and dining district on scooters and bikes, and they could easily call an Uber or Lyft to get places. The house they chose was filled with "Instagramable moments," including great walls prefect as a backdrop for content, a rooftop deck with a hot tub, and a pool area, which are the type of things that make sense for the content they're creating.

However, what doesn't make sense for SDI is to pay $30,000 a month to rent a house, particularly when their strategy is to have multiple houses. So they're scouting property to purchase and renovate that fits with what they need for their content houses, including more bedrooms and production space. "It's a great investment to not be paying rent to some other landlord not in the business, but to build a real estate portfolio that we know will be utilized by not only our content houses but future content houses or just future collectives of creatives living together," says Vanias.

Normalizing Diversity

SDI is a diverse agency, so the projects they do are going to be diverse by nature. The agency wants the houses to represent how the country and world look, but it doesn't want to use that diversity as a promotion tool. Vanias says, "We knew people had eyes and could see. We wanted to normalize diversity versus making it something special to us. You should be doing articles as to why the other houses are all white or that they add someone here or there to check boxes. That to us is odd."

Some houses have been the subject of controversies involving a lack of diversity. Rave Vanias says she went to one of those content houses, and "it wasn't a good experience." When asked to elaborate on why it was uncomfortable, she cites running into a person with a history of scandals, especially one involving race that included having people of color kicked out of the house.

Being Brand Friendly

In order to achieve long-term success, a content house should be what is termed brand friendly, but achieving that is not an off-the-cuff process; indeed, it's a particular challenge when running what is, in essence, a 24-7 production set. Vanias says, "Houses are not as easy as they look. That's why the majority of houses you see [don't succeed]." They often lack structure, marketing savvy, the knowledge and discipline to manage talent, and the ability to deliver quality content.

Brand reps with a $100,000 budget came to SDI and said that they chose the Vault because they liked the diversity and the variety of content, as well as the fact that other houses—but not the Vault—are known for getting in trouble and doing things they shouldn't. Vanias insists, "We built all of our houses to be brand friendly, and that was intentional. You don't see our kids throwing parties, doing drugs, getting in trouble, getting arrested, and all of those sorts of things."

Another aspect of making themselves amenable to brands is building houses with every tier of influencer that brands would normally do collaborations with outside of a house. Brands want to see influencers across different platforms and in different stages of their career. They want microinfluencers just starting out, midtier influences, and influencers with millions of followers.

According to Vanias, a big appeal of content houses right now is a return to more traditional product placements—those that have withstood the test of time, like opening a refrigerator and seeing a certain brand of water, or showcasing a certain high-end car in the driveway. For a while now, the social media audience has been bombarded with "next to your face" advertising, where the influencer holds up a product and says, "I use this!" However, Vanias believes this model is beginning to wear on audience and talent agency alike. She predicts a shift to more subtle and subliminal product placements within content houses. It's where "the industry needs to go and will go."

A TYPICAL DAY IN THE VAULT

Vault member Rave Vanias describes a normal day in a content house, starting when they wake up, which is about 10 to 11 AM, but, depending on the day, may creep up from there: "We get ready, and then we start filming for a couple of hours. I would say from 1 to 4 or 5 [PM]. I specifically film between those times because I love the sunlight. That's my whole thing; I love sun and the golden hour. . . . Somewhere in between there we're definitely eating. We love eating. Then we eat again after filming because we're always hungry. And then, depending on what we have to do, we'll go shopping. We'll either meet up with other creators or do something fun. We'll do something all together, like go to the beach or some sort of activity. . . . And then we come back, we all hang out, maybe do some random filming, chill, watch movies. We love to watch movies together, do that kind of stuff, and then we go to sleep around 2 or 3 [AM]."

After their main filming period, in the evening, people are still taking pictures, posting pictures, or coming off their "lives," which allows them to interact with their audience in real time. Rave says, "The closer you get to 11 PM, no one's really doing anything. We might still be responding to comments or on our phones, but we're not posting or we're not actively doing anything for that kind of thing, because no one's really waiting for you to post at 12 AM." Asked about how much time she spends on her phone a day, Rave scrolls for the average: about ten hours a day.

Between the content for the house across platforms and all of the influencers' individual platforms—it's a lot of content to put out. This is why there is a house manager, who is tasked with being the keeper of the schedule and the calendar, so everything runs smoothly and everything gets done.

In the mix of a typical day are parties and events, of which there are many. Other than company or brand parties, red-carpet birthday parties for actors or popular influencers top the event list. For Rave, dressing up and wearing heels to these events is pretty much a must—heels with skirts, heels with dresses, heels with pants. It's no small effort traipsing up hills and driveways to reach the end goal.

Rave says, "I went to a lot of Boohoo or Fashion NOVA events, and you would literally go get a whole bunch of clothes." During events like these, she enjoys the food, takes pictures, gets the products, and then can leave. How much fun Rave has at an event depends on the product or who is throwing the party. "At the end of the day, I'm getting free stuff afterwards. I'm not that mad about it!" she laughs, adding that it "drains a little bit of my social battery . . . but I definitely like talking with people."

How often does she go to these parties and events? At least once a day, if not twice. "There's definitely ones where we would be jumping from event to party, event to party, and there'd be like four or five in a night. You would go say hi to the people you knew, say hi to anyone that came up to you, get your stuff, and you would leave. You'd be there for like thirty minutes or so, and then you'd go to the next one," Rave says.

In terms of relationships within the Vault, Rave describes them like a family. She acknowledges competitiveness with other houses, but she says that within the Vault, they try to uplift one another. If someone's views are a little low that week, everyone will pitch in to get them back to where they need to be.

Because content houses are artificial spaces populated with real people, they are a curious blend of artifice and truth, like PRomances—that is, fake relationships between influencers that are designed to capture the audience's attention. Rave says that fake romances are a lot more common than people think, but sometimes it turns into something real.

The constant negotiation and overlap of what's real and what isn't is a constant theme for influencers in their lives. Rave is careful to point out an important reality behind the production: "At the end of the day, we're on camera and yes, some of the things we post aren't exactly real, like, you might have a fake boyfriend, or this isn't really your real name, or you go out and it's not really how you act—whatever the case is—you do skits and this is not your real life—whatever the case is. We are still people. The same kids that are watching us—we're still kids too." Even though everything on screen isn't necessarily real, an influencer's underlying emotions most certainly are.

ATHLETE INFLUENCERS

How the Game Is Played

Athlete influencers are in a class all their own. Engagement rates with their audience are through the roof, but so are the challenges that come with navigating the world of sports and athlete endorsements.

Historically, a big reason brands moved toward everyday people as influencers, as opposed to athletes and celebrities, is the complexity, not to mention the big costs, associated with them. Joe Gagliese, of Viral Nation, says he and his partner started out wanting to see if athletes' social media was monetizable at a time when it wasn't being done. "We signed a couple of NHL players and some other athletes, started working on that, and realized that it was too tough, because the athletes made too much money for where the market was in terms of social. So even if we could get an athlete a social deal, it wasn't enticing enough to get them to dedicate their time to it," he recalls. That's when they started looking at influencers.

Times have changed. Even though an athlete's valuable audience comes at a price, many brands deem it a price worth paying. The challenge for athletes, who are not marketers first and foremost, is to find a way capitalize on their engagement.

THE HUG BETWEEN FANS AND THEIR TEAM

Why is an athlete's endorsement so special? Daniel Rascher says it's about the "mad passion" fans have for their favorite players and teams: "The fans and the teams are hugging each other, so to speak . . . and the brands try to get in on that hug." They realize it's a powerful relationship and want to be a part of it.

Sports manager Jeff Chilcoat adds that there is a premium on athletes because "they have reached the pinnacle of something that we all wish we could do." It's one part passion, one part Freudian wish fulfillment, and one part admiration, equaling lots of audience engagement. A study of worldwide Instagram influencer engagement rates throughout 2019 showed that sports was the second most engaged-with influencer category, at 3.08 percent (interestingly, topped only by photography, at 3.3 percent).[1]

Personal characteristics such as likability help boost an athlete's endorsement potential, but outside factors like exposure also help drive money an athlete's way. The frequency with which an athlete appears on screen depends on what sport they play and whether it's a team or individual sport. When they're on screen, is the camera focused on them, or is it on the team? Rascher, who has done research trying to understand what drives athletes' endorsement earnings, says, "Individual sport athletes like golfers and tennis players, when they're top twenty, top thirty, top fifty, they can earn a lot of money and endorsements—often much more than they earn playing their sport . . . while you sort of flip that over in baseball and football. Now, baseball players play lots of games, but the amount of time the individual player appears on camera is not that much. And football players have a helmet on. That even makes it more difficult. So those athletes, other than the stars, don't typically earn very much money in endorsements. Basketball players are sort of in between. The cameras are on them a lot. They don't have helmets on. The cameras focus in on them closely. Basketball players are very marketable from that perspective, simply because of their exposure."

COMPLIANCE ISSUES

Nonathlete influencers don't have a governing body over them dictating a specific set of rules and regulations. When a brand takes on an athlete influencer, it also takes on all the influencer's compliance issues.

Sometimes sponsorships and individual influencing go hand in hand, but there are also times when they are at odds with one another. In terms of pro team sports, T. Bettina Cornwell looks at sponsorships like layers of an onion. The more layers that are added, the more difficult it is for an athlete to have individual influencer relationships. Types of sponsorship layers may include the arena or stadium being sponsored, league-level sponsorship, team-level sponsorship, and cheerleader sponsorship. Athlete influencers and their representatives are required to peel back all these layers to get to the core of their own personal influence. Athletes who are part of a team need to tear though more layers.

Blake Lawrence says that unlike regular influencers, many athlete influencers "are limited by the fact that they are part of a team." He makes the distinction between dealing with soft challenges, like the impact on locker room dynamics when an athlete is out influencing on his own, versus hard challenges, like the actual conflict that exists with team sponsors, especially when the brands are from competing categories.

Lawrence says, "If you are wearing Nike on the field but you're an Adidas athlete off the field, how do you promote and support the brand that's chosen you? Well, oftentimes sharing content of you wearing a competing brand on your own channel, so that's an interesting thing. And then you have group licensing rights and agreements." He goes on to give an example using Pepsi and Coca-Cola as the hypotheticals. "What if Pepsi is the official sponsor of the NFL? That means they would have ability to leverage every NFL player at any rate that they want on their social channels. But let's say that six athletes get approached to be a part of a Coca-Cola advertising campaign. The rub is that non-NFL sponsors can only activate five NFL players before they are in violation of the group licensing agreement. This would land the players a cease-and-desist order because they're participating in a campaign that competes with the sponsor."

Limitations placed on athletes often depend on exclusivity agreements negotiated as part of the contract. For instance, a player might not be able to wear a competing brand on game day but is allowed to individually promote a competing brand two days later. It all hinges on the agreement.

There are many different, nuanced ways that pro athletes such as NFL players can make money via team sponsorships and individual influencing. For example, Jeff Chilcoat says, "Every player in the NFL is going to get a piece of all of the licensing deals that the Players Association does with various corporations. But then you could also give your image rights to do deals of six or more through the Players Association, you get additional funds, and then you can also do your own individual stuff on the side, outside the Players Association, and make money that way." It revolves around compliance issues.

Of course, it's not just the NFL and pro sports. Take Olympic athletes, who must make sure they're adhering to Rule 40 of the Olympic Charter, which states: "Competitors, team officials and other team personnel who participate in the Olympic Games may allow their person, name, picture or sports performances to be used for advertising purposes during the Olympic Games in accordance with the principles determined by the IOC [International Olympic Committee] Executive Board."[2] This is a relaxed version of a previous rule, which didn't allow Olympians to have their image or performance used in advertising during the games without permission.

In 2021, a major change rocked the world of student athletes when the National Collegiate Athletic Association reversed course on its belief that student athletes should not receive payments. They adopted an interim policy allowing NCAA student athletes to benefit from their name, image, and likeness, opening up a new world of endorsement and influencer opportunities.

Within the last few years, players' associations have been reducing their restrictions around alcohol, gambling, and CBD sponsorships and endorsements, but there is still policy to maneuver around.

Another important difference between influencers and athlete influencers is that nonathlete influencers own the content they create. Not necessarily so for athlete influencers. Blake Lawrence says, "So much of the content that athletes create that fans want to see that keep them connected and engaged, they have no rights to." For instance, if a player performs well in the fourth quarter of the Super Bowl and wants to share it, he has no legal right to the video because the content belongs to the NFL. In an industry where money is tied to churning out content, it can leave athletes at a loss in terms of what to put out.

THE BUSINESS OF SPORTS INFLUENCE

Blake Lawrence also looked toward influence and social media after football, but in a different way. He started out in Nebraska playing college football, only to have his career cut short by recurring concussions. He says, "I woke up starting linebacker and when I went to bed—I could never play football again. And that is something that everyone in life has, a moment where what you thought you'd be doing or what you're doing is no longer a reality or possible, and you've got to figure out what's next. So for me, I fortunately started using this thing called Twitter. . . . I thought to myself, I will never be able to play in front of these fans again, but I've got this connection." He stepped away from football in 2009, and social media was right in front of him. Lawrence leaned in further and further.

In spring 2011, Lawrence got a phone call from one of his best friends, Prince Amukamara, who was a New York Giants first-round draft pick. The three questions that Amukamara asked Lawrence during that call helped shape the mission for Opendorse, which specializes in athlete influencer marketing.

Question 1: What Is My Audience Worth?

Amukamara had explosive growth the day he got drafted, going from something like 10K followers to more than 100K followers across channels. After looking over the analytics that Lawrence and his business partner were using for businesses, they realized that Amukamara's audience was ten times more engaged than the local businesses or brands they were working with at the time. It was "an incredibly valuable audience."

Question 2: How Do I Grow My Audience?

To answer this question, Lawrence and his partner looked at what traditional influencers and creators were doing to grow their audience. They boiled down the main tactic to posting on a consistent basis, which drives up engagement, and "more engagement leads to more followers. More followers leads to more value and everybody wins," Lawrence says. The problem? They quickly realized that his friend, and other athletes, were really bad at sharing content. Lawrence says of his friend, "He would post like, once a week, and the average influencer is posting, like, once every couple hours, and so we saw an opportunity here—that if we could help him increase his activity, we could help him grow his audience much faster."

Question 3: How Do I Monetize My Audience?

This is when Lawrence and his partner got introduced to the world of agents, managers, and marketing reps, coming face-to-face with all the complexities that come along with athletes: group licensing rights agreements, professional sports players associations, unions, and so on. They also saw a gap in the existing technology to help athletes answer these questions.

In answering these three questions, Opendorse uses two revenue models. First is the model of software as service, where they sell their solutions to sports team leagues' athletic departments. Second is a marketplace model, where brands pay a transaction fee to Opendorse in order to build out endorsement campaigns with athletes.

Jeff Chilcoat noted around 2015 that it was the first time a deal ended because their client wasn't social media savvy enough. The athlete had a three- or four-year relationship with the brand, but because of a lack of followers, the brand dropped him. At that time, Chilcoat remembers, "We started to think, OK, we have to make this front and center."

In talks now, social media is always front and center. Just before our conversation, Jeff Chilcoat assessed a proposal. Two of the questions from the brand were, in essence, "Outline the personality of your athlete from a social media standpoint," and "Give us all the numbers of followers and on which platform."

When they were getting started with social media marketing, one-off deals were more common, but now they hold less appeal because ongoing relationships offer a partnership mentality, giving athletes more say in what they're promoting than with one-off endorsements. Deals where brand and athlete look out for each other are ideal; but that's not necessarily the case when athletes are handed a script and told to read it, and the deal is done.

One of the reasons Chilcoat thinks that social media has become so popular with brands is because you can put a number on it. He says, "You can quantify social media. You can't quantify eyeballs on TV typically. For instance, in golf, you can know what the ratings are, but you don't know necessarily what the ratings were at the moment your athlete was viewed, or if they were viewed at all."

ARE ALL SPORTS EQUAL IN INFLUENCING?

Not all sports are equal in influencing. There's a hierarchy. Lawrence said Opendorse analyzed over 36,000 Instagram posts published on behalf of over 3,200 sponsors in sports and found that athletes from different sports have different propensities in their use of social media. For instance, during a ten-month period between April 2019 and February 2020, the average NBA player shared eighty-three posts on their social channels, while the average NFL player shared eighty-nine. This is not a huge difference. The drop-off starts with the Major League Baseball player, whose average is forty. Then the plummet happens with the average NHL hockey player, who shares fourteen posts—an average of about 1.4 per month.

Lawrence has a theory about why we see these numbers, and why there's so much variation between sports in terms of which athletes post a lot and which don't. It has everything to do with the culture surrounding the sport. Lawrence says, "NBA players, when they're in high school, are treated like kings, like they are the best player in their city, some of the best on the planet; they get recruited, courted, and they're told that they are a superstar. And they get to college. There, they act like superstars. They're very into themselves. They just happen to be part of a team. NFL players, same thing. They are highly recruited, they go to college, they're part of a team. They stand out. They get drafted—so they're used to talking about themselves."

The shift in culture comes with Major League Baseball players. Lawrence says that they are "often standouts in high school, but the number one draft going to Major League Baseball gets drafted and [could be] immediately sent to the minor leagues. He sleeps in motels you and I wouldn't want to stay in, travels in buses that we don't care about. And this is a guy who is making $10 million a year and his bonus and whatnot, and he gets drafted, but he's humbled very quickly."

ATHLETE SUPERSTAR OR NEWBIE?

For brands, there are pros and cons to working with athlete superstars and newbies alike. Perhaps counterintuitively, the age and experience of star athletes can work against them. Rascher explains that they can get "stale" after they've been on the scene for a while: "They have a lot of followers and everything, but sometimes the brands want that fresh new face, just as something new to be able to push." However, there's less risk associated with solid veterans from the standpoint of having a built-in follower base, and also it's less of a chance in terms of losses. With every athlete there is a risk of injury, but with athlete influencers, brands also need to consider the risk of being associated with someone who loses. Rascher says that brands sometimes try to insulate themselves from this risk by doing humorous campaigns rather than ones that center around the athletes' talents. But in the end, for athlete influencers, their power wanes when the wins run out.

#TRENDING

We are the midst of the influencer era. Content creators/influencers have been legitimized, and digital-first content is at a premium, not an afterthought. What will be trending next? What does the future of the influencing industry look like?

It looks like it's here to stay, and then some. Most of the industry professionals we talked with believe that influencer marketing will become a larger slice of overall marketing budgets. Nechelle Vanias says, "It's too entrenched, it's too necessary within moving product and building brands on social media that influencer marketing is not going away." She also acknowledges that the industry will mature, morph, and change, but in the end, there's an underlying stability.

Influencing is not just a part of the culture; it's entrenched in it. Joe Gagliese says, "Influencing and having a social audience and power and clout has become the norm in our society, and I don't think you can ever strip it away." It's a pastime as well as something now integrated into professions as diverse as athletics, music, acting, and politics.

In terms of the future, we asked our interviewees what their thoughts were on both short-term and long-term influencing trends. Here's what they said.

POWER SHIFT: CHOOSING MANY OVER ONE

The Great Seal of the United States features the Latin phrase "E pluribus unum," which translates as "out of many, one." It symbolizes the many states that came together to form one nation. The future of social media influencing is likely to mirror that in some ways, as the industry will become more democratized as a result of the influx of many new influencers. Mark Cuban says he believes the social media influencer industry is "becoming more democratic. That everyone is an influencer, and they aggregate it; have more impact than (just one) high-follower influencer."

For brands, that might mean moving away from some of the high-dollar campaigns that use one influencer with millions of followers, instead replacing them with one large campaign made up of dozens or hundreds of influencers with smaller follower bases. Daniel Rascher also sees this happening as the number of influencers surges, giving brands more choices, which also could lead to their being able to pay less for the same campaigns. Rascher says, "Imagine you're a brand and all of a sudden there's 10,000 athletes that have 100,000 or more followers that sort of fit your category; you're going to be able to pay them a lot less than if there were only a few."

EMPIRE BUILDING

For influencers, the sky is the limit. Sarah Penna believes that we are going to see "big empire building" from content creators, who more and more will take their digital influence and use it to create clothing or makeup lines, other kinds of merch and other businesses. She also predicts, "I think you're going to continue to see less, the next movie star came off of TikTok, and more, the next Kardashian came off of TikTok."

It's easy to get a feel for the empire building firsthand when talking with Max Levine about plans for what he calls their personality-driven media company. Because nonfungible tokens, or NFTs, are a big thing at the moment, it's something they're looking into creating. Put simply, NFTs are unique digital artworks or collectables. Levine gives the example of musician Shawn Mendes's selling a digital guitar and YouTuber Jake Paul's putting out a boxing match NFT, as well as Tampa Bay Buccaneer Rob Gronkowski's NFT Collection, commemorating his championships with four limited-edition NFT trading cards.

Another possible venture on Levine's plate: a restaurant brand. "Have you heard of MrBeast Burger?" he asks, referencing the megastar YouTuber and his delivery-only fast-food restaurant chain. "We're talking to the people that created that to create our own restaurant brand, or food and beverage brand. I think the future of this is you can really do anything—if you want to get into the restaurant space; if you want to launch a shoe; if you want to launch an app; if you want to invest in start-ups and take equity in companies—you can really do anything."

Levine clearly plans on harnessing the power that comes with influencing, and believes industry leaders will continue to do so. "I think media companies of the future are going to be run or fueled by these content creators who have these rabid communities and powerful platforms."

SOLOPRENEUR

Today, people want more control over their financial situation, along with being able to create the work–life balance they want. Often this means leaving the traditional safety net of a large company and venturing out on their own. The Covid-19 pandemic only hastened this trend. Jessy Grossman says she's seeing more and more people, women especially, choosing to work for themselves, or at least getting solo curious, because even though it's online, the influencer industry is basically a relationship-based business, which lends itself to solopreneurship.

As pioneer solopreneurs pave the way, the stigma and fear of leaving large companies with prestigious names is vanishing. It's hard for many to leave a job with a steady paycheck, but it's getting easier. Grossman believes, as do most in the industry, that the core of influencer marketing is being able to pivot quickly and react to new trends on the spot. That's one of the biggest advantages of not being tied up in the red tape and "too many cooks in the kitchen" of a large company.

One of the main things she advises people who want to go out on their own in other layers of the influencing profession, including management, is to focus on branding themselves. It's not only influencers who need to focus on being the brand. When people first wade into the profession and get into the weeds of it, they sometimes lose focus of the bigger picture and getting the message of who they are out there. You can be the best professional for the job, but if no one knows it thanks to a lack of branding, it's all for nothing.

A great example of the importance of personal branding and solopreneurship are journalists who become influencers. Stephanie McNeal talks about the trend of following individual reporters rather than media outlets: "People are now gravitating towards personalities over a brand, besides a couple of brands like the *New York Times* or something like that, because the habits of millennial and Gen Z consumers of journalism are not to go to the front page of CNN or go to the front page of the *New York Times*. Instead of just getting the paper and reading what's in it, they're seeking out news based on their own biases and interests. And I think that naturally lends itself to following reporters rather than following brands." McNeal says that reporters are becoming independent by podcasting on their own, blogging, and going on sites like Substack, which enables writers to start newsletters that make money from subscriptions. She says there's a "new push for people to be like, I am an independent journalist, and I write about X, and if you follow me, you can support me directly."

Since the influencer space is newer and seems like an enigma to some companies, the trust part of the relationships is key. They want someone self-assured to lead them through that space. Grossman believes that's what makes individuals stand out from the larger company backing them. "For women who assert themselves and become experts in the space and exude that confidence, like 'I'm your trusted partner,' that's worth its weight in gold," she says.

Grossman also sees enough money in the industry for people to go solopreneur. She notes, "You can build an entire business because you have, literally, one massive client. To be honest, there's just that much money in it, and I'm speaking from all sides of it—from the agency side, meaning the ad agency or PR person; or you could have just a brand that does that much influencer marketing, that there's absolutely that much work to be able to manage for a bunch of people in a company. And certainly, if you're managing talent, there are influencers, like pretty average, middle-of-the-road influencers, who are making half a million dollars a year, so 20 percent of that is a really nice paycheck. And that's literally with one influencer. So there's just so much money being thrown around that you don't need twenty clients and twenty brands."

From the influencer side, Mae Karwowski thinks that "more influencers are gonna start their own companies as a way to be more in control of their own image and their own trajectory."

Grossman does issue a caution regarding solopreneurs' choosing their own path and striking that seemingly elusive work–life balance. She sees people in the industry who dream about the right work–life balance as solopreneurs, but then they don't or aren't able to follow through. Just as with a larger company, solopreneurs can fall into an all work–no balance pattern.

OFFLINE EXPERIENCES AND
COMMUNITY BUILDING

In the future, online is going to merge with offline more and more. Influencers see that their audiences have commonalities and want to get them to connect on the basis of those commonalities through their platforms and in the real world. Kristina Zias says, "I am such a people person, and I value my audience so much. I want to bring value to them. And so much comes with meeting people in real life and in person and building a community." Toward this end, Zias started the Confidence Collective, a community and podcast with the goal of inspiring members to live their most confident life. Events have included free biweekly fitness events in LA for women, as well as a partnership with Nike to lead a group of women running their first half marathon in LA.

Zias believes that the future of influencing will include the experiential. She says, "I think that people want to feel part of something and are really longing and looking for that. And that's where I think that influencers can bring value and should bring value." Still, her focus on the virtual community is strong, with plans to grow stronger, because there's power in online neighborhoods. Zias is working on building out a Facebook group as a result of the amount of recommendations and questions she gets from people. "This person from Texas who follows me who asked me this question; the person from Maine asked the same question—these people should connect. I think it's about bringing your community together. This is a goal of mine. I want us to be one big happy family."

LIFESTYLE OVER BEAUTY

Followers want more from their influencers than surface beauty. As engagement goes up, so do connections between influencers and their audience. The person behind the influencer is growing in importance. Aysha Harun has noticed the shift and expects it to continue. She says, "I feel like before, beauty had its moment. And now when I post a beauty tutorial or something beauty related, it doesn't get as much traction as lifestyle, and I feel like that's just kind of where the internet is now. People want to see more personal things, vulnerability, what you're doing in a day-to-day life because that's what they relate to the most. . . . Just sharing things like that and honestly, I've been experimenting with more mental health–focused content and sharing life advice and all of that, and I think that has also been gaining a lot more traction, which is different than any type of content that I've done."

GAME ON!

Gaming influencers are a big part of what's now and a big part of what's next. Influencers we talked with expect games to continue to dominate, but with story mode coming back huge because story lines and role-playing keep people engaged by being less rote and repetitive.

Lachlan Power says that the tournament trend has been big for a while, and he expects it to continue. He also sees group gaming content creation having more of a place: "That's why we're investing a lot of PWR to kind of be on the forefront of that one. Yeah, I think just based on the analytics that I'm seeing that that's definitely a healthy trend that's growing, and I'm interested to see how that keeps on going."

QUICK AND LIVE

The popularity of Vine and TikTok have shown that there is an appetite for short-form content. Of course, there will always be demand for long-form content, but the influencers we talked with were all about the short form as a current and future trend. Aysha Harun describes the addictive quality of short forms like TikTok as being like "a dark hole that you creep into once you start." She wants to do more of it because she believes "quick, digestible content" is the future.

Influencers also see livestreaming as a big part of their future—and a great way to get creative and connect deeper with their audiences. For example, Nikki Glaser is a comedian, podcaster, and influencer who loves having a close relationship with her "besties" (the name for her fans) and uses Instagram Live to its fullest, from speed dating to playing guitar.

THE SPACE GETS MORE INCLUSIVE

Despite the continued presence of an inordinate amount of hate online, influencers from marginalized communities aren't letting that stop them from having their voices heard, and it's a trend that will continue in both the short and long term. There's too much value in it. For instance, Lolo Spencer says, "I have noticed that more and more people with disabilities want to enter the influencing space. More and more people with disabilities want to start sharing their stories, and make content, and talk about their lives and their experiences. So that's something that's really exciting and is needed. . . . And I'm seeing more and more brands involved in disability representation in their content. And in their campaigns. It's still very few and far between. But I am starting to see it on a more regular basis—like I'm starting to see a lot more than I ever had before."

THE STAYING POWER OF MICROINFLUENCERS

Over and over again, influencers and industry professionals talk about the power of microinfluencers and niche influencers. Perez

Hilton believes that their proven success will continue into the future and things will get even more focused: "Not just, OK, I'm a cooking influencer, but it's become even more fragmented. It's like, I specialize in barbecues, I specialize in ten-minute meals, I specialize in this, I specialize in that. The more niche influencers are the ones that can make more money than, like, a cute twenty-year-old that's hot and gets a lot of followers just because they're hot and sexy."

THE POWER OF SHAPE-SHIFTING

Because of the nonlinear, immediate nature of influencer marketing, organizations need to learn how to bend without breaking. Rigid organizational hierarchies aren't going to cut it when it comes to influencer marketing. Tressie Lieberman says, "More than ever, you have to be extremely flexible. And you have to be ready to hustle and you have to have the structure, the strategy, and the team to move on things and collaborate and make decisions. I continue seeing that to be a critical part of how an organization is structured." There are brands that still view flexibility and collaboration as a loss of control; they aren't able to respond with agility to what's trending.

AUTHENTICITY ON TOP OF AUTHENTICITY

There wasn't a single influencer or other industry professional who said that the thirst for authenticity would go away anytime soon. Lieberman believes it's going to become even more important, adding that unpaid publicity is going to be critical: "I think having to build those relationships and harness them over time and also finding the right way to amplify those relationships will be important. So word-of-mouth marketing and earned [media] will reign."

Sarah Penna calls getting a peek into influencers' personal lives and authenticity "the de-Instagramableness of Instagram." She says,

"People are kind of sick of the fake—the fakeness. And I do like that trend, because I think while we all bought in on the fakeness, it was hard to compare yourself to all these beautiful, perfect—whatever. There will always be that corner of the internet, but I think the tribe of Gen Z [is] sharing realness and being in the sort of Billie Eilish thing of like, I don't care what I look like and I'm gonna show me and all of my flaws."

But people won't only want to see authenticity from influencers; they'll also want to see it in the brands they love. That's where brand action becomes important. Lieberman says, "What you do as a brand and what you're standing up for, and the people that you partner with, are going to be very important."

Along with the idea of authenticity, people want honesty about influencer income, not rumors about shady backdoor deals with brands and influencers. Consultant Jolie Jankowitz says, "We're starting to see more transparency from influencers about how they make their money, what the breakdown of that is. People want to know that. They want full transparency." Mark Cuban stresses the importance of influencers, who are being paid to promote products, disclosing that it's a financial relationship.

HATE AND EXTREMISM

Among all the influencers and influencing professionals interviewed, hate seems to be reluctantly accepted as part of the online atmosphere, and no one expects that to change anytime soon. Colin Wayne Leach maintains that the norms about what's acceptable to say have shifted over the past several years, and extremism online is an existing trend.

Extremism is a strongly held belief, including political or religious, that is far outside of the mainstream value system. Extremists often use radical methods, including violence, to perpetuate their beliefs.

Past behavior being the best predictor of future behavior, and with nothing to slow it down, extremism will be part of what's next online. A literature review on violent extremists' use of the internet notes, "There is no doubt that the internet will remain of utmost importance to extremist causes across the ideological spectrum for decades to come. . . . It cannot be inoculated from extremism: history shows that, as technology improves, extremists will adapt their approaches to optimally reflect the new operational environment and elude the measures working to undermine them. While the menace they present cannot be eradicated, it can be mitigated through informed policy choices."[1]

The implications for influencers are many. They will continue to be targets of haters and trolls; some influencers will dish out hate; and in some cases, influencers and extremism will become linked. For instance, during the Covid-19 pandemic, as part of a disinformation campaign, French and German influencers say they were asked to disparage the Pfizer vaccine by a mysterious PR agency in London that had ties to Russia.[2]

Both the policy and cultural choices societies make will determine to what extent online hate and extremism belong to the future.

PLATFORM PROLIFERATION

Influencers and platforms have a reciprocal relationship; each helps shape the other. Influencers create trends, as do the platforms they use to showcase themselves. Raina Penchansky likes the fact that there are always multiple places for content and that it will continue to grow "because it allows different kinds of creators to bubble up and you see different kinds of content and more diverse content to support."

The industry and proliferation of platforms are fluid, which makes them difficult to predict. Joe Gagliese notes, "It's going to continue to change as the influencers change as people and as the platforms change. . . . The big powerhouses in social, they run that market." But there is volatility in that powerhouse. For instance, "There could be another Instagram in ten years that our kids will be like, you're a loser for having Instagram," Gagliese laughs, then adds, "These are the types of things that change and every one of those changes will impact the influencer industry differently."

Platforms constantly modify their models to lure more influencers by offering them different ways to monetize. The following are a few examples.

- Community allows influencers, for a fee, to connect instantly and market directly to their audience via text messaging.
- OnlyFans allows influencers to monetize without advertisers by having users subscribe to their content.
- Cameo is a video-sharing app enabling influencers to get paid for virtual appearances.
- Patreon is a membership platform with a subscription-style payment model that gives fans access to exclusive content from influencers for a monthly fee.
- With the Substack app, influencers can send digital newsletters to subscribers and get paid for it.
- With Kajabi, influencers can get paid directly by offering classes and coaching.

The big, established apps are also in the mix, trying to entice influencers and their fans by providing customizable features and allowing influencers to directly cash in. For instance, in 2021, Twitter rolled out Twitter Blue, their first subscription offering. Also in 2021, Snapchat paid more than $250 million to Snapchat Spotlight creators.

User-friendly commerce features are a future must for scaling social commerce, such as the e-commerce platform Shopify's introducing new shopping experiences on TikTok. In a January 2022 report, global IT company Accenture stated that social commerce is going to surpass other retail options, including e-commerce, by 2025, bringing in $1.2 trillion worth of global sales within the next three years.[3]

REGULATION

You can't talk about the future of social media without looking at the prospect of regulatory changes that could dramatically shape the digital platforms themselves, as well as how the billions of people who use social media interact with them. There has been a debate going on in legal and government circles for a number of years now, and the voices for new, more strict regulation of social media companies are only getting louder. In fact, the US Supreme Court was asked to weigh in on whether people should be able to block other users on Twitter from interacting with their posts; the lawsuit involved Donald Trump, who blocked people from being able to comment on his posts on Twitter. The Supreme Court dismissed the suit, but in his concurring opinion in the case, Justice Clarence Thomas sent a shot across the bow of the social media companies. He pointed out that the companies have an unprecedented amount of control over the many voices on their platforms, then added, "We will soon have no choice but to address how our legal doctrines apply to highly concentrated, privately owned information infrastructure such as digital platforms."[4]

However, some states have tried to enact laws that would restrict what social media companies can do in regard to banning individual users and what they say are politically motivated actions. Florida and Texas both took aim at the digital companies, but federal courts have struck down those laws so far.[5] New York has also proposed a bill that would attempt to regulate speech on social media platforms;

the bill was predominantly meant to help eliminate false statements that could harm public health. The bill is targeting vaccine misinformation, but some suspect that it will also be shot down by the courts on First Amendment grounds.

Others are calling for more strict controls over social media—not for political speech, but for what they say are too lenient controls over cyberbullying, which has led to some teenagers committing suicide.[6] There have been a number of lawsuits against some of the top social media platforms in cases related to suicides by youth.

The debate continues, with freedom of speech often cited as a reason not to regulate social media platforms or to push them to go even further in regulating what their users post. Although many in the social media industry are closely watching the debates and efforts by state and federal legislators to push for new and more strict regulations, none of the efforts for more severe restrictions has taken hold.

IS THE METAVERSE THE FUTURE?

The future of influencer marketing, and perhaps social media in general, is likely going to be quite different from today. In fact, in a sense, it might not even be "real." That's because the metaverse is expected by many in the tech world to be where everything, from commerce to entertainment to our personal lives, happens in the future. What exactly is the metaverse? While the metaverse doesn't exist in full yet, there are some forms of it around. Ultimately, it is a form of cyberspace where virtual reality offers people the chance to interact in a virtual world that continues to exist even when people are not actively in it.[7]

So why should we care about the metaverse, and are we sure it will even come to fruition? Well, it's already being tested in some ways, at least in concept, and it shows some amazing results. Luxury retail brand Gucci hosted an event in Roblox, a current virtual world similar to what the metaverse may become, in May 2021. That event, known as the Gucci Garden exhibition, drew more than 19.9 million people to take part.[8]

Also, the popular musician Travis Scott hosted a concert using his avatar to perform virtually in the popular video game *Fortnite* in April 2020, which drew 12 million people and made $20 million—for the single concert.[9]

These are just two early examples of this kind of event, which can draw millions of people—people who never actually have to leave their home to attend the event. Money is being made; its potential seems limitless. For influencers, this means a vast opportunity, but it also presents a new challenge: holding on to an audience in an uncertain world, where the eventual hot platform of the future likely hasn't even been invented yet. Many brands are already experimenting with virtual influencers and their own lifelike avatars, which are being used to post on social media sites that could potentially steal away business from certain types of influencers who work with some of the brands, particularly in the fashion business. But as the future unfolds, it's likely that the metaverse will be where influencers will increasingly need to have a presence as they continue to expand their own personal business and expand their audience.

MATURATION OF AN INDUSTRY

Just like any new industry, what we can expect for the influencing industry is for it to grow up. Stephanie McNeal sees it maturing in a way that renders it more regulated and less volatile. She sees there being "more standards for pay rates and less exploitation of creators. . . . When influencers go to negotiate with a brand now, there's a lot more people in the room to advocate for them on both sides. And brands are starting to realize that they have a large swath of influencers at their disposal. They don't have to just go for the person with 2 million followers; they can go for someone with 50,000 followers, because that's a really engaged audience. And I think that's a sign of the industry maturing. I think eventually there'll be some restrictions on kids on Instagram, from a legal standpoint." Overall, McNeal's take seems to be in a positive direction, with influencing "growing into a more equitable space."

LIST OF INTERVIEWEES

The following is a list of our interviewees, along with some info about them, including, as relevant, number of followers or subscribers as of mid-2022, as well as interview date.

Liza Anderson—President and founder of Anderson Group Public Relations. March 5, 2021.

Isabella Avila—Fun facts and gaming influencer (@Onlyjayus, 18.2M on TikTok). September 27, 2020, and January 12, 2022.

Jacques Bastien—Cofounder of Shade, influencer marketing agency for diversity-focused campaigns. September 2, 2020.

Shanicia Boswell—Influencer/writer, founder Black Mom's Blog (@shaniciaboswell, 31.7K on Instagram). September 10, 2020.

Mike Brooks, PhD—Licensed psychologist, speaker, coauthor of *Tech Generation: Raising Balanced Kids in a Hyper-connected World.* January 7, 2021.

Danielle R. Busby, PhD—Licensed clinical psychologist, vice president of professional relations, liaison/cofounder Black Mental Wellness Corp. April 23, 2021.

Paula Carozzo—Influencer/Miami disability activist (@pauuzzo, 23.7K on Instagram). November 22, 2021.

Jeff Chilcoat—Founder Sterling Sports Management. October 16, 2020.

T. Bettina Cornwell, PhD—Academic director Warsaw Sports Marketing Center; Philip H. Knight chair holder and head of department of marketing, Lundquist College of Business, University of Oregon; coauthor of *Influencer: The Science behind Swaying Others.* November 12, 2020.

Mark Cuban—Billionaire entrepreneur (@mcuban, 8.8M on Twitter). June 30, 2020.

Dana L. Cunningham, PhD—Licensed clinical psychologist, vice president community outreach and engagement, cofounder Black Mental Wellness Corp. April 23, 2021.

Paul Desisto—Founder of Paul Desisto Talent Management. November 5, 2020.

Eli Erlick—Influencer, writer, speaker, transgender rights activist (@elierlick, 42.2K on Instagram). February 16, 2021.

David Ewoldsen, PhD—Professor, Department of Media and Information, Michigan State University. September 29, 2020.

Lisa Filipelli—Partner, Select Management Group. January 25, 2021.

Mary Fitzgerald—Costar of Netflix's *Selling Sunset,* real estate agent (@themaryfitzgerald, 2.2M on Instagram). December 4, 2020.

Joe Gagliese—Co-CEO/cofounder of Viral Nation, influencer marketing agency. July 27, 2020.

Judy Gold—Stand-up comedian, actress, podcaster, Daytime Emmy Award–winning writer, producer, author of *Yes, I Can Say That: When They Come for the Comedians, We Are All in Trouble* (@jewdygold, 64.1K followers on Twitter). February 24, 2021.

GloZell Green—Comedy influencer/YouTube star (4.6M on YouTube). December 8, 2020.

Jessy Grossman—Founder, president WIIM: Women in Influencer Marketing, influencer talent manager, social influencer consultant. February 8, 2021.

Kim Guerra—Influencer, writer, activist, creator of brand Badass x Bonita (@badassxbonita, 126K on Instagram). December 3, 2020.

Jared Haibon—Influencer, contestant on several series in ABC's Bachelor franchise, host of iHeart's *Help! I Suck at Dating with Dean, Jared & . . .* podcast (@jaredhaibon, 700K on Instagram). November 6, 2020.

Aysha Harun—Beauty, lifestyle, fashion influencer (@ayshaharun, 337K on Instagram). January 12, 2021.

Kyle Hernandez—Comedy influencer (@kyleblockbuster, 1.7M on TikTok). September 15, 2020.

Perez Hilton—Influencer, gossip blogger, PerezHilton.com, media personality, author (@theperezhilton, 789K on Instagram). July 16, 2020.

Ashley Iaconetti Haibon, aka Ashley I—Influencer, journalist, contestant on several series in ABC's Bachelor franchise, host of iHeart's *The Ben and Ashley I Almost Famous Podcast* (@ashley_Iaconetti, 1.2M on Instagram). November 6, 2020.

Logan Isbell—Influencer/TikToker (@loganisbell, 880.7K on TikTok). September 21, 2020.

Jolie Jankowitz—Influencer marketing consultant; former senior director, influencer marketing and talent partnerships at FabFitFun. January 8, 2021.

Johnny Jet—Money and time-saving travel influencer (@johnnyjet, 28.4K on Instagram). December 17, 2020.

Tim Karsliyev—Owner/founder of Daily Dose (@dailydose, 1.6M on Instagram). July 30, 2020.

Mae Karwowski—CEO/founder of Obviously, influencer marketing agency. August 19, 2020.

Kevin Kreider—Influencer, costar of Netflix's *Bling Empire* (@kevin.kreider, 543K on Instagram). January 29, 2021.

Lorraine Ladish—Yoga, wellness, pro-aging influencer/blogger; publisher of Viva Fifty, a bilingual community that celebrates your best age (@lorrainecladish, 34.9K on Instagram). December 2, 2020.

Blake Lawrence—CEO/cofounder of Opendorse, influencer marketing organization, providing technology to the athlete endorsement industry. October 9, 2020.

Colin Wayne Leach, PhD—Professor of psychology and Africana studies, Barnard College, Columbia University. April 8, 2021.

Naomi Lennon—President/founder Lennon Management. October 27, 2020.

Max Levine—Cofounder Amp Studios (Generates 1 billion views per month on social media). March 23, 2021.

Tressie Lieberman—Vice president, digital marketing and off-premise, Chipotle Mexican Grill (Named to 2021 Business Insider Power List of top influencer marketers at brands). September 17, 2020.

Ray Ligaya—Head of talent at Viral Nation; musical artist/influencer known as Mansuki (@rayligaya, 96.2K on Instagram). July 31, 2020.

Chloe Long—Costar of MTV's *Siesta Key,* influencer; video coaching, conceptbychloe.com (@chloe.long, 470K on Instagram). October 28, 2020.

Aditi Oberoi Malhotra—Fashion/beauty influencer, CEO/founder of NFTartpedia.com and BusinessofNFT.com, entrepreneur (@aditioberoimalhotra, 777K on Instagram). February 18, 2021.

Stephanie McNeal—Journalist, senior culture reporter for BuzzFeed News; writes about internet culture and influencers, hosts podcast *The Rise and Fall of LuLaRoe.*

Douglas O'Neal Middleton Jr.—NFL veteran safety, mental health advocate/influencer, founder of dreamtheimpossible.org (@36dm_era, 8,885 on Instagram). March 24, 2021.

Tim Montgomery—Comedy influencer/TikToker (@timsmontgomery, 437.2K on TikTok). September 23, 2020.

Tyler Moss—Influencer/43 YouTube channels (TMossBoss 28.4K on YouTube). October 8, 2020.

Ooreofe Oluwadara—Fashion influencer, entrepreneur (@oreofay, 131K on Instagram). March 16, 2021.

Raina Penchansky—CEO/cofounder Digital Brand Architects, an influencing marketing agency acquired by United Talent Agency in 2019. August 19, 2020.

Sarah Penna—Senior manager, creator launch, at Patreon,

cofounder of Frolic Media, cofounder of Big Frame. December 7, 2020.

Cindy Pham—Booktuber, travel influencer, blogger (withcindy, 475K on YouTube). March 7, 2021.

Lachlan Ross Power—Australian YouTuber, professional gamer, founder of lifestyle brand and gaming organization PWR (Lachlan, 14.8M on YouTube). April 6, 2022.

Rey Rahimi—Influencer, online gossip (HotTea, 182K on YouTube). October 5, 2020.

Mary Lynn Rajskub—Actress, comedian, costar of FX/FXX's *It's Always Sunny in Philadelphia* and Fox's *24* (@marylynnrajskub, 162.5K on Twitter). February 19, 2021.

Daniel A. Rascher, PhD—Professor and director of academic programs for the sport management program at the University of San Francisco, president of SportsEconomics. October 19, 2020.

Gigi Robinson—Influencer, mental health/chronic illness, Gen Z thought leader (@itsgigirobinson, 132.9K on TikTok). March 3, 2021.

Larry Rosen, PhD—International expert in the psychology of technology and author/coauthor of numerous books, including *The Distracted Mind: Ancient Brains in a High-Tech World*. October 7, 2020.

Michael Schweiger—CEO Central Entertainment Group, influencer marketing. August 27, 2020.

LaToya Shambo—CEO/founder of Black Girl Digital, influencer marketing agency specializing in a Black female audience. September 1, 2020.

Brian Carey Sims, PhD—African media psychologist, associate professor, department of psychology, Florida A&M University. March 30, 2021.

Lauren "Lolo" Spencer—Disability lifestyle influencer and actor, HBO Max *The Sex Lives of College Girls;* Film Independent Spirit

Award–nominated actor for *Give Me Liberty* (@itslololove, 58.5K on Instagram). November 17, 2021.

Alexa Stabler—NFL agent and lawyer; founder of Stabler Sports. October 16, 2020.

Joshua Suarez—Influencer, comedy and pranks (@kingkidjoshua, 14.3M on TikTok). January 2021.

Brittani Louise Taylor—YouTuber well known for music video parodies, sketch comedy, and vlogs; actress and author (Brittani Louise Taylor, 1.38M on YouTube). December 14, 2020.

Nechelle Vanias—Chief solutions officer/cofounder Six Degrees of Influence, an influencer marketing, media, and talent management agency. January 6, 2021.

Rave Vanias—Influencer/actor, part of TikTok collective the Vault (@thevaultla 1.5M and @ravevanias 425.6K on TikTok). January 2021.

Celeste Viciere, LMHC, aka Celeste the Therapist—Therapist, mental health influencer, author, *Celeste the Therapist* podcast host (@celestethetherapist, 5,620 on Instagram). April 7, 2021.

Erin A. Vogel, PhD—Social psychologist, senior research associate, University of Southern California Keck School of Medicine. February 24. 2021

Laura Vogel, JD—Owner, Winged Pup Productions, social media marketing, online fund-raising, merchandising, original video content. February 7, 2021.

Dan Weinstein—Cofounder/partner of Underscore Talent, former president/cofounder of Studio71. December 14, 2020.

Joey Zauzig—Influencer, men's fashion, fitness, skin care, LGBTQAI+ (@joeyzauzig, 265K on Instagram). September 16, 2020.

Kristina Zias—Curve model, fashion influencer, blogger; cofounder @confidentcollective community and podcast (@kristinaZias, 269K on Instagram). September 11, 2020.

NOTES

CHAPTER 1

1. Kevin Roose, "Don't Scoff at Influencers. They're Taking over the World," *New York Times,* July 16, 2019, https://www.nytimes.com/2019/07/16/technology/vidcon-social-media-influencers.html.

2. "Global Influencer Marketing Platform Market, 2021–2028: Changing Content Consumption Trends Are Offering Promising Growth Opportunities," *PRNewswire,* September 15, 2021, https://www.prnewswire.com/news-releases/global-influencer-marketing-platform-market-2021-2028-changing-content-consumption-trends-are-offering-promising-growth-opportunities-301377539.html.

3. LEGO Group, "LEGO Group Kicks Off Global Program to Inspire the Next Generation of Space Explorers as NASA Celebrates 50 Years of Moon Landing," *PRNewswire,* July 16, 2019, https://www.prnewswire.com/news-releases/lego-group-kicks-off-global-program-to-inspire-the-next-generation-of-space-explorers-as-nasa-celebrates-50-years-of-moon-landing-300885423.html.

4. NU Athletic Communications, "Huskers and Opendorse Announce Groundbreaking Partnership," *Huskers,* March 10, 2020, https://huskers.com/news/2020/3/10/athletics-huskers-launch-first-ncaa-program-to-maximize-value-of-individual-brands.aspx.

5. Sara Cook, "White House Briefs Social Media Influencers on Ukraine Crisis," CBS News, March 11, 2022, https://www.cbsnews.com/news/ukraine-russia-tiktok-white-house/.

6. Taylor Lorenz, "The Real Difference between Creators and Influencers: It's Not a Gender Thing," *Atlantic,* May 31, 2019, https://www.theatlantic.com/technology/archive/2019/05/how-creators-became-influencers/590725/.

7. Josh Horton, "Are You Smarter than a Basketball YouTuber Trivia Challenge!," YouTube, June 8, 2020, video, 15:01, https://www.youtube.com/watch?v=5dz7jfBjD5k.

8. "Daily Time Spent on Social Networking by Internet Users Worldwide from 2012 to 2022," Statista, March 21, 2022, https://www.statista.com/statistics/433871/daily-social-media-usage-worldwide/.

9. Sarah Ware, "Instagram Marketing: Does Influencer Size Matter?,"

based on a report from influencer marketing platform Markerly, April 12, 2016, https://markerly.com/blog/instagram-marketing-does-influencer-size-matter/.

10. Kaya Ismail, "Social Media Influencers: Mega, Macro, Micro or Nano," *CMSWire,* December 10, 2018, https://www.cmswire.com/digital-marketing/social-media-influencers-mega-macro-micro-or-nano/.

11. Helen Langan, "New Research Shows Micro-influencers Drive Consumer Buying Behavior at Much Higher Rates than Previously Thought," based on a report from ExpertVoice, October 29, 2019, https://www.expertvoice.com/new-research-shows-micro-influencers-drive-consumer-buying-behavior-much-higher-rates-previously-thought/.

CHAPTER 2

1. Natalie Jarvey, "VidCon at 10: How a 'Thrown-Together' Event Gave Rise to the Influencer Era," *Hollywood Reporter,* July 13, 2019, https://www.hollywoodreporter.com/news/general-news/vidcon-at-10-how-a-thrown-together-event-gave-rise-to-influencer-era-1224136/.

2. Matthew Lasar, "How TV's 'Vast Wasteland' Became a Vast Garden," *Wired,* March 19, 2011, https://www.wired.com/2011/03/tv-became-a-vast-garden/.

3. "TikTok under Investigation for Possible Facilitation of Human Trafficking and Child Privacy Violations," ABC 13 Eyewitness News, February 18, 2022, https://abc13.com/tiktok-human-trafficking-ag-paxton-child-privacy-violations/11578195/.

CHAPTER 3

1. Statista Research Department, "Number of Influencer Marketing Agencies and Platforms Worldwide, 2015–2020," Statista, August 23, 2021, https://www.statista.com/statistics/1257471/number-influencer-marketing-agencies-worldwide/.

CHAPTER 5

1. Kerry Flynn, "Inside the Black Market Where People Pay Thousands of

Dollars for Instagram Verification," *Mashable,* September 1, 2017, https://mashable.com/article/instagram-verification-paid-Black-market -facebook.

2. Taylor Lorenz, "Perez Hilton vs. the Fan Armies," *New York Times,* December 14, 2020, https://www.nytimes.com/2020/12/14/style/perez-hilton -tiktok-ban.html.

3. Arvind Hickman, "More than Half of Instagram Influencers 'Engaged in Fraud,' with 45 per cent of Accounts 'Fake,'" *PRWeek,* April 15, 2021, https://www.prweek.com/article/1712976/half-instagram-influencers -engaged-fraud-45-per-cent-accounts-fake.

4. Linkr Editorial Team, "Fake Followers—How Big Is the Problem?," *Linkr,* June 25, 2020, https://linkr-network.com/en/blog-collection/fake -followers-how-big-is-the-problem/.

5. "Attorney General James Announces Groundbreaking Settlement with Sellers of Fake Followers and 'Likes' on Social Media," press release, New York Attorney General, January 30, 2019, https://ag.ny.gov/press-release/2019 /attorney-general-james-announces-groundbreaking-settlement-sellers -fake-followers.

6. "Instagram Richlist: Official Hopper HQ List," 2018–2021, *Hopper,* https://www.hopperhq.com/instagram-rich-list/.

7. Werner Geyser, "Influencer Rates: How Much Do Influencers Really Cost in 2022?," *Influencer Marketing Hub,* November 26, 2021, https://influencermarketinghub.com/influencer-rates/.

CHAPTER 6

1. Insider Intelligence, "Influencer Marketing Stats: How Creators Have Impacted Businesses in 2021," *Business Insider,* May 17, 2021, https://www .businessinsider.com/influencer-marketing-important-for-brands-2021-5.

2. Amanda Perelli, "YouTube Star David Dobrik Has Been Dropped by 13 Brands Including HelloFresh, EA Sports, and Honey," Yahoo! News, March 25, 2021, https://news.yahoo.com/youtube-star-david-dobrik -dropped-120700415.html.

CHAPTER 7

1. Association for Psychological Science, "Social Media 'Likes' Impact Teens' Brains and Behavior," news release, Association for Psychological Science, May 31, 2016, https://www.psychologicalscience.org/news/releases /social-media-likes-impact-teens-brains-and-behavior.html.

2. Hae Yeon Lee, Jeremy Jamieson, Harry Reis, et al., "Getting Fewer 'Likes' than Others on Social Media Elicits Emotional Distress among Victimized Adolescents," *Child Development* 91, no. 6 (2020): 2141–59, https://doi.org/10.1111/cdev.13422.

3. Dave Itzkoff, "Melissa McCarthy Goes over the Top," *New York Times,* June 13, 2013, https://www.nytimes.com/2013/06/16/movies/melissa -mccarthy-goes-over-the-top.html.

4. Leadership Conference Education Fund, "Online Hate Speech Is Pervasive. Here's How to Start Combating It," Civil and Human Rights News, February 9, 2017, https://civilrights.org/edfund/resource/combat-online -hate-speech/.

5. Fatih Ozbay, Douglas C. Johnson, Eleni Dimoulas, C. A. Morgan III, Dennis Charney, and Steven Southwick, "Social Support and Resilience to Stress: From Neurobiology to Clinical Practice," *Psychiatry (Edgmont)* 4, no. 5 (2007): 35–40.

6. Zach Barnett, "Joe Burrow's Advice to Young Athletes: 'Work in Silence,'" *Footballscoop,* February 7, 2022, https://footballscoop.com/news /joe-burrow-work-in-silence.

CHAPTER 8

1. Nicole Wetsman, "Facebook's Whistleblower Report Confirms What Researchers Have Known for Years," *Verge,* October 6, 2021, https://www .theverge.com/2021/10/6/22712927/facebook-instagram-teen-mental-health -research.

2. Erin A. Vogel, Jason P. Rose, Bradley M. Okdie, Katheryn Eckles, and Brittany Franz, "Who Compares and Despairs? The Effect of Social Comparison Orientation on Social Media Use and Its Outcomes," *Personality and Individual Differences* 86 (2015): 249–56, https://doi.org/10.1016 /j.paid.2015.06.026; Erin A. Vogel, Jason P. Rose, Lindsay R. Roberts, and Katheryn Eckles, "Social Comparison, Social Media, and Self-Esteem," *Psychology of Popular Media Culture* 3 (2014): 206–22.

3. Patti Valkenburg, Ine Beyens, J. Loes Pouwels, Irene I. van Driel, and

Loes Keijsers, "Social Media Use and Adolescents' Self-Esteem: Heading for a Person-Specific Media Effects Paradigm," *Journal of Communication* 71, no. 1 (2021): 56–78, https://doi.org/10.1093/joc/jqaa039.

4. Gina Wurtz, "Kim Kardashian Accused of Photoshopping Now-Deleted Instagram Photo," *Screen Rant,* January 26, 2022, https://screenrant.com /kim-kardashian-photoshopped-instagram-pictures/; Laura Rizzo, "Kourtney Kardashian Deletes Photo of Her Backside after Getting Called Out for 'Bad' Photoshop," *Life and Style,* January 28, 2022, https://www.lifeandstylemag .com/posts/kourtney-kardashian-deletes-photo-gets-slammed-for-bad -editing/; Stephanie Soteriou, "Khloé Kardashian Fans Are Claiming They've Spotted a Hilarious Photoshop Fail in Her Latest Instagram Post after She Was Left 'Embarrassed' When an Unedited Bikini Picture Went Viral," *BuzzFeed News,* January 14, 2022, https://www.buzzfeednews.com/article /stephaniesoteriou/khloe-kardashian-photoshop-fail-instagram.

5. Jia Tolentino, "The Age of Instagram Face: How Social Media, FaceTune, and Plastic Surgery Created a Single, Cyborgian Look," *New Yorker,* December 12, 2019, https://www.newyorker.com/culture/decade-in-review /the-age-of-instagram-face.

6. Alex Hawgood, "What Is 'Bigorexia'?," *New York Times,* March 5, 2022, https://www.nytimes.com/2022/03/05/style/teen-bodybuilding-bigorexia -tiktok.html.

7. Lisa Rapaport, "Some Teens Who Exercise to Build Muscle Might Have Eating Disorders," *Physicians Weekly,* July 10, 2019, https://www .physiciansweekly.com/some-teens-who-exercise.

CHAPTER 9

1. William Cummings, "'That's Not Bringing about Change': Obama Advises 'Woke' Young People Not to Be So Judgmental," *USA Today,* October 30, 2019, https://www.usatoday.com/story/news/politics/2019/10/30/barack -obama-tells-woke-youth-get-over-quickly/4095362002/.

2. Brett M. Pinkus, "The Limits of Free Speech in Social Media," in special Spring 2021 issue on "Constitutional Law," *Assessable Law,* April 26, 2021, https://accessiblelaw.untdallas.edu/limits-free-speech-social-media.

3. Marie-Andrée Weiss, "Regulating Freedom of Speech on Social Media: Comparing the EU and the US Approach," research project, Transatlantic Technology Law Forum, Stanford Law School, accessed March 3, 2022,

https://law.stanford.edu/projects/regulating-freedom-of-speech-on-social
-media-comparing-the-eu-and-the-u-s-approach/.

4. David L. Hudson Jr., "In the Age of Social Media, Expand the Reach of
the First Amendment," *Human Rights Magazine* 43, no. 4, October 20, 2018,
https://www.americanbar.org/groups/crsj/publications/human_rights
_magazine_home/the-ongoing-challenge-to-define-free-speech/in-the-age
-of-socia-media-first-amendment/.

5. Evelyn Douek, "Governing Online Speech: From 'Posts-as-Trumps'
to Proportionality and Probability," *Columbia Law Review* 121, no. 3 (2021),
https://columbialawreview.org/wp-content/uploads/2021/04/Douek-
Governing_Online_Speech-from_Posts_As-Trumps_To_Proportionality_And
_Probability.pdf.

CHAPTER 11

1. Adam Mosseri, "Ensuring Black Voices Are Heard," Instagram, June 15,
2020, https://about.instagram.com/blog/announcements/ensuring-black
-voices-are-heard.

2. Susan Wojcicki, "My Mid-year Update to the YouTube Community,"
YouTube, June 11, 2020, https://blog.youtube/inside-youtube/susan-wojcicki
-my-mid-year-update-youtube-community/.

3. Safiya Umoja Noble, *Algorithms of Oppression: How Search Engines
Reinforce Racism* (New York: NYU Press, 2018), 1.

4. Nicol Turner Lee, Paul Resnick, and Genie Barton, "Algorithmic Bias
Detection and Mitigation: Best Practices and Policies to Reduce Consumer
Harms," Brookings Institution, May 22, 2019, https://www.brookings.edu
/research/algorithmic-bias-detection-and-mitigation-best-practices-and
-policies-to-reduce-consumer-harms/.

5. "We're Leading a Cultural Movement towards Equitable and
Accountable AI," mission statement, Algorithmic Justice League, accessed
March 24, 2022, https://www.ajl.org/about.

6. Sarah Frier, "Marketers Are Underpaying Black Influencers while
Pushing Black Lives Matter," *Bloomberg Businessweek,* March 11, 2021,
https://www.bloomberg.com/news/features/2021-03-11/marketers-are
-underpaying-black-influencers-while-pushing-black-lives-matter.

7. "MSL Study Reveals Racial Pay Gap in Influencer Marketing,"
PRNewswire, December 6, 2021, https://www.prnewswire.com/news-releases

/msl-study-reveals-racial-pay-gap-in-influencer-marketing-301437451.html.

8. Lena Young, "How Much Do Influencers Charge?," *Klear,* May 16, 2019, https://klear.com/blog/influencer-pricing-2019/.

9. "Influencer Agreement Fact Sheet," SAG-AFTRA, accessed March 26, 2022, https://www.sagaftra.org/influencer-agreement-fact-sheet.

10. Dan Gordon, "Discrimination Can Be Harmful to Your Mental Health," UCLA News, January 13, 2016, https://newsroom.ucla.edu/stories /discrimination-can-be-harmful-to-your-mental-health.

11. Esther Akinola, "Why Black Twitter Matters for Brands," *PR Week,* February 21, 2020, https://www.prweek.com/article/1674744/why-Black -twitter-matters-brands.

CHAPTER 12

1. Lacey Rose, "Jennifer Aniston Has No Regrets," *Hollywood Reporter,* December 8, 2021, https://www.hollywoodreporter.com/feature /jennifer-aniston-interview-morning-show-friends-murder-mystery -sequel-1235058142/.

2. Kat Tenbarge and Tyler Sonnemaker, "YouTube Is Temporarily Demonetizing David Dobrik's Channels Following a Rape Allegation against His Former Vlog Squad Cohort Dom Durte," *Insider,* March 25, 2021, https://www.businessinsider.com/youtube-demonetizing-david-dobrik -following-vlog-squad-scandal-2021-3.

3. Emma Nolan, "What David Dobrik and Seth Francois Video Shows as Allegations Made against YouTuber," *Newsweek,* March 17, 2021, https://www .newsweek.com/david-dobrik-seth-francois-video-sexual-assault-allegations -youtube-1576856.

4. Zoe Haylock, "James Charles Says He's Sorry He 'Flirted' with Underage Fans," April 1, 2021, *Vulture,* https://www.vulture.com/2021/04/james-charles -apology-video-grooming-allegations.html.

5. Andreea Cristina Bolbea, "The Relentless Horror of Being Stalked as an Instagram Star," *Vice,* November 19, 2018, https://www.vice.com/en/article /j5zeb4/andreea-cristina-instagram-stalker-blog.

6. Kate Lyons, "Japanese Assault Suspect 'Tracked Down Pop Star Via Eye Reflection in Selfie,'" *Guardian,* October 10, 2019, https://www.theguardian .com/world/2019/oct/11/japanese-assault-suspect-tracked-down-pop-star-via -eye-reflection-in-selfie.

7. Erin Van Der Meer, "Kim Kardashian Believes She Was Stalked by Thieves Prior to Paris Robbery," *Grazia,* accessed March 26, 2022, https://graziamagazine.com/articles/kim-kardashian-stalked-paris-robbery/.

8. Amanda Krause, "Beauty Influencer Bretman Rock Is Begging Fans to Stop Visiting His Home to Take Photos with Him, Especially during the Coronavirus Pandemic," *Insider,* April 16, 2020, https://www.insider.com /bretman-rock-begs-fans-to-stop-visiting-his-house-2020-4.

CHAPTER 13

1. Abram Brown, "Founders Feud at Hype House Gets Nasty: An Armed Guard, a New Lawsuit—And a Breakaway Group of TikTok Stars," *Forbes,* March 26, 2020, https://www.forbes.com/sites/abrambrown/2020/03/26 /founders-feud-at-hype-house-gets-nasty-an-armed-guard-a-new-lawsuit -and-a-breakaway-group-of-tiktok-stars/.

2. Dakota Smith, "TikTok Stars Charged with Misdemeanors Related to Hollywood Parties during Pandemic," *Los Angeles Times,* August 28, 2020, https://www.latimes.com/california/story/2020-08-28/tiktok-stars-charged -with-misdemeanors-for-huge-hollywood-parties-during-coronavirus.

3. "TikTok Stars Bryce Hall, Jaden Hossler Arrested for Drug Possession: Reports," Fox 7 Austin, May 27, 2020, https://www.fox7austin.com/news /tiktok-stars-bryce-hall-jaden-hossler-arrested-for-drug-possession-reports.

4. Jodi Guglielmi, "TikTok's Sway House Is Officially Over—But Its Message 'Will Never Die,'" *People,* February 8, 2021, https://people.com/tv /tiktok-sway-house-is-officially-over/.

CHAPTER 14

1. "Engagement Rate among Instagram Influencers Worldwide 2019, by Category," Statista, October 19, 2021, https://www.statista.com /statistics/1123056/instagram-influencers-engagement-rate-world-category/.

2. US Olympic and Paralympic Committee, "Athlete Marketing for the Olympic and Paralympic Games, Tokyo 2020, Rule 40—Guidance for the United States," TeamUSA, October 7, 2019, https://www.teamusa.org/USA -Judo/Athletes/Rule-40.

CHAPTER 15

1. Charlie Winter, Peter Neumann, Alexander Meleagrou-Hitchens, Magnus Ranstor, Lorenzo Vidino, and Johanna Fürst, "Online Extremism: Research Trends in Internet Activism, Radicalization, and Counterstrategies," *International Journal of Conflict and Violence* 14, no. 2 (2020), https://www.ijcv.org/index.php/ijcv/article/view/3809/3868.

2. Liz Alderman, "Influencers Say They Were Urged to Criticize Pfizer Vaccine," *New York Times,* May 26, 2021, https://www.nytimes.com/2021/05/26/business/pfizer-vaccine-disinformation-influeners.html.

3. "Shopping on Social Media Platforms Expected to Reach $1.2 Trillion Globally by 2025," news release, Accenture, January 4, 2022, https://newsroom.accenture.com/industries/consumer-goods--services/shopping-on-social-media-platforms-expected-to-reach-1-2-trillion-globally-by-2025-new-accenture-study-finds.htm.

4. Joseph R. Biden Jr., President of United States, et al. v. Knight First Amendment Institute at Columbia University, et al. (2021), 593 No. 20-197, Supreme Court of the United States, p. 2, https://www.supremecourt.gov/opinions/20pdf/20-197_5ie6.pdf.

5. Eric Cervone, "What Is the Future of Social Media Regulation?," *Regulatory Review,* July 12, 2021, https://www.theregreview.org/2021/07/12/cervone-future-social-media-regulation/.

6. Bryan B. Menegus, "Meta and Snap Sued by Mother over Alleged Role in Her Daughter's Suicide," *Engadget,* January 2, 2022, https://www.engadget.com/facebook-snap-suicide-lawsuit-selena-rodriguez-213057362.html.

7. Eric Ravenscraft, "What Is the Metaverse, Exactly?," *Wired,* April 25, 2022, https://www.wired.com/story/what-is-the-metaverse/.

8. Kati Chitrakorn, "What Influencer Marketing Looks Like in the Metaverse," December 7, 2021, *Vogue Business,* https://www.voguebusiness.com/technology/what-influencer-marketing-looks-like-in-the-metaverse/amp.

9. Gergo Csiszar, Peter Varga Szilagyi, and Renata Milicevic, "How the Metaverse Will Shape the Future of Business, Marketing and Consequently Influencer Marketing," *Influencer Marketing Hub,* January 21, 2022, https://influencermarketinghub.com/metaverse-influencer-marketing/amp/.

INDEX